WHISKY·JAPAN

THE ESSENTIAL GUIDE TO THE WORLD'S MOST EXOTIC WHISKY

DOMINIC ROSKROW

FOREWORD BY
MIKE MIYAMOTO

WHISKY • JAPAN

THE ESSENTIAL GUIDE TO THE WORLD'S MOST EXOTIC WHISKY

DOMINIC ROSKROW

FOREWORD BY
MIKE MIYAMOTO

Published by Kodansha USA, Inc.
451 Park Avenue South, New York, NY 10016
www.kodanshausa.com

Distributed in the United Kingdom and continental Europe
by Kodansha Europe Ltd.
www.kodansha.eu

Copyright © 2016 Fine Wine Editions Ltd.

All rights reserved. No part of this publication may be reproduced, stored in a retrieval system or transmitted in any form or by any means, electronic, mechanical, photocopying, recording or otherwise, without the permission of the copyright holder.

Library of Congress Cataloging-in-Publication Data

Names: Roskrow, Dominic, author.
Title: Whisky Japan : the essential guide to the world's most exotic whisky / by Dominic Roskrow.
Description: New York, NY : Kodansha USA, [2016] | "A Quintessence book." Includes bibliographical references and index.
Identifiers: LCCN 2016020022 | ISBN 9781568365756
Subjects: LCSH: Whiskey—Japan—Guidebooks. | Whiskey industry—Japan—History.
Classification: LCC TP605 .R65 2016 | DDC 663/.520952—dc23 LC record available at https://lccn.loc.gov/2016020022

ISBN: 918-1-56836-575-6

This book was produced by
Fine Wine Editions Ltd.
6 Blundell Street
London N7 9BH

Project Editor	Sophie Blackman
Editor	Henry Russell
Design concept	gradedesign.com
Designer	Michelle Kliem
Picture Researchers	Sophie Blackman, Mattisse Cover, Michelle Kliem
Translation	Naho Iguchi
Production Manager	Anna Pauletti
Editorial Director	Ruth Patrick
Publisher	Philip Cooper

10 9 8 7 6 5 4 3 2 1

Color reproduction by Bright Arts, Hong Kong.
Printed in China by C&C Offset Printing Co., LTD.

CONTENTS
/
コンテンツ
・

FOREWORD BY MIKE MIYAMOTO
08

INTRODUCTION
12

022   **ONE / 一**
THE HISTORY OF JAPANESE WHISKY

034   **TWO / 二**
MAKING JAPANESE WHISKY

060   **THREE / 三**
THE WHISKY DISTILLERIES OF JAPAN

112   **FOUR / 四**
TASTING NOTES

138   **FIVE / 五**
THE RISE OF JAPANESE WHISKY

156   **SIX / 六**
JAPANESE WHISKY BARS

182   **SEVEN / 七**
BARS AROUND THE WORLD

234   **EIGHT / 八**
WHISKY COCKTAILS AND FOOD PAIRINGS

246   **NINE / 九**
THE FUTURE OF JAPANESE WHISKY

A TOURIST'S GUIDE TO JAPAN
262

WHISKY DIRECTORY, ACKNOWLEDGMENTS, BIBLIOGRAPHY, GLOSSARY, INDEX, PICTURE CREDITS
276

FOREWORD

MIKE MIYAMOTO

•

GLOBAL BRAND AMBASSADOR
FOR SUNTORY WHISKY

If I could ask one person his thoughts on the current status of Japanese whisky in the global market it would be Shinjiro Torii; one of the founders and pioneers who started it all. He wanted to create a whisky that would appeal to, and resonate with, more delicate palates, and be accessible to everyone.

Although it is now a global sensation, just ten years ago, whisky from the Far East was viewed as a knock-off. When I was the Distillery Manager of Yamazaki (2004–10), domestic consumption of whisky was in the midst of a twenty-five-year-long slump. Production was cut back, and I was filled with dread that the very existence of Japanese whisky was at risk.

We didn't give up, however, and after countless efforts and experiments, our skilled blenders created a variety of malt whiskies that have since become the Yamazaki Single Malt and the Hibiki Blended Whisky. With these in hand, we ventured to the United States in 2006 to showcase Shinjiro's dreams. Having won the Gold Award with our Yamazaki 12 Year Old at the International Spirits Challenge (ISC) in 2003, I was quite sure of our success.

Overcoming initial remarks such as "Japanese whisky? Is it made of rice?" we nudged the non-believers into taking their first sip. I cannot forget the surprised looks on their faces. I suppose the phrase "tasting is believing" epitomizes that moment.

Ever since, we have had amazing support from around the world. Wherever I visit, be it Europe, the United States of America, or Asia, I see both men and women enjoying our whiskies. Our convictions paid off, and I'd like to use this opportunity to thank each and every person who has supported Suntory and the Japanese whisky industry.

I believe that the smooth, well-balanced, yet complex character of Japanese whisky is what captures the hearts of many consumers across the globe—even more so for those who have never enjoyed whisky before.

However, there hasn't been much reading material that has delved into the craft, industry, and phenomenon that is Japanese whisky, so I am sure that this new book will enlighten those who would like to know more about its characteristics, flavor, and manufacturing techniques, as well as those who are new to the whisky in general. Dominic Roskrow has written this book at the perfect time. His long career as an esteemed whisky writer, and his great insights and understanding, will guide those who are interested in Japanese whisky and will convert those who are still unsure about it. I sincerely hope you enjoy our whisky along with this book.

SUNTORY WHISKIES_ The Hakushu 12 Year Old, Yamazaki 12 Year Old, and Hibiki 17 Year Old have all won international whisky awards.
NEXT PAGE_ Whisky casks maturing at Yamazaki Distillery in Osaka.

INTRODUCTION

Mention Japanese whisky to people with even a smattering of knowledge of the drinks industry, and it will provoke a number of reactions. Most will be aware that Japan makes whisky; a good number will know that the product is highly rated, but few will have tried it, be able to name any Japanese brand, or give any insight into what causes the excitement that surrounds it. Like Japan itself, Japanese whisky can be an exotic and mysterious source of intrigue.

Japan's whisky industry, like so much else in that amazing and beautiful country, is complex, exciting, dynamic, and currently in a state of flux. Although Japanese whisky has a long history it is still regarded by many people worldwide as new, and some commentators have tried to explain it over-simplistically.

When outsiders are confronted by a culture as complex and nuanced as that of Japan, alienated by a language that uses a totally different alphabet and includes words for which they have no equivalents—not so much lost in translation as with no accurate translation at all—it's easy for people to fall back on simplistic generalizations. As a result, the West has been guilty of adopting a largely meaningless cultural shorthand, full of lazy stereotypes. Meanwhile, the huge economic miracle that took place in Japan has led to a monstrous assault on the traditional ways and customs of the nation's rural areas.

In breaks from writing this book, I watched the television documentary *Off the Rails: A Journey Through Japan*, in which correspondent and author Ramsey Zarifeh compared the decline of Japan's regional rail network with the country's ever more sophisticated high-speed trains. During his travels on the old-style railroad system, he introduced the viewers to eccentric musicians who impersonate trains: for example "Train Idol," a woman who lives her life dressed as a conductor and surrounded by railroad memorabilia, and a cat that saved a station from closure by becoming a tourist attraction. Zarifeh also showed the latest maglev train that travels on a cushion of air and is capable of a top speed of 375 mph (600 km/h).

The old and new of the railroads were contrasted side by side, and Zarifeh questioned whether Japan would be diminished by losing the regional lines that have held local communities together, and having them replaced by ever faster trains that link megacities in record times.

Which brings us to whisky. The changes to the railroads—the uneasy balance between the old and the new—are reflected in Japan's whisky industry. The country's biggest producer, Suntory, now finds itself a long way from its roots and from the days when its founders were looking to Scotland for inspiration. Suntory was once a Japanese company serving its domestic market, but it has grown and made overseas acquisitions that have turned it into one of the biggest drinks companies in the world.

Suntory has two distilleries in Japan, but also under its wing are the two huge Jim Beam plants and Maker's Mark in the United States; and Laphroaig, Ardmore, Glen Garioch, Bowmore, Auchentoshan, and the blended whisky Teacher's in Scotland. Suntory's interests these days stretch way beyond its homeland.

There is no right or correct way to read a whisky label. Outside Scotland, whisky producers use terms and descriptors loosely and Japan is no exception. For example, you cannot use the word "pure" in Scotland but it is used regularly in Japan. For this reason whisky labeling can be confusing and can imply that a company makes a particular whisky when in fact they do not. This book has attempted as far as possible to make whisky names consistent for the reader, and the major whiskies mentioned are listed in the Whisky Directory on pp. 276–79.

YAMAZAKI 12 YEAR OLD_This classic Japanese whisky first came onto the market in 1984 and continues to be popular today.

There is nothing new about Japanese whisky. Japan has made its own since the 1920s, and its fascination with the spirit goes back to the 1850s, when a U.S. fleet arrived to negotiate a treaty that would force Japan to end its long period of isolation and begin trading with other nations.

The commodore of that fleet brought with him a barrel of American whiskey and another 110 gallons (416 liters) of liquor to present to the Emperor. It was then that the die was cast—Japan's obsession grew from that small and modest beginning.

Japan has had a long and steady relationship with alcohol. Sake, its increasingly respected rice wine, and the distilled spirits shōchū and awamori, have been produced and perfected over hundreds of years. So perhaps it should come as something of a surprise that the country took to a spirit made from malted barley, a grain not readily available in Japan. Although Japan has made beer for some 400 years, for most of that period this drink was either prohibitively expensive, or else was called beer but in fact was something totally different, a product almost certainly unacquainted with malted barley. For most of the twentieth century, Japanese government-approved beer was a dull, fizzy lager.

The search for whisky began sixty or seventy years before the legendary Japanese whisky pioneer Masataka Taketsuru traveled to Scotland in 1918 to learn how to distill "proper" single malt whisky, or Suntory founder Shinjiro Torii built the country's first distillery in 1923.

There is evidence that, in the second half of the nineteenth century, all kinds of concoctions were passed off as "whisky," often labeled "Scotch whisky," so it was only a matter of time before someone set about doing it properly. Nevertheless, for most of the twentieth century, Japanese whisky served only the domestic market, and when interest in the drink grew among young, fashionable Japanese, they looked to Scotland, not to their own local products.

Japanese whisky had to overcome numerous hurdles to reach the exalted status it enjoys today. Despite all the evidence to the contrary, there are still scores of people who won't accept that any whisky, let alone Japanese whisky, could ever match what Scotland produces. Japan's whiskies have an extra problem not faced by the likes of Ireland and the United States: they are whiskies that are made the same way as Scotland's, making direct comparisons unavoidable.

Let us tackle the question of impersonation right away. It is true that Japan was considerably inspired by Scotland and adopted the Scottish spelling of whisky as opposed to the Irish and American one, whiskey. It would be wrong to pretend that Japan's whisky industry hasn't been vastly influenced by the whiskies of Scotland. The whole story of the "birth" of Japanese whisky is based on a whisky education in Scotland, and the sites for the distilleries of Japan were chosen because they reflected many of the conditions found in Scotland. More than that, while other countries, particularly the United States, have whisky industries that are diverse, and make whiskies with a range of grain and in a range of different styles, Japan has stayed close to the Scottish whisky blueprint—single malts, vatted malts, blended whiskies, and occasional grain whiskies.

There are other reasons why comparisons between the whiskies of both countries are understandable. Although Japan has some barley—mugicha is a popular tea made with roasted barley—it imports Scottish barley for whisky making and uses mainly traditional oak casks that previously held bourbon or sherry. Then there's Japanese blended whisky. To make a top-quality, blended whisky, you need to have a lot of different malts to provide the complex array of flavors. In Scotland, there is an arrangement between whisky producers to exchange spirits, so that each blender has the broadest possible choice. That simply doesn't happen in Japan. It's the nature of business there not to share with rivals. Even if that were not the case, Suntory and Nikka own only two Japanese distilleries each. There are only two ways to get over

TONKOTSU, LONDON_ This bar has a selection of more than sixty Japanese whiskies, which customers can match with the ramen dishes on offer.

that problem: either you equip your distilleries with stills in different shapes and sizes, and of different types, use a range of yeasts, and mature the various spirits in different styles of casks; alternatively, you can bring in the spirit from overseas. In Japan, both solutions have been adopted. The distilleries owned by Suntory and Nikka are incredibly complex, and they are capable of producing dozens of different malts. It is the second way of improving their range that has raised eyebrows.

Japan is not alone in importing malt whisky from Scotland and using it in what it calls blended whisky: India has any number of such whiskies; Canada permits its distillers to add other liquids to their creations, and some—owned by distilling companies in Kentucky—add bourbon. Destilerias y Crianza, Suntory Beam's distillery in Spain, adds Laphroaig and Ardmore to its domestic blends. However, since the huge success of Japanese whiskies in international competitions put them well and truly into the spotlight, some commentators have suggested that the practice is wrong and should be abandoned.

It is far too simplistic to dismiss Japanese whiskies as little more than "me too" Scotches. Those working in Japanese distilleries analyze and improve to the point of perfection, and Scotland has clearly served as their major influence. However, from the outset, Suntory founder Shinjiro Torii aimed to create whisky suited to the Japanese palate, and the more you taste Japanese whisky, the more you realize how diverse and varied it is, how complex many of the spirits are, and how many of the aromas and flavors can be found nowhere else. If whisky can vary so significantly across Scotland, or between Sweden and Australia, then it is almost inevitable that Japanese whisky will be something else again.

In broad terms, there are two basic ways of making whisky: either the same way as the Scots—in which case it needs to be very good, because they have been doing it for a long time—or by doing something different, as with bourbon and some of the experimental grain whiskeys coming out of the United States.

LAPHROAIG DISTILLERY
This distillery on Islay, Scotland, is one of several world distilleries owned by Suntory Beam.

INTRODUCTION 17

TOP: POT STILLS_These are used during the traditional method of making single malt whisky in both Scotland and Japan.
BOTTOM LEFT: BARLEY_Most Japanese distilleries use imported grain. **BOTTOM RIGHT: BLENDING**_Samples for blending whisky.

PEAT_This is used to make Japan's smoky whisky. **WOOD**_Ex-bourbon and ex-sherry wood is used in Japan.

Let's drill down a little farther. All styles of whisky are made with grain, yeast, and water. Making whisky can be done in one of two ways—by using a pot still, or by using a column or continuous still. Japan makes use of both methods, and so does Scotland. There are five styles of whisky—single malt, vatted malt, blended malt, single grain, and multigrain. Japan makes all of them. Again, so does Scotland. The other two major contributors to a whisky's flavor are the peat used to dry the barley, and the wood in which the malt spirit is matured. Here again, both Japan and Scotland follow pretty much the same path.

These are critical times for Japanese whisky. In 2015, after years of shortages, crisis point was reached, and Nikka announced that it was scrapping age statement whisky for expressions with no age on the label, which allows for the producers to bottle whisky younger to meet escalating demand. This has happened a lot across the whisky world.

There is nothing wrong with that in principle, and so far both Suntory and Nikka's un-aged releases have maintained the high standards expected of them. New distillery Chichibu has released whiskies that were aged for only three or four years, but which have been of a consistently high standard.

The limits on choice imposed by Nikka on consumers by removing several components of its range aren't good, but they also signal a much more serious problem for the company. Nikka said it had made the changes to avoid running out of whisky and having to close down altogether. Suntory, too, has faced big supply problems. It could well be that between 2001 and 2016, the period this book seeks to document, those of us who were lucky enough to have had access to Japanese whisky were enjoying a "golden window," through which the very best Japanese whiskies were readily available. That window is now closed, and it may be years before it reopens—and even then, perhaps only partly.

So where does that leave Japanese whisky in the future? With the exception of a small number of whisky writers and a handful of other experts, many of them featured in this book, there has been little attempt to move beyond the shorthand and to understand the sophisticated, considered, and beautifully executed qualities of Japan's fine single malts, vatted malts, and blended whiskies. Japanese whisky has only relatively recently started to emerge from the fog of ignorance, but it remains an enigma and a curiosity.

Why? Partly because, while it has a history stretching back more than a century, the average non-Japanese consumer would still consider it "new." Partly because, while most people have heard of Japanese whisky, few have actually seen it, and fewer have tasted it. Partly because the Japanese whisky industry has not marketed itself well.

I have many fond memories of my encounters with Japan and its whiskies, but one of the greatest was a day tasting whiskies with Suntory's global brand ambassador Mike Miyamoto and listening to his amazing insights. In one afternoon and over every expression of Yamazaki and Hakushu, he took me on a journey to the heart of what Japanese whisky is all about. He explained the reasons for the complexity and diversity, and he provided a fascinating insight into the immense amount of thought that Japanese whisky makers put into perfecting their malts and blends.

Yet I have not been under any illusion as to what I was taking on with this book and what my limitations would be. When I finally started writing, in September 2015, I contacted several people with far more knowledge than I will ever have. Early on, I received an email from Stefan Van Eycken, chief editor of the excellent and essential Japanese whisky website Nonjatta. He described the idea as "ambitious," and said I was a brave man for undertaking it. I suspect he thinks I'm a little crazy.

Had I been trying to write the definitive guide to whisky production, and an insider's view of the complex distilleries in Japan, he would have been correct: to do the technical side of the Japanese whisky industry justice is the writer's equivalent of climbing Mount Everest. There have been extensive attempts to do this in English in the past, and they have not all ended well. There will no doubt be ambitious attempts to try to do this in the future, too. Stefan tells me that he has spent two years working on such a project, and I still hope he completes it. There is a clear need for an accurate "techie" book on Japanese whisky.

However, this book is not it. *Whisky Japan* is a work of investigative journalism. It sets out to look at where Japanese whisky came from and how it got to where it is. It's a "zero to hero" story, an attempt to explain how a whisky nation went from being all but a secret beyond its own shores to being honored and exalted as the world's most exotic and exciting producer.

Along the way, I've looked at the country's distilleries, highlighted the best Japanese whisky bars and restaurants in Japan and abroad, and spoken to many of the people who made the Japanese whisky revolution happen. I have also provided tasting notes for a selection of the finest malts that made it from Japan into the outside world.

However, while researching this book, I also came across a number of whiskies made intermittently, and often only in tiny quantities. They are occasional diversions by sake and shōchū producers. These products, known as "ji-whisky," are defined by the blog website of Tokyo's leading retailer Dekantā as "whisky made by small local distillers that is usually not sold nationwide, but only sold in the local area in which it is produced. In Japanese, the term is written as '地ウィスキー,' in which the '地' denotes 'local' or 'area.' It is, in other words, the Japanese word for what are commonly called local whiskies in English."

Ji-whisky is often made on the same equipment as that used for sake and shōchū, and much of it tastes decidedly different from whiskies made by large producers. There are some excellent whiskies in this category, but anyone trying them is urged to approach with an open mind.

The blink-and-you'll-miss-them nature of bottlings such as these, as well as the large number of whiskies produced exclusively for the domestic market, suggest that it would be almost impossible to compile a comprehensive list of such bottlings, and it is to Dekantā's credit that its website is as thorough as it is, but these whiskies have not been included in this book.

I hope that I have provided a sense of the sophistication, nuance, and quality of Japanese whisky, and created a starting point for many who have heard of it but are yet to be seduced by it. This book doesn't provide any of the technical answers or unlock the secrets of this unique country's multifaceted whiskies, but I hope that it at least raises plenty of questions.

So what sets Japan apart and makes its whiskies different? As we will see, there are a number of factors, starting with Japan's location, its exposure to the elements, the way its distilleries operate, and the way the spirit is matured. First of all, however, let's take a look at how the Japanese started drinking whisky.

Kampai!

STRAIGHT FROM THE BARREL_ Matured whisky ready for tasting, then bottling, at the Yamazaki Distillery.

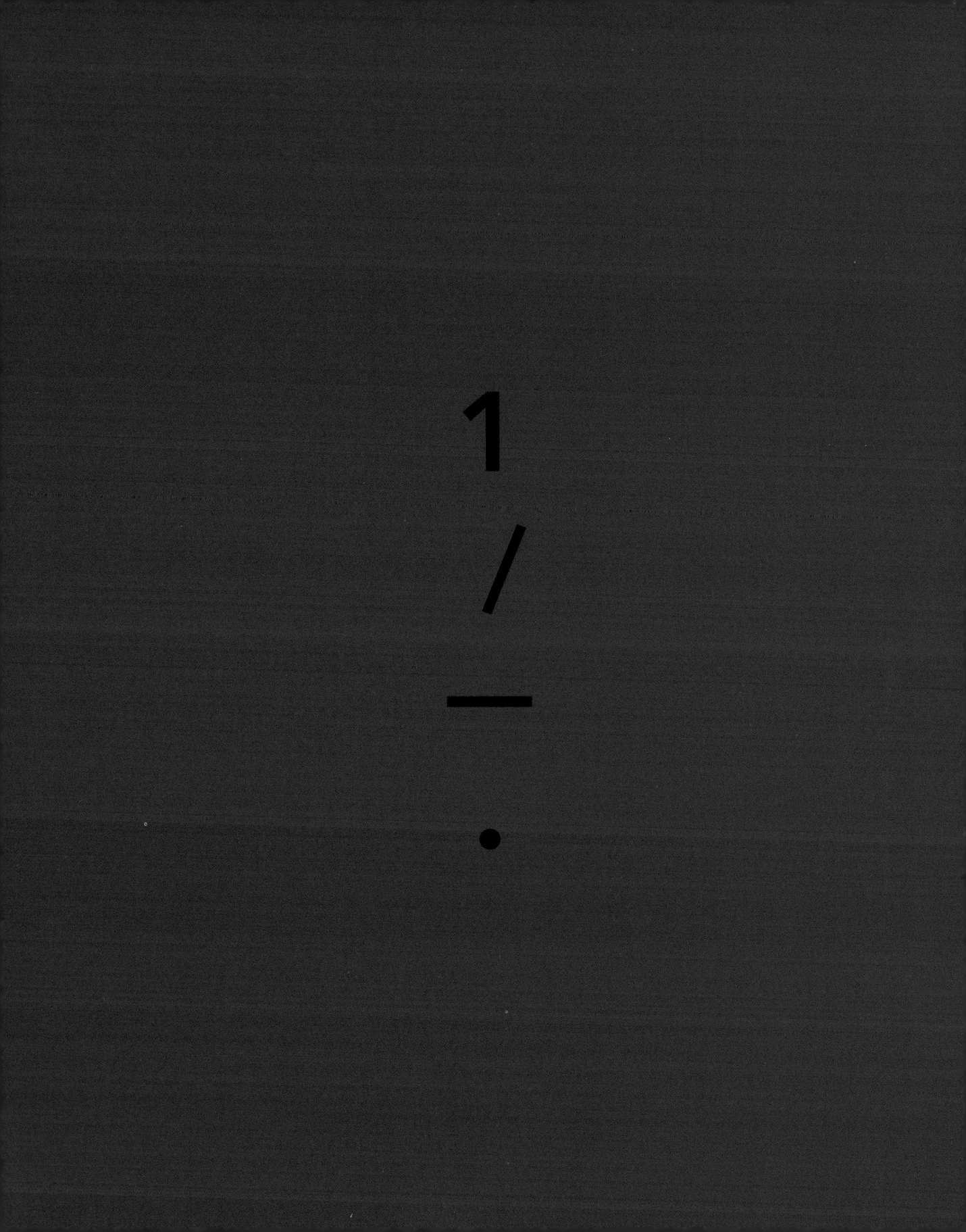

CHAPTER ONE

•

THE HISTORY OF JAPANESE WHISKY

日本のウィスキー史

Suggest to some people that Japan is one of the five traditional or established whisky nations, and you'll be faced with a few raised eyebrows. However, within whisky circles it is recognized as such, and Japanese distillers are proud of their place among the whisky world's biggest hitters.

For many, Japanese whisky is considered new for a number of reasons, not least because of its relative scarcity. Out of sight has not only meant out of mind; it has meant that, for many people, Japanese whisky is still at the stage of percolating its way through into our lives, and has not yet fully achieved its place on our whisky shelves.

It is true that its history in the West is relatively new, and goes back only to the start of the current millennium. Yet whisky within Japan has a long and colorful history stretching back well over 100 years. It's just that the vast majority of it has stayed within Japan's borders.

What information you will find on the subject has come mainly from the country's two main producers, Suntory and Nikka. And both companies have been selective in their recollection of the country's formative whisky years. They point to the 1920s as a starting point but, as we shall see, this isn't the whole story; far from it. For political reasons, there are periods when the whisky thread becomes all but invisible, and you have to dig pretty deep. But it's always there, and it tells a unique story of the flexibility, foresight, passion, and skill of generations of whisky makers who developed an industry that served the tastes of a drink-loving nation, and eventually extended its appeal to fans across the world.

Here, then, is an account of how Japanese whisky took a few embers from Scotland's whisky industry and went on to set the world on fire.

SHINJIRO TORII AND MASATAKA TAKETSURU

The importance of Shinjiro Torii and Masataka Taketsuru in the birth of genuine Japanese whisky is well documented, and most of the details are beyond dispute. With the passage of time, however, their story has become rather two-dimensional. The central characters seem to appear as if by magic in the early part of the twentieth century, seemingly with a passion, acquired overnight, to produce whisky in the same way as the Scots. More than that, the interpretation of events by the leading companies involved in the story—Suntory and Nikka—is selective in the extreme. And "selective" may be putting it kindly. Here is Suntory's take on events: Shinjiro Torii headed a company named Kotobukiya, which launched Akadama, a fortified wine; the product became a big hit. According to the Suntory website:

"Based on the money earned by the success, Shinjiro was determined to create a whisky which suits the delicate Japanese palate. Although such a challenge was believed to be impossible to achieve, he was propelled to create an authentic Japanese whisky."

Those early efforts weren't very good, and considerable investment of time and money was channeled into improving and perfecting the blending and distilling process before a whisky the company was satisfied with was ready for release in the year 1929. The Suntory Whisky Shirofuda was described as the first authentic whisky ever made in Japan, and so pleased was Suntory with it that the company announced that it had made a whisky on a par with true Scotch, an accomplishment that was showcased in newspaper advertisements declaring that there would be "no more imports needed." The whisky did not sell well, but this failure prompted the release of the Kakubin whisky in 1937, which was much more successful.

SUNTORY IN THE EARLY DAYS_ The company worked hard to improve its blending process after the initial failure of Suntory Whisky Shirofuda.

SHINJIRO TORII_ The founder of Suntory, who set out to make whisky for the Japanese palate.

Nikka regards the history somewhat differently. Its take on the story has Masataka Taketsuru, a young man intending to take on the family sake business, studying as a chemist and then getting the chance to go to Scotland. While there, Taketsuru became fascinated with Scotch whisky, and as he learned more about it, he decided that making whisky would be his calling. He enrolled at the University of Glasgow and became the first Japanese person to study the art of whisky making. He took chemistry courses at the university and apprenticed at the distilleries, where he learned firsthand from craftsmen. Masataka would later become a master blender.

That Scotland should have had such a major influence on the Japanese whisky industry is in large part a consequence of the efforts of Jessie Roberta Cowan, known as Rita, who married Masataka Taketsuru in Scotland, returned to Japan with him, and then spent nearly forty years at his side, supporting him as he built his business and earning the title of "mother of Japanese whisky." A daily TV soap opera featuring Rita has won a large following in Japan, and without doubt she was a rock through several turbulent years, including the duration of World War II, when there was a national reaction against anything or anyone from the West. These were difficult times for Westerners in Japan, but Rita stood firm alongside her husband.

ABOVE_TORII FAMILY
Their modest family business has now become one of the world's biggest drinks companies.

ABOVE RIGHT_MASATAKA TAKETSURU AND RITA COWAN
Taketsuru traveled to Scotland to study distilling, where he met and married Jessie Rita Cowan, who returned with him to Japan and lived there for forty years.

ANCIENT ROOTS AND WESTERN INFLUENCE

Read the previous two stories closely, and you'll find omissions or half-truths in both. So where does the real truth lie in all of this? Well, first, Japanese whisky didn't exactly become an overnight sensation. Japan has a long relationship with alcohol that goes back centuries, and Japan's drinking culture is complex. Sake, wine, and beer are consumed in vast quantities; dignified spirits, such as shōchū and awamori, have complex, nuanced histories.

However, Japan's thirst for spirits isn't slaked domestically, and in his authoritative guide *Drinking Japan,* Chris Bunting makes a compelling case for why Japan is the best place in the world to drink alcohol, on the grounds that its top-grade bars offer great selections of the finest drinks from across the world, including single malt whisky, as well as offering scores of domestically produced drinks. Nowhere, he argues, brings so many different alcoholic drinks together better than Japan does. This interest in, and passion for, Western-style alcoholic products is not new.

BELOW LEFT_AWAMORI
A distilled Japanese alcoholic drink originally from Okinawa.

BELOW_WESTERN-STYLE JAPANESE BEER
Japan has a long history of alcoholic drinks, and no other country offers more variety to its visitors.

TOP_COMMODORE MATTHEW PERRY
He arrived in Japan in 1854, bringing whiskey from the United States.

ABOVE_THE OPENING OF JAPAN
A painting re-creates the historical opening of Japan, when Perry met with the Imperial Commissioners at Yokohama and, on March 31, 1854, the Convention of Kanagawa was signed.

Nikka's account of history includes the sentence: "Scotch whisky captured the young man's imagination, as well as the interest of a few other enterprising Japanese of that day." Japan was well aware of what was happening elsewhere, and of the quality of Scotch whisky. Even when Japan was "closed" to Western trade, news of whisky was getting through.

"The Japanese kept close tabs on things foreign through their experts in 'Dutch studies' and through Dutch traders given limited rights to trade," reports Japanese blog website Nonjatta. "What is certain is that whisky, or rather whiskey, arrived simultaneously with Japan's opening to the West. When Commodore Matthew Perry came in his black ships to negotiate a treaty with Japan in 1854, he brought with him a barrel and 110 additional gallons (416 liters) of American whiskey as a gift for the Emperor and his subjects."

It would be another sixty years before anyone from Japan traveled to Scotland to learn distilling officially, but in that time, interest in whisky from North America had transferred to whisky from Scotland. Perhaps the interest was fueled by the growing number of trade missions in the second half of the nineteenth century, although how much interaction there was between the visiting sailors and the local population is a moot point. In *Life of a Sailor*, Admiral of the Fleet Sir William May breaks from his narrative to report darkly on his visit to Tokyo:

"In those days the Japanese had an intense dislike for all foreigners, and even in Yokohama one had to be careful not to offend any of the Japanese. When we visited Tokyo, the capital (then called Yeddo), we had to have an escort of cavalry."

In his definitive *The World Atlas of Whisky*, Dave Broom identifies the year and even the brand that may well have opened the door, not just for Scotch whisky, but for Western-style spirits in general: the arrival in 1872 of a case of Old Parr with the Iwakura Trade Mission.

SHINJIRO TORII AND MASATAKA TAKETSURU

RIGHT_LONGMORN DISTILLERY
This distillery in Speyside is the first place Masataka Taketsuru worked in Scotland.

BELOW RIGHT_SUNTORY STAFF
Suntory workers pose for a photograph at the company's first distillery.

Certainly, from this period there is evidence that some Japanese companies were turning to the laboratory to produce Western-style spirits. Bottles claiming to be whisky were found to contain grain spirit mixed with fruit juice, spices, and perfume. Bottles with the words "Old Scotch" or "Scottish liqueur" were in circulation. Both Torii and Taketsuru worked for companies involved in the manufacture of Western-style spirits.

Broom rightly makes the point that it is "fundamentally wrong" to point to these laboratory spirits and conclude that Japan merely copied what Scotland was doing, and that Japanese whisky was conceived primarily through science and not through the environment.

What happened next demonstrates this perfectly. Given the divisions in language and culture that still exist today, consider how amazing it was that Masataka Taketsuru took it upon himself to travel to Glasgow to become the first Japanese person to study distilling, and then knock on distillery doors until he was taken on to train, first at Longmorn and then at Hazelburn, and to spend a few months learning blending at Bo'ness.

There's another thing, too. While writing this book, I was sent a picture from the family behind La Alazana Distillery in Argentina. Pictured alongside the distillery owners was legendary Scottish distiller Jim McEwan, now retired. It struck me that perhaps we don't highlight enough the hospitality and generosity of Scottish whisky folk, and their willingness to help and share. It's a trait that clearly stretches back 100 years, and it is still in evidence today.

Taketsuru found lodgings with the Cowan family while in Scotland, and within a couple of years had married Rita, who traveled back to Japan with him in 1920. Rita was to play an essential role in the development of Taketsuru's business in the following years.

YAMAZAKI DISTILLERY
An early photograph of the Yamazaki Distillery, which first opened in 1923, in the Vale of Yamazaki.

Initially, Taketsuru worked for Torii's company, Kotobukiya, which had made a lot of money with reinforced and sweet wines. Torii was, from the outset, determined to find a whisky that suited Japanese palates, and he identified a site on Honshu that was perfect for whisky making. It included a source of fresh water and the climate was humid.

Taketsuru had other ideas, however. He wanted to create a distillery with a geography and climate closely aligned to those of Scotland.

Both views had everything to do with the location and environment, and although Taketsuru helped Torii open Japan's first whisky distillery, Yamazaki, and to launch the country's first proper whisky, the partnership was destined not to last. In 1934, Taketsuru split to create his new company Dainippokaju, later renamed Nikka, and to set up the Yoichi Distillery on the northern island of Hokkaido.

ECONOMIC FLUX

All this occurred at the start of an unpredictable and potentially fatal period for Japan and its industries. In 1937, open fighting between China and Japan broke out, and, in 1941, Japan entered World War II, with disastrous consequences. Bizarrely, however, while the Japanese people were living in poverty and hunger, Japan's whisky distilleries were given preferred military status. Throughout the 1930s and 1940s, the Imperial Navy, in particular, took whisky as its drink of choice, and Yoichi even became a naval base.

In purely economic terms, this was just as well, because Nikka had lost a lot of money in the early 1930s. Taketsuru and Rita worked hard to keep the business running, and as antipathy toward the West grew, life became difficult as Rita was subject to abuse and suspicion from the people among whom she lived.

The extreme poverty continued after World War II, but again it was the military that saved Japanese whisky, this time in the form of the occupying U.S. forces. When some wealth did return to the economy, Japan's youth drowned their memories of the country's past by drinking whisky in booming bars. By the mid-1950s, Suntory had established 1,500 "Torys bars" to take advantage of the trend of company workers—known as "salarymen"—to drink whisky after work, a practice that has been ingrained in Japanese culture ever since.

What goes up must come down; the boom times didn't last. Japanese vacationers and businessmen started traveling abroad more, and more women entered the workplace, as well as the clubs and bars. Younger drinkers turned their backs on the strong taste of Japanese whisky and replaced it with cocktails and fruit-based drinks. As a result, Japanese whisky was badly hit. A new generation of younger drinkers either dismissed it as an old person's drink, or if they did seek out whisky, it was Scottish single malt.

However, the blog website Nonjatta firmly makes the point that the seeds were already sown for the rise of Japanese whisky well before Shinjiro Torii and Masataka Taketsuru "wrote" the early chapters in Japanese whisky's story. It's also equally true that Japanese whisky didn't require the involvement of Westerners to succeed.

ABOVE_A TORYS BAR
Suntory set up bars to serve its whiskies to thirsty salarymen.

RIGHT_U.S. FORCES
The thirst of occupying American forces in Japan saved the flagging Japanese whisky industry after World War II.

GAI-ATSU

While Japanese whisky makers have proved adept at making and selling their product, a leading retailer uses the Japanese term "gai-atsu" to describe the industry. This refers to the fact that, in order to succeed, Japan needs pressure from foreigners. It derives from the belief that Japan's political leaders wouldn't take tough decisions unless they were pushed to do so by overseas influence, because of an overwhelming fear of the shame of failure.

It's a term that you could apply to the "gunboat diplomacy" that led to Japan opening its borders for trade in the 1820s, and simultaneously introduced the first taste of American whiskey to the Japanese. It's arguably of equal relevance to Japanese whisky in the first few years of the current millennium. Japan created its whisky, all on its own. It learned quickly through trial and error, all on its own. The two main producers had successfully brought Japanese whisky to the domestic market, and had correctly predicted the trends toward premium whisky, and to single malt, and to blended malt whisky, all on their own.

It took gai-atsu to create the success story that is Japanese whisky today. Over the following pages, there will be a considerable number of Western people taking up the narrative, but that's because in the period during which Japanese whisky went from unknown to the most-feted drink of its kind in the world, it took a number of Westerners to lead the way. This in no way devalues the incredible whisky-making skills of the distillery workers, warehousemen, distillers, and blenders in Japan, but it is an acknowledgment of (and a nod of gratitude to) the fact that, throughout the golden period of 2001 to 2016, a relatively small number of people tapped into a rich seam of quality whisky, and through their love and passion they were able to overcome the barriers that Japanese culture and language put in the way. They also make a neutral and objective case for why it's worthwhile to seek out the bars and restaurants that promote and sell Japanese whisky, to pay a little extra to taste some of the whisky delights from the East, and perhaps even learn more about the country and travel to its distilleries.

CHAPTER TWO

•

MAKING JAPANESE WHISKY

日本のウィスキーづくり

It has been said that there are two ways to make whisky: like the Scots do, in which you had better be very good, or some other way. Japanese distillers make whisky the Scottish way. And they are very good at it.

Japanese whisky makers are quick to acknowledge the influence of Scotland on all their output. They point proudly to the fact that their pioneer whisky makers learned their trade directly from the Scots, and pay homage to the influence the country has had on them ever since. When a Japanese whisky was voted the best whisky in the world by the world's leading experts in 2001, its producers took enormous satisfaction in being considered alongside the finest Scotches.

However, it would be a big mistake to assume that Japanese whisky is simply a pale copy of what the Scots are doing. It is much more than that.

The process of making single malt whisky, grain whisky, and blends is pretty much the same wherever whisky is made. Yet, as we shall see, Japan has examined the process, and tweaked it to suit the tastes of its home market. And while the process is pretty much the same, the way Japanese distillers combine stills of different sizes and types into an elaborate jigsaw puzzle is distinctly different.

The main Japanese distillers make scores—possibly hundreds—of different malts and grain whiskies, and combine them in different ways to make their blended whiskies. They mature their spirits in different casks, including some made from the country's unique mizunara oak, to produce single malts that are distinctively not the same as Scottish equivalents. The results are whiskies that fans of Scottish single malts can appreciate and cherish, but which take the drinker on new and exciting journeys.

JAPAN'S GEOGRAPHY AND CLIMATE

Much is made among whisky connoisseurs of geography and location, and, increasingly, distillers are starting to talk about "terroir" in the same way as the wine industry does. But technological progress means that there is now greater flexibility than ever before on where whisky can be made. For example, it is no longer essential to be next to a soft water source, and extremes of heat cannot only be overcome, they can be harnessed into a force for good. Water is the main requirement. Lots and lots of it, and ideally, icy cool.

Japan has a complex geography and climate, but it ticks the right boxes when it comes to distilling. Japan consists of hundreds of islands but is dominated by four of them: Hokkaido, Kyushu, Shikoku, and the largest of them all, Honshu, where the capital Tokyo lies. Tokyo faces the Pacific Ocean on the eastern side of the country, while to the west, the Sea of Japan separates Japan from its nearest neighbors: South Korea, North Korea, China, and Russia.

When you see the country on a map alongside its huge Asian neighbors, Japan seems tiny. In fact, it covers about the same land area as California. Much of the country is inhabitable. More than 50 percent of the country is mountainous and covered by forests. Rivers, many of them unnavigable, cut across the land.

Japan's distilleries are stretched across the main island of Honshu, with four clustered in the center of the island, one to the north of the island, and two farther south. The sites they occupy have been chosen because of the favorable climate, an abundance of water, and their proximity to the population centers, in particular, Tokyo.

TOP AND ABOVE_MOUNT FUJI
Two views of famous Mount Fuji on the island of Honshu. Conditions in this region are ideal for whisky making.

RIGHT_HAKUSHU DISTILLERY
Suntory's second distillery—known as "the forest distillery"—is one of the world's prettiest.

There are distilleries removed from the urban centers, too. At the other end of Japan, on the island of Hokkaido, one distillery, Yoichi, is in operation and another, Akkeshi, is planned. Here, there are conditions considered to be closest to those found in Scotland, with snowy winters, plenty of water, and peat beds that may offer potential in the future. The advantage here, of course, is that there is plenty of water to make the whisky, and plenty of cool water to recondense the evaporated whisky spirit once it has been distilled.

Because there is such a great distance from north to south, the climate varies substantially. To put it in context, Japan's northernmost islands are located on a similar geographical latitude to Portland, Oregon, and almost directly across from Yoichi is Vladivostok. At the other extreme, the country's southernmost islands are on the same latitude as the Bahamas.

ABOVE_PEAT BEDS
Most peat is imported, but distilleries, such as Chichibu, are eager to use only local resources.

RIGHT_FRESH WATER
Japan is blessed with an abundance of cold and clean water.

The climate in most of the major cities, including Tokyo, is temperate to subtropical and consists of four seasons. The winters are mild, and the summers are hot and humid. There is a rainy season in the early summer, and typhoons hit parts of the country every year during late summer. Whisky production is affected by these factors, because heat speeds up maturation, and humidity affects the amount of spirit that is lost in the production process.

The climate of the northern island of Hokkaido and the Sea of Japan coast is colder, and snow falls in large quantities. In Okinawa, on the other hand, the mean January temperature is a moderate 63°F (17°C). Cold weather will slow down maturation, and variations in temperature will accelerate it.

Latitude and longitude are not the only considerations that influence climate, however. Ocean currents, such as the Kuroshio and Tsushima currents from the south, warm the islands on the Pacific side, and those near the Korean straits, especially toward the south. Meanwhile, the cold Kurile current, coming southward toward Hokkaido, brings plentiful nourishment to the coastal waters and improves the fishing. Again, any influence on temperature will affect whisky maturation.

Cold winds from northern Asia blow east over the Sea of Japan, bringing deep, heavy snowfalls to the northwestern coasts. There is a big difference between winters on the coast facing the Sea of Japan, known as Japan's "snow country," and the clear, crisp winters on the eastern shore, with little snow at all, leaving dry winters on the more heavily populated side of the main islands.

CLIMATE VARIATION IN JAPAN

SAPPORO | HOKKAIDO
- **Rain:** 312,000 gallons (1,180 kiloliters) a year
- **Humidity:** 70.8% annual humidity, rising to 80% in July
- **Snow:** 131 days a year

OSAKA | HONSHU
- **Rain:** 494,000 gallons (1,870 kiloliters) a year
- **Humidity:** 65.4% humidity
- **Snow:** No snow throughout the year

FAR LEFT_MOUNT ECHIGO-KOMAGATAKE
View of Mount Echigo-Komagatake at Ginzandaira, in the Koshinetsu Region, Uonuma.

LEFT_JAPANESE COAST SASAGAWA-NAGARE
The Sasagawa-Nagare coastline facing the Sea of Japan. Winters can be cold here.

ABOVE AND NEXT PAGE_LAKE KAWAGUCHI AND MOUNT FUJI
Mountain snow ensures that plenty of water is available for distillation and recondensation.

Temperature averages in Sapporo on Hokkaido near Yoichi are 23°F (-5°C) in January and February to 72°F (22°C) in August, whereas at Osaka, close to Yamazaki Distillery, the temperature varies from 39°F (4°C) in January to 82°F (28°C) in August. Temperatures may climb into the 90s°F (mid-30s°C).

Even on the eastern shores, however, Japan has abundant rainfall, because seasonal winds carry moisture into the country from its surrounding waters. In fact, in addition to the four seasons similar to those of the U.S. temperate zone climate, there is a rainy season, lasting about a month in June, followed by a hot summer.

All these factors affect the country's ability to make whisky. An abundance of fresh, cold water that runs off the mountains, copious amounts of snow, and variations in temperature all influence fermentation, distillation, and maturation. There is a big difference between the climates faced by Yoichi in the far northwest and those of Miyashita and Yamazaki in the south. There are significant climatic differences within Honshu, too, with Hakushu in the mountainous regions in the north and west, and White Oak and Yamazaki facing down to the Pacific.

MAKING SINGLE MALT WHISKY

The process of making single malts is more or less identical wherever it is used. What makes it so extraordinary is the fact that it produces so much variety. Every cask of finished whisky is different, and the magic of malt is that no one can fully control the final aromas and flavors, and these will vary significantly not just from country to country, or region to region, but from one cask to another, even when they have been filled with exactly the same spirit from the same run, and stored next to each other for exactly the same length of time.

It should come as no surprise, then, that after nearly a century of making whisky, Japan's distillers have taken their whiskies into new and uncharted territories.

The process of making single malt whisky is a simple one. To summarize it in one sentence: It is a batch process, which means that the distiller starts with raw ingredients, makes a distiller's beer through fermentation, distills it into malt spirit, stores it in wood barrels to mature, and then starts all over again.

THE THREE INGREDIENTS
These are the three essential ingredients needed for making whisky. Left: yeast; above: water; right: dried grain before it is ground into flour; far right: flour made from dry grain.

INGREDIENTS
Single malt whisky is made with three basic ingredients: grain, yeast, and water.

GRAIN
Throughout the years, grain has been upgraded to produce higher yields, however, considerable experimentation is going on across the industry to assess the impact of lower-yielding grains on overall quality, and to analyze regional variations in grain production.

YEAST
Yeast affects flavor, and, in Japan, the use of yeast is complex and secretive. Each distillery has several yeasts, and information about them is closely guarded.

WATER
There is a lot of romance surrounding the water used to make whisky. You'll often hear it said that the soft water of the Spey is best suited to making soft, fruity whisky, but it isn't quite that simple. Water can be treated, so hard water is now less of a challenge. Whisky is made from beer, and beer brewers know that beer fermentation is best suited to hard water. Japan has both soft and hard water, and, of course, what the water has passed through plays a role in the mineral content of the whisky. The most important aspects of water are its cleanliness and purity, and the fact that there is a lot of it at a sufficiently low temperature to recondense the whisky spirit back into liquid.

MALTING AND MASHING

Malting is the process by which the barley is "tricked" into growing by the addition of warm water. Then, after a few days, the growing process is ended by heating the grain. When making a peaty whisky, it is at this stage that the flavor is imparted by drying some of the barley over peat fires.

When the barley starts to grow, the shoots break the grain's husk, giving access to the starches and enzymes needed to make alcohol. After this process has taken place for a few days, it needs to be stopped, and this is done by drying the barley. These days, this is accomplished with electric heaters, but if the distiller is looking to make a peaty whisky, then this is the part of the process where the peat flavor is imparted by drying the barley in the traditional way, over a peat fire.

After drying, the barley is crushed into flour and put into large mash tuns, where hot water is added. The process is not unlike making a cup of tea. The waters release the starches and enzymes, and eventually the liquid can be separated from the husks. The resulting liquid, known as wort, is dark and sweet, and it is transferred to another holding vessel, known as a wash back.

BELOW LEFT_BARLEY
Malted barley that has started to grow.

BELOW_BURNING PEAT
The smoke will impart the whisky with its characteristic smoky, peaty taste.

TRADITIONAL METHOD
This is a traditional wooden wash back at Chichibu Distillery. Here, yeast is added to the wash to start the fermenting process.

FERMENTING
To this wort is added the yeast, which feeds off the sugars and starches to form carbon dioxide and alcohol. This fermentation process may take anywhere from 45 hours to 145 hours, and, when it is complete, the product is known as distiller's beer, or wash. It will have an alcoholic strength of 7–11%, and it is sour, like a Belgian lambic beer. It differs from brewery beer in that it is purposely prepared in unsterilized conditions, and this is important, because the bacteria it contains are crucial to the distilling process.

Fermentation times can vary massively, depending on the conditions in which a distillery operates. Traditionally, Scottish distillers have paid less attention to this part of the process, but that is changing. Distilleries are increasingly looking to the beer industry. The quality, type, and temperature of water will affect the rate of fermentation, and therefore the qualities and taste of the wash created. The Speyside region of Scotland, for instance, has benefited from the rich, soft water of the Spey River and its tributaries.

DISTILLING

The wash is next placed into the first of two pot stills, known as the wash still. Pot stills are made of copper and are used to separate alcohol from water by boiling. The spirit passes up the copper still until it reaches a pipe toward the top of the still, known as the lyne arm.

The spirit passes into the lyne arm, where it is recondensed. On this first run, all the spirit is collected and then passed on to the second still, known as the spirit still.

This time around, the distiller wants to save only the part of the run that will be matured into whisky. When the spirit is heated, the first alcohols are the most volatile; they are also the strongest, the most dangerous, and the least pleasant. These are diverted and stored in their own tank. When the distiller is ready to collect the heart of the run, the spirit will be redirected into a central holding tank. This is known as "the cut." Eventually, after a certain amount of time, the alcohols will become too weak and grainy to be worth collecting, and they, too, will be directed elsewhere.

It's similar to cutting up a fish. You remove the unpleasant head, you keep the fleshy body, and you cut off the bony tail. Although the process is pretty much the same in every single malt distillery, subtle differences can make all the difference to the spirit produced.

The bigger the cut, the greater the number of flavor components that will be retained in the new-make spirit, and the richer and fruitier the spirit at the end. Some distilleries keep a relatively small amount of the body; others want a weightier, fuller spirit and make a bigger cut.

The three ingredients—grain, yeast, and water—will, of course, have some effect. However, there are other key factors, too, such as the shape and size of the still. Copper is used in distillation because it is a rough metal, and, as the spirit passes over it, fattier and oilier components in the spirit will be held back. The bigger the still, the longer the contact between the copper and the spirit, the more that will be removed, and the lighter the final spirit. Short, stubby stills make for heavier, more characterful spirits. Copper will react with sulfur in the spirit to form copper sulfate—again "cleaning up" the final spirit by removing a negative component.

All of these factors will influence the new-make spirit before it even goes into the cask.

POT STILLS_These are effectively huge copper kettles in which the wash is boiled, separating the alcohol from the water.

MAKING SINGLE MALT WHISKY 49

MATURATION

Up to three-quarters of the final flavor of a single malt whisky comes from its maturation. Nearly all whisky is matured in oak casks (although there are some exceptions), and that's because it's the perfect wood for the task. It's strong but pliable, it's porous but not leaky, and it lets air pass through it, allowing for oxidation during maturation. Four processes take place when whisky spirit is in the cask:

1. **THE SPIRIT GAINS FLAVOR AND COLOR:** With even mild temperature changes, the spirit will move inside the cask, where it expands and contracts. When it expands, it is forced into the wood, where it picks up color and flavor, partly from the wood and partly from the residue that has been left in the wood from the cask's previous use.
2. **COMPOUNDS ARE REMOVED:** The wood also works the other way around, too, removing some flavors from the spirit, often negative ones.
3. **CHEMICAL REACTION:** The wood and the spirit will react with each other, creating complicated flavor compounds that remind us of fruits, spices, or nuts, and so on.
4. **OXIDIZATION:** Finally, this takes place between the air coming into the cask and the spirit within it.

These elements make the process fairly homogenous, but there are a number of variants to take into account:

ABOVE_CASK VARIETIES
A selection of casks of different ages and sizes, all of which would be used to store whisky.

ABOVE RIGHT_MIZUNARA OAK
The tree that gives us Japan's unique mizunara oak, *Quercus mongolica*.

TYPE OF OAK USED

Oaks from different parts of the world vary enormously. European oak (*Quercus roba*) will absorb liquid in a totally different way from American oak (*Quercus alba*). French oak is different again, and Hungarian and East European oaks are highly porous. Australian oak can't be used for whisky making because it leaks. Japan has its own unique oak, mizunara (*Quercus mongolica*), which most certainly adds a unique quality to Japanese whisky.

WHAT THE CASK CONTAINED BEFORE

It is rare to make single malt whisky in a new cask made of virgin oak, because maturation in oak takes a long time, and the natural spiciness and flavors of the wood will quickly dominate and effectively destroy the subtle flavors of the malt spirit. So casks that have previously been used for something else are used. Normally, the cask has contained bourbon or sherry. A cask that previously held sherry will affect the taste of the spirit in a totally different way from one that held bourbon, both in terms of taste and color. Casks that previously held bourbon or sherry are most commonly used for whisky maturation. Various other spirits and wines have been used for maturation, some of them unique to one country. Japan has used casks that had previously contained sweet plum wine.

MIZUNARA OR JAPANESE OAK (*QUERCUS MONGOLICA*)

Japan has a unique species of oak, called mizunara. It has been used since the 1930s and was introduced in response to a shortage of oak from elsewhere. The war with China from 1937 and entry into World War II meant supplies of oak stopped, and Japan hardened its attitude to anything that was considered Western.

Mizunara gives whisky a unique set of flavors. The wood has extremely high levels of vanillins (phenolic aldehydes) but is soft and porous, which means that casks made with it are delicate, easy to damage, and potentially leaky. Like every other commercial distiller, Suntory and Nikka tend to use predominantly sherry and bourbon casks, but a proportion of their spirit will go into mizunara casks. Japanese companies have also responded to a worldwide interest in the characteristics that make their whisky unique. Some commentators talk about a mushroomy taste in old Japanese whisky—sometimes described as "umami," although this is misleading—others remark on the fruity, spicy, almost incenselike flavor associated with mizunara oak. Mizunara wood is sometimes used for finishing a whisky, and Suntory has experimented with the wood, releasing as a separate whisky the mizunara component of its Yamazaki 12 Year Old in 2014. In 2015 it brought three mizunara casks to Bowmore, Islay, and matured Scottish peaty whisky in the wood, with stunning results.

➤ Other descriptors you might see associated with this type of oak are honey, apples, pears, nutmeg, and cloves.

MAKING SINGLE MALT WHISKY

NUMBER OF TIMES THE CASK HAS BEEN USED BEFORE
A cask being filled with malt spirit for the first time after being used for sherry will have a greater effect on that spirit than one that is being filled with spirit for the second or third time.

THE SIZE OF THE CASK
There is a considerable difference in size between an American bourbon barrel, a port pipe, and a sherry butt. This matters, because the more contact the spirit has with the wood, the bigger the effect on the final product. For this reason, small quarter casks accelerate maturation.

AIR TEMPERATURE
The higher the temperature, the faster the chemical reaction in the cask. More than that, extremes of temperature, from very cold to hot, will also have an effect. When Indian distiller Amrut made Greedy Angels, an eight-year-old whisky, three-quarters of the malt was lost through evaporation (the spirit lost to the elements is known as "the angel's share," hence the name). But the whisky had a delightful "whisky rancio" flavor, which you don't find in Scottish single malt under twenty-five years old.

HUMIDITY
The amount of moisture in the air will affect whether water leaves the cask during maturation, making the spirit stronger, as happens on the higher floors of the bourbon distilleries of Kentucky, or whether it remains, as in Scotland, weakening the whisky spirit over time.

INNOVATION
Whisky makers have tinkered with all the above factors, and more beside. As we will see, Japan has its own approach to whisky making. Some whisky makers have gone farther, using different drying methods and woods other than oak for their casks. In Japan, they have experimented with different wood types—not least, by using the country's unique oak.

Japan has also experimented with the distillation process, making single malt whisky in the kind of still normally used for making grain whisky, known as the Coffey or continuous still. This process makes a different type of spirit from that which emerges from a pot still, because it doesn't separate the alcohol from the water by boiling the liquid but by using high-temperature steam under pressure. The result is a stronger, and distinctly different, spirit.

ABOVE LEFT_VIRGIN CASKS
New and frequently filled casks wait to be stored in a maturation warehouse.

LEFT_COLD TEMPERATURES
Extreme changes in temperature between the seasons can speed up the maturation process.

ABOVE_MATURATION
A typical maturation warehouse with stacked casks. The wood itself adds flavor to the whisky.

NEXT PAGE_USED BARRELS
These barrels have been used to mature whisky. Barrels are often charred before they are used for maturation.

DESCRIBING WHISKY THROUGH TASTING NOTES

All the above factors will provide flavors in a finished single malt whisky that have not been added by the distiller. There are no apples or cinnamon added—all of the flavors occur naturally and give us the wonderful and varied world of malt whisky.

In the tasting section of the book (see pp.112–137), a simple flavor wheel has been used to help you understand what to expect from a given whisky. The headings used—peat, fruit, wood, spice, and sherry—are, of course, oversimplistic. "Fruit" could be broken down into orange fruit, green fruit, and red fruit, for example, and then into individual fruits. There are scores of spices, and so on.

Of the five different headings we have used, four relate to the maturation process. Fruit is the only exception.

BLENDED MALT AND BLENDED WHISKY

The worlds of single malt production in Scotland and Japan run in parallel, but it's a different story when it comes to making blended malt and blended whiskies.

These are two distinct styles of whisky. Blended malt whisky is a mix of single malt whiskies from different distilleries. A blended whisky is a mix of single malts from different distilleries mixed with grain whisky. This is the style that dominates Scotch whisky, accounting for more than 90 percent of sales. In Japan, the process takes a new twist.

YAMAZAKI WHISKY LIBRARY
Several thousand bottles of unblended malt whisky are stored here in the Yamazaki Distillery. A quality blend is made up of dozens of different whiskies.

TOP_WHISKY BLENDING
Suntory's chief blender, Seiichi Koshimizu, working at Yamazaki Distillery.

ABOVE_WHISKY SAMPLES
Blending samples ready for nosing.

When defining a single malt whisky, the word "single" refers to the fact that the whisky is from only one distillery. A single malt whisky is not a whisky from one cask, although single cask whiskies are released. In fact, a single malt whisky will most often be a combination of a lot of casks, of different sizes and types, and aged for different periods of time. These are brought together in batches, with each batch intended to taste as close to the last batch as possible, so that the end drinker does not notice an inconsistency.

A Yamazaki single malt whisky is put together in the same way as a Lagavulin. However, let's start by questioning our conventional definitions. Add grain whisky and you have a blended whisky. But what if the grain is from the same distillery as the single malts? This is still a blend, but you could also call it a single blended whisky, because it's all from one distillery. If there is only one grain and one single malt, you could call it a Double Single, as Compass Box in London did. Or you can't, because Compass Box has trademarked the term. As we will see, Japan takes the whole definition issue several steps farther.

To make a good blend, a blender needs as many different flavors as possible. Blends can contain whiskies from dozens of distilleries. To make this happen, the distillers of Scotland swap their spirits with each other. With well over 100 single malt distilleries in Scotland, that provides the platform for the wonderful blended whiskies for which Scotland is renowned around the world.

This doesn't happen in Japan, which is known for fierce corporate rivalry within its domestic market—its global success partly results from it—and the whisky industry is no different. Since their initial fallout, the original heroes of Japanese whisky, Suntory and Nikka, have been bitter rivals and have had virtually nothing to do with each other. The idea of cooperation is completely alien to both of them, and they share any information that could aid a competitor reluctantly, preferring to operate behind a veil of secrecy.

Even if by some miracle that situation were to change, these two companies dominate Japanese whisky production, and they only have two distilleries each. So what to do?

There are only two ways around a problem such as this. One is to bring in whiskies from other parts of the world, and the other is to produce a considerable number of different styles of whisky within your existing distilleries. Suntory and

Nikka have done both, importing Scottish single malts to use in their blends and designing distilleries that are capable of making a lot of different whisky styles under the same roof.

All whisky companies are cagey when it comes to the composition of their blended whiskies, so it should come as no surprise to find that the big Japanese players are reluctant to give too much away. In the past, however, they have been criticized for a practice that puts a question mark over whether some Japanese blends are worthy of the title at all.

Thankfully, the alternative approach—of making as many different styles of new-make spirit as possible in each distillery and then maturing them in myriad different ways—is the normal way that Japan's producers overcome their limitations. As a result, Japan's biggest distilleries are highly sophisticated and complex, with an assortment of column and pot stills, yeast strains, and cask types, and each of the distilleries can produce dozens of different whisky spirits.

Japanese whisky has therefore taken a Scottish blueprint and quite deliberately tweaked it to suit a Japanese palate. It just happens that those tweaks have resulted in a range of whiskies that appeal equally to Western palates. They have been richly rewarded in world whisky competitions and feted by a growing body of whisky drinkers across the world.

Given that there are so few producers, the diversity among Japanese whisky styles is extraordinary. These styles range from huge, plummy, sherry-soaked, battering-ram oak, and industrial-strength peaty whiskies at one end, to whispering, delicate, floral, and throat-caressing gossamer at the other. And pretty much everything in between.

Over the following pages, we'll look at the main distilleries across Japan, and provide some information on how to get to them. These distilleries encompass practically everything you are likely to find in any bar or restaurant in or outside Japan.

WHISKY BLENDING
Japan has developed its own particular way of blending. Distilleries either bring in whiskies from other parts of the world or make different styles of whisky in the same distillery.

CHAPTER THREE

•

THE WHISKY DISTILLERIES OF JAPAN

日本のウィスキーの蒸留所

These are heady times for whisky worldwide, not only from Japan but also from a number of other countries, including many—such as Argentina, Taiwan, Israel, and Italy—that you might not associate with whisky. Many of the new distilleries start off small, and it's one of the quirks of the whisky industry that, once the publicity over announcing a new distillery, building it, and then operating it has died down, things go quiet for years, as the producers set about the lengthy task of maturing their new spirit into fine whisky. It's possible that, in any country, a whisky industry is acting like a submarine, working hard out of sight, and one day it will burst to the surface. This has happened in Australia and is happening in Sweden. It is yet to happen in Japan, although it might be stirring. So far, only Chichibu has stood up to the plate. While there are rumors of a submarine under the waters, sightings have been intermittent and are unconfirmed.

Why is this? Perhaps because of the obstacles that all distillers face and that are exaggerated in Japan. The wooden casks needed to mature whisky are rare anywhere on the planet, but are tougher to find in the East. Mostly barley has to be imported. The money required to buy land, even if a suitable site is found, is immense. Although Chichibu has bucked the trend, the bar is set particularly high in Japan, with aged and weighty whiskies expected. Ichiro Akuto was able to bring young Chichibu to market, but he had built up a cult following and an enviable record for quality whisky from Hanyu and Karuizawa. There is also the route to market and the difficulties of carving out a niche when two giants, Nikka and Suntory, dominate the whisky landscape. However, slowly and surely, new distilleries are appearing and, by the mid-2020s, Japanese whisky may have entered a new phase.

MAP OF JAPAN'S DISTILLERIES

For many people, Japan is a very long way to travel simply to visit a whisky distillery or two. Throughout this book, therefore, we have linked the distilleries to the cities they are in, or near, and have highlighted some points of interest and tourist attractions for potential visitors. This map shows the locations of the principal distilleries and the cities in Japan that are covered in the Tourist's Guide (see p. 262).

■ DISTILLERIES INCLUDING ESTABLISHED DISTILLERIES AND NEWER WORKS IN PROGRESS

01 AKKESHI DISTILLERY
➡ SEE P. 64

02 YOICHI DISTILLERY
➡ SEE P. 106

03 MIYAGIKYO DISTILLERY
➡ SEE P. 96

04 KARUIZAWA DISTILLERY
➡ SEE P. 90

05 CHICHIBU DISTILLERY
➡ SEE P. 66

06 HANYU DISTILLERY
➡ SEE P. 92

07 MARS SHINSHU DISTILLERY
➡ SEE P. 94

08 HAKUSHU DISTILLERY
➡ SEE P. 76

09 FUJI GOTEMBA DISTILLERY
➡ SEE P. 72

10 SHIZUOKA DISTILLERY
➡ SEE P. 100

11 YAMAZAKI DISTILLERY
➡ SEE P. 82

12 WHITE OAK DISTILLERY
➡ SEE P. 102

13 MIYASHITA SHUZO DISTILLERY
➡ SEE P. 93

● CITIES (FEATURED IN CHAPTER SIX AND TOURIST'S GUIDE)

Otaru SEE P. 274
Sapporo SEE P. 181, P. 272

Sendai SEE P. 266
Tokyo SEE P. 158, P. 263

Kyoto SEE P. 179
Osaka SEE P. 176, P. 268

Okayama SEE P. 270
Fukuoka SEE P. 180

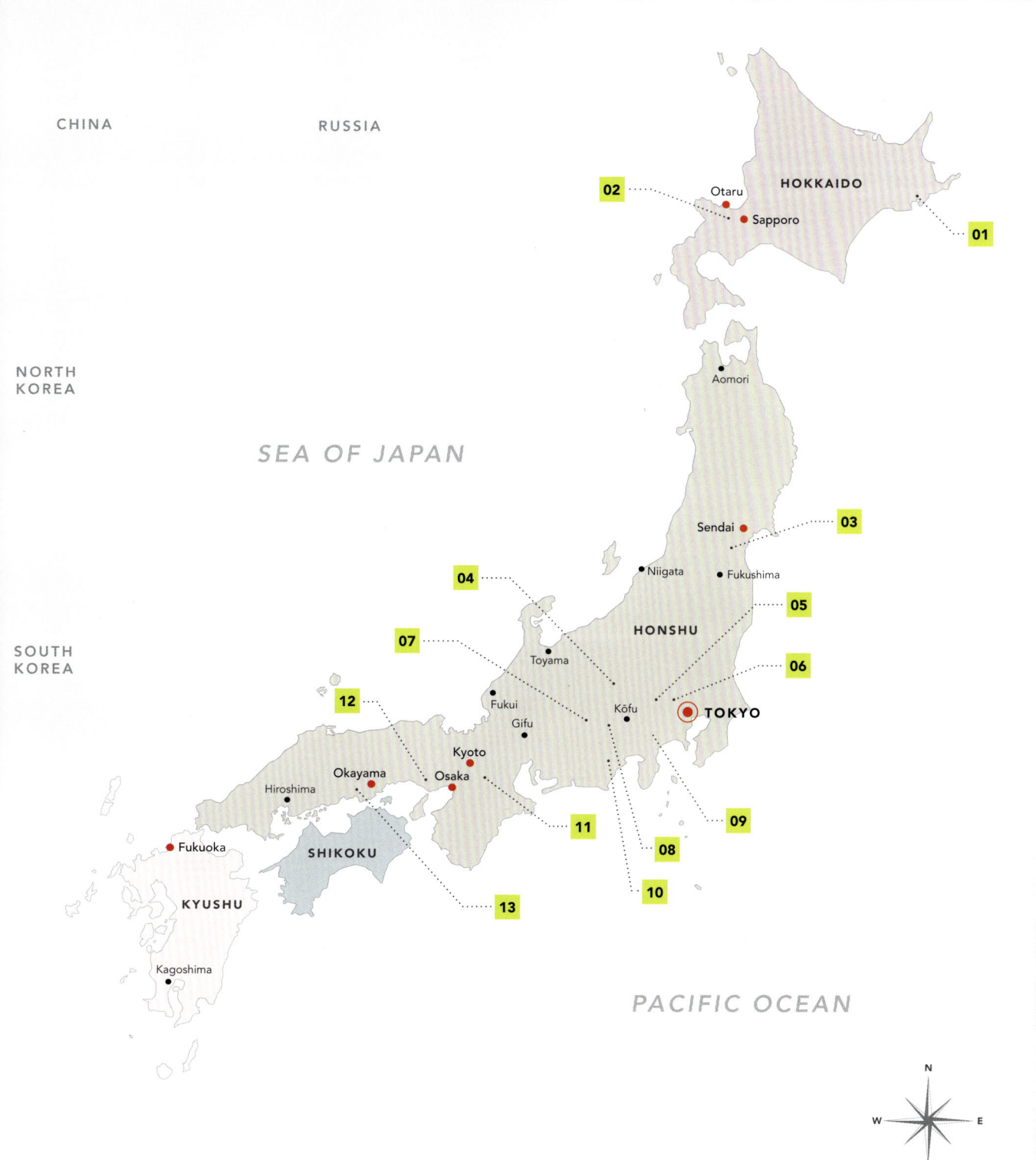

MAP OF JAPAN'S DISTILLERIES

AKKESHI DISTILLERY

LOCATION
HOKKAIDO, NORTH JAPAN

OWNER
KENTON COMPANY, LTD.

FOUNDED
2014

CAPACITY
79,000 GALLONS (300,000 LITERS)

RANGE
N/A

VISITOR FACILITIES
NO FACILITIES

TEST MATURATION WAREHOUSE
This warehouse was constructed in order to determine what effect the climate and terrain in this area would have on maturing whisky.

It is fitting that we start this section with Japan's newest distillery—so new, in fact, that the chance to sample whisky from it is still some years away.

The history of whisky is littered with failed distillery projects, and it's always risky writing anything before the spirit starts flowing. But the company behind the project, Kenton Company, Ltd., has launched an extensive website in English as well as in Japanese, and it contains a wealth of in-depth information about the new distillery. Akkeshi is in a remote area of Hokkaido in Japan's north, in a coastal location. It was chosen because the owners feel that the region is reminiscent of Scotland's home of peaty whiskies, Islay. Salty fog rolls in from the sea, and the area has a variety of different peat bogs, which is uncommon for Japan. Although initially the barley will be imported, the plan is to find land to grow domestic barley, and then to experiment with peat types to create an Islay-style whisky. The owners are hoping for a distinctively original Akkeshi characteristic, too.

Output from the distillery is planned to eventually be around 79,000 gallons (300,000 liters) a year, produced in two pot stills built for the company by Forsyths in Scotland. Special steps have been taken to construct the distillery on soft, boggy land. The distillery will consist of just two buildings—the distillery itself and an office building. The company has planned for production by buying in new-make spirit from two other distilleries and experimenting with maturation times. The temperature in this part of Japan can dip to as low as -4°F (-20°C) in winter, and peak in the low 70s°F (low 20s°C) in the summer, so the range of temperatures is extensive. The experiments suggest maturation will be relatively fast here.

"One of our unwavering principles is dedication to the traditional distilling methods of Scotland," explains Kenton Company's representative director, Keichi Toita. "At the same time, we intend to make whisky that is unmistakably a product of the Akkeshi Distillery.

"I have been a whisky devotee since my youth, and over the years I have tasted whiskies from many different whisky distilleries. I had a dream of someday creating whisky with my own hands. I knew it would be something like those Islay malts. No one is more excited than me to taste the finished product. I think we have something in the works for whisky lovers far and wide to look forward to."

The owners of Akkeshi are hoping that their whisky will go well with local delicacies, especially oysters and cheese.

MATURING CASKS_ Within the test maturation warehouse, fifteen whisky casks of various sizes have been maturing since 2013.

CHICHIBU
DISTILLERY

LOCATION
CHICHIBU CITY, SAITAMA PREFECTURE, HONSHU

OWNER
VENTURE WHISKY

FOUNDED
2004

CAPACITY
21,000 GALLONS (80,000 LITERS)

RANGE
THE FLOOR MALTED 3 YEAR OLD, CHICHIBU PORT PIPE, CHICHIBU PEATED

VISITOR FACILITIES
TOURS CAN BE ARRANGED BY APPOINTMENT

If Japanese whisky were a soap opera, the story of Chichibu and its founder, Ichiro Akuto, would be a sensational subplot that has gripped an increasingly growing audience, desperate to hear about the next twist. Akuto has introduced innovation and a healthy freshness that stands in stark contrast to the Suntory-Nikka monolith, which has dominated the Japanese whisky industry for the last 100 years or so.

Chichibu is tiny, but in a short period of time it has shaken up the local whisky industry, overcoming considerable odds to pump new thinking and ideas into Japanese whisky. As a result, anything with Ichiro Akuto's signature on it—and he is responsible for a number of different projects—has become massively sought after and is highly collectable.

Akuto comes from a family with a long history of making alcohol stretching back some 500 years. For most of that time they produced sake and shōchū. They started distilling whisky at Hanyu in the 1980s, but the distillery lasted less than twenty years, because the market for whisky collapsed. Akuto managed to salvage 400 casks of Hanyu, and since the turn of the millennium, there have been regular releases, including the sought-after Card series, where each release had the label of a playing card, with higher numbers indicating older casks.

Akuto's real desire, however, was to return to distilling, and in 2008 malt spirit started flowing at Chichibu.

CHICHIBU THE FIRST
As the name suggests, this was Chichibu's first whisky. It matured for three years and was released in 2011. It also features in Chapter Four (see p.114).

CHICHIBU CASKS_ The distillery is using oak casks that have previously contained a range of different spirits including Cognac and rum.

"I'M EXCITED BY THE POSITIVE INTERNATIONAL RECEPTION FOR MY WHISKY. I WILL CARRY ON MAKING THE VERY BEST SINGLE MALT I CAN. AS LONG AS PEOPLE CONTINUE TO LIKE WHAT I DO, I AM OPTIMISTIC." — ICHIRO AKUTO

Chichibu has built up an enviable reputation for quality whisky. Since 2011, there have been a series of releases in various styles. Bottled under the collective name "Ichiro's Malt," there have been heavily peated whiskies and light fruity ones. Ichiro has also released a malt and grain whisky. All of the whiskies have been released to widespread critical acclaim, and so successful has the distillery been that, by 2015, it had already expanded. The distilling operation here is more labor intensive and manual than at many other distilleries. Akuto and his small team of willing youngsters are involved at every stage and they don't rely on technology. The mash is stirred manually before the used grains are drained away. The spirit is tasted from every batch before any of it is saved for whisky making.

Despite its modest size, Chichibu is proving adept at making a large range of different whisky styles. Three different distillates are made at the distillery, and the spirit is being matured in casks that have previously contained Cognac, rum, and Madeira, as well as the more conventional ex-bourbon casks.

The longer-term aim of Akuto is to produce a 100 percent Japanese whisky. Chichibu is attempting to be a craft distillery in the truest sense of the term, with a growing percentage of local barley being used, which is almost unheard of in Japan. The distillery is peating some of its own barley, too. The distillery has is own cooperage, and a number of casks are cut down to quarter size. Akuto has also invested in mizunara oak as ex-bourbon casks become rarer. Akuto is unsure whether Chichibu will develop its own house style, but is clear that he wants to continue to explore different styles of whisky.

"I wanted flexibility when I set up the distillery," he says. "I'm excited by the positive international reception for my whisky. I will carry on making the very best single malt I can. As long as people continue to like what I do, I am optimistic."

Whatever the future may hold, Akuto is already thinking long term, and his aim is to bottle a twenty-year-old Chichibu when the time comes. He'll have to resist the temptation to release all his stock, even though the demand is there. Whatever he does, he has overcome considerable obstacles to bring new and exciting Japanese whisky to a growing body of fans.

WHISKY INSPECTION
Employees inspect Ichiro's malt whiskies at Chichibu Distillery.

PRODUCTION AT CHICHIBU_ The distillery is a low-tech craft distillery in the truest sense.

INTERVIEW

ICHIRO AKUTO

FOUNDER AND OWNER OF
CHICHIBU DISTILLERY

•

The unlikely hero of a new wave
of Japanese whisky drinkers

Japanese whisky pioneer Ichiro Akuto believes the future will be bright if Japan's new distillers focus on quality. When he decided to take the plunge and build his own distillery, he had no idea that Japanese whisky was about to become the toast of whisky connoisseurs around the world—or that he would become the unlikely hero of a new wave of Japanese whisky drinkers. He comes from a family with a history of alcohol making stretching back to the seventeenth century, when they produced traditional Japanese drinks such as sake. His father, Yutaka Akuto, owned Hanyu Distillery, which started making whisky in the 1980s.

"Traditional pot stills were installed at Hanyu Distillery in the 1980s, and it followed the traditional Scottish way of making whisky," Akuto says. "However, at that time, rather than enjoying single malt on its own, people unfortunately preferred to drink whisky 'Mizuwari' style [with ice and a lot of water], which doesn't emphasize the character much. In the late 1990s, business was not good. The sake brewing business was especially bad, and, sadly, my father decided to sell the company in 2004. Worse still, the new owner was not interested in the whisky business, and tried to throw away the stocks from Hanyu Distillery.

"I decided to leave the company, and set up a whisky company by myself. I asked many companies to store the Hanyu casks. However, it wasn't easy. Finally, Mr. Yamaguchi from the sake-brewing company Sasanokawa Shuzo listened to me, and gave a helping hand. I understood the stocks from Hanyu Distillery would be gone someday, and I felt the need to leave something for future generations, too, so I built Chichibu Distillery in 2008. But I was very surprised with the growth of interest in Japanese whisky. When we started the Chichibu Distillery in 2008, I didn't foresee the situation as it is now. I'm glad to hear that our Japanese whisky has been accepted by many people, and hope they taste and enjoy our whisky, not just buy it as an investment."

Ever since the first bottlings of Chichibu were launched, they have been excellently received, and although they're obviously much younger than the classic old and rare single malts that built Japan's reputation for whisky, they have picked up the quality baton. So what makes these whiskies so special?

"First of all, I think it's to do with the environment of Chichibu," Akuto says. "The summer can be extremely hot, and the winters extremely cold. I believe that whisky

maturation is greatly influenced by the nature of the place. To be honest, we are just trying the traditional way that many distilleries used to do, including the challenges of floor malting, and building our own cooperage. But, of course, our passion for whisky making makes our whisky special. Actually, we think about whisky all day."

It's the emphasis on quality that will ensure the future. Akuto is hoping that new distillers won't cut corners and compromise on standards.

"New distilleries are of course a good thing," he says. "It's great that so many people started having an interest in whisky, and we hope it goes well so that we can all build a strong Japanese brand. What we are hoping for from the new distilleries is quality. Because of that, we are happy to help them. We have to ensure the Japanese brand as a quality brand." So despite the shortage of Japanese whisky, does he think the future is bright?

"I believe so," he says. "The reputation of Japanese whisky is good now, but it doesn't mean we should stop our search for better quality. We are still working hard for the future generations; that's how the whisky business should be."

FUJI GOTEMBA
DISTILLERY

LOCATION
GOTEMBA, SHIZOUKA PREFECTURE, HONSHU

OWNER
KIRIN

FOUNDED
1973

CAPACITY
528,300 GALLONS (2,000,000 LITERS)

RANGE
SINGLE MALT 18 YEAR OLD, SINGLE GRAIN 25 YEAR OLD, FUJISANROKU 50 YEAR OLD

VISITOR FACILITIES
TOURS, TASTINGS, AND A STORE

FUJI GOTEMBA DISTILLERY
The distillery is situated in a picturesque location 2,000 feet (610 meters) above sea level.

Due to the fact that it takes years to mature premium malt whisky, Nikka and Suntory have been facing stock issues that will last well into the 2020s. With so many obstacles to new distilleries entering the market, there is little chance that new players will fill the shortfall. So the role of existing distillers, such as Fuji Gotemba, which is owned by Kirin, becomes more pertinent.

This distillery, which makes both malt and grain whisky, has been something of a misfit and somewhat impervious to the surge of interest in Japanese whisky. It was originally built in 1973 as a joint venture between major drinks companies Kirin and Seagram, and Kirin eventually took full ownership in 2002. However, while Japan's other whisky producers started to turn their eyes toward international markets, and Kirin had a direct route to the North American market through its ownership of the Kentucky bourbon brand Four Roses, Kirin stuck to the domestic Japanese market, with much of it targeted at the budget end.

The market, however, might be changing. The Japanese whisky blog website Nonjatta reports that the company has said that there will be more releases of Fuji Gotemba in the future. The distillery itself is a large "one-stop shop," unusually producing grain and malt whisky, and includes a bottling plant and visitor facilities on its huge site.

The distillery lies at the base of picturesque Mount Fuji and is set among trees close to the main road into Gotemba. The flatlands tend to be hot and humid during the summer months, but the distillery lies at nearly 2,000 feet (610 metric) above sea level, so its temperatures are relatively low.

Spirit is distilled in pot stills, kettles, and a range of column stills, and, as in other Japanese distilleries, there is scope to make a wide range of different spirits. Not surprisingly, given the link with the brand Four Roses, the spirit is matured in ex-bourbon barrels.

The distillery does allow visitors, but it advises that you should ring in advance. Some English is spoken here, and visitors are permitted to follow a planned route unaccompanied, viewing whisky production through glass. There are posters along the route to explain the process.

Fuji Gotemba single malt whisky is marketed under two names: Fuji Gotemba and Fujisanroku, and both are eighteen-year-old malts. A grain whisky is also available, but it is rare so you are unlikely to come across it. The malts are sweet, soft, and easy to drink.

17 YEAR OLD SINGLE MALT_More expressions for export from Fuji Gotemba are in the pipeline.

INTERVIEW

JOTA TANAKA

CHIEF BLENDER AT THE
FUJI GOTEMBA DISTILLERY

•

At the vanguard of the movement to produce
quality whisky for Japan

While most of the interest in Japanese whisky has been focused either on the leading two companies, Suntory and Nikka, or on the innovative efforts of the small players, such as Chichibu, a handful of other manufacturers have stayed below the radar. This is because they have tended to concentrate on the domestic Japanese market. However, with demand so high for Japanese whisky across the world, this situation has been changing. One of the companies with its eyes firmly fixed on exports is Kirin, owner of the Fuji Gotemba Distillery, sited close to Mount Fuji in the heart of Japan. According to chief blender Jota Tanaka, the site was chosen for three reasons.

"Firstly, the distillery is located at 2,000 feet (610 meters) above sea level at the foot of Fuji in the city of Gotemba," he says. "It's cool with an average temperature of around 55°F [13°C], and the high humidity throughout the year is ideal for whisky maturation. Secondly, the production water is taken from underground streams that flow beneath Mount Fuji. The water is extremely clean and soft, and is filtered through Mount Fuji for more than 50 years.

"And finally the location is in the middle of Japan, and so it is logistically good for distribution throughout Japan."

Kirin has been producing whisky, first as Kirin-Seagram in partnership with Chivas Brothers, and then on its own, since 1973. The operation at its distillery is similar to distilleries elsewhere in Japan; that is, the plant has the capability to make a range of different single malt whisky styles as well as three contrasting styles of grain whisky: light, medium, and heavy.

The whisky itself, however, is a little different from that of other Japanese distilleries. "The quality policy for our whisky is 'clean and estery,'" says Tanaka. "We aim to make our whisky very smooth, with a rich, fruity flavor, and with sweet notes.

"Our goal has always been to produce quality whisky products for Japanese consumers to enjoy by using the most modern technology, equipment, and the top know-how available in the whisky industry, not only from Scotland, but also the United States and Canada. We have been producing a wide variety of whisky products."

The distillery makes an estimated 63,000 gallons (238,500 liters) a year of grain and single malt whisky, nearly all of it for the domestic market. This, however, is in the process of changing. So does that reflect the belief that world demand will remain high for Japanese whisky?

"The world, including the people here in Japan, have discovered just how good Japanese whisky is," says Tanaka. "The current boom might be due to drinkers craving something new, and the fact that it is scarce. To keep the momentum and to establish the category, we as whisky producers need to continue to show our commitment in offering genuine products. I am sure there will be ups and downs in the future. But in the long run, we at Kirin think the future for Japanese whisky is very promising."

HAKUSHU DISTILLERY_ The general manager of Hakushu, Takeshi Ono, stands next to some of the pot stills in the distillery.

HAKUSHU
DISTILLERY

LOCATION
TORIHARA, YAMANASHI PREFECTURE, HONSHU

OWNER
SUNTORY

FOUNDED
1973

CAPACITY
1,057,000 GALLONS (4,000,000 LITERS)

RANGE
HAKUSHU NAS, HAKUSHU 12 YEAR OLD,
18 YEAR OLD, 25 YEAR OLD, HEAVILY PEATED

VISITOR FACILITIES
TOURS, TASTINGS, MUSEUM, RESTAURANT, STORE

Hakushu Distillery prides itself on the way it merges with its beautiful environment, and it incorporates a bird sanctuary and nature reserve. Owner Suntory offers visitors the chance to birdwatch within its extensive and verdant grounds, and to spot scores of rare species. There is a network of pathways to explore, too, making it a walker's paradise. Hakushu is Suntory's second distillery, and both the distillery itself and the land it occupies are huge. Warehouses sprawl over a tree-covered and mountainous landscape, a perfect example of how technological production and natural beauty can exist side by side.

Hakushu is located about two-and-a-half hours by high-speed Shinkansen train from Tokyo. It's Japan's highest distillery, located in the country's southern alps. It is a relatively new distillery, built in the 1970s, and it was substantially updated in 1983. Its principal role is to provide whisky to meet the seemingly insatiable thirst among businessmen for blended whisky. The blended whisky Suntory Royal became the biggest-selling whisky brand in the world at one time and was moving 15 million cases in Japan alone.

At its peak, Hakushu was producing 7.9 million gallons (30 million liters) of spirit a year; for a while, it was the biggest distillery in the world. As it turned out, however, the demand for blended whisky was satiable. By the 1990s, the boom had come to an end and production was cut back.

Hakushu is really two distilleries in one, with an east site and a west site linked by a bridge. The west site ceased production during the slump of the 1990s, but the east site was expanded in 2015 in response to renewed demand for Japanese whisky as a single malt, and for the blended whisky Hibiki. The warehouses are crammed with casks, and the total stored through the estate's scattered warehouses runs to not far short of half a million. Hakushu is sited partly for its proximity to Tokyo but also because of the quality of its water—soft, and suited to malt distillation. It is so good that Suntory bottles it, and it has become the country's top-selling mineral water. Should you so desire, you can tour the distillery, and you can also visit the substantial water bottling plant.

Hakushu is as complex as a distillery can be. Much of the flavor of the spirit is defined by its distillation. The size and shape of the stills, and the direction of the lyne arm, will all influence the spirit produced. So the stills are of all shapes and sizes, and the distiller has the option of any number of permutations to vary the spirit. There are also various different barley styles in use, and maturation happens in an array of casks, so you'll see that there is huge scope for a range of different spirits. A column still was added in 2010, so grain whisky has also been made on the site.

THE HAKUSHU RANGE
Single Malt Hakushu whiskies—10, 12, 18, and 25 year olds, along with the Sherry Cask and Heavily Peated varieties.

IF HAKUSHU WERE A COLOR, IT WOULD BE AS GREEN AS THE REGION IN WHICH IT IS LOCATED, AND AS GREEN AS THE BOTTLE IT COMES IN

THE INNER WORKINGS_The distillery houses imposing stills of all shapes and sizes.

HAKUSHU DISTILLERY_The site includes a restaurant, a fully stocked bar, and a museum showcasing the Suntory story.

DISTILLERY LOCATION_ The region's water is so pure that Suntory bottles it and it has become Japan's best-selling mineral water.

HAKUSHU SINGLE MALT
The range includes peated and honeyed varieties, but in general the whiskies are fresh, clean, and fruity.

Hakushu Distillery is home to a first-class restaurant, and in the bar you can enjoy the whole range of Suntory's whiskies, both from Japan and from its increasing portfolio across the world. There is also a sizable museum spread over three floors. The museum explains how whisky is made and the science behind its production, looks at whiskies from across the world, and gives an extensive Suntory view of the history of whisky making in Japan. There are also reproductions of an English bar and a Parisian cafe, as well as one of the definitive "Tory bars," where Japanese businessmen went to drink Suntory blends in the late 1950s and early 1960s. You get a superb view of the whole distillery and the nature reserve from the observation platform, whereas the rare whiskies offered in the tasting room help you to understand just what today's Japanese whisky drinker is missing out on.

Although there exist heavily peaty versions, and whiskies rich in vanilla and honey notes from maturation in former bourbon casks, Hakushu malt tends to be fresh, clean, and fruity. If Hakushu were a color, it would be as green as the region in which it is located, and as green as the bottles it comes in.

YAMAZAKI
DISTILLERY

LOCATION
SHIMAMOTO, OSAKA PREFECTURE, HONSHU

OWNER
SUNTORY

FOUNDED
1923

CAPACITY
1,849,000 GALLONS (7,000,000 LITERS)

RANGE
NAS, 12 YEAR OLD, 18 YEAR OLD, 25 YEAR OLD, LIMITED EDITION BOURBON, MIZUNARA, AND SHERRY CASK BOTTLINGS

VISITOR FACILITIES
TOURS IN JAPANESE AND ENGLISH, MUSEUM, WHISKY LIBRARY, STORE WITH UNIQUE BOTTLINGS

Japan's oldest customized distillery is the place where the modern-day Japanese whisky story started, and it retains a special place at the heart of Suntory's expanding drinks empire. This is where Shinjiro Torii set about making genuine Japanese single malt whisky, and where Masataka Taketsuru worked with him to create the early Suntory whiskies. It was here that the first tentative steps were taken to create a whisky that was both true to the Scottish model that Takesuru had learned about during his time in Scotland, and to develop it into a spirit suited to the Japanese palate.

One look at the stillroom is sufficient to understand that Japanese whisky is a replica of Scottish single malt in only the loosest sense, and see that it is something else again. To understand even the basics of the distillation system on show at Yamazaki is to appreciate that there are hundreds of nuances and sophistications designed to make a complex, cultivated, and uniquely Japanese product.

Yamazaki is big and modern, but it cuts no corners when making quality spirit. If ever there was a distillery that proved that it is absolutely possible to combine quantity with quality, this is it. There are question marks over its exact output, but the figure is thought to be in the region of 1.05 million gallons

CASK MANAGEMENT
Billions of dollars have been spent improving facilities at the Yamazaki Distillery.

ONE IN A MILLION_ Suntory employee Hiromitsu Tsuji shows off Yamazaki's most expensive cask, one out of approximately one million stored here.

SPIRIT STILL NO.8_The distillery has an impressive sixteen stills of various types.

LEFT_FILLING THE BARREL
Barley-base single malt whisky is poured into a 12-gallon (45-liter) barrel.

BELOW_IDEAL LOCATION
Yamazaki Distillery is surrounded by mountains, and the moisture in the air enables the whisky to mature at a slow pace.

YAMAZAKI 1979
This rare Japanese whisky was matured for twenty nine years in mizunara oak casks, which gave it a cinnamon flavor with hints of pineapple and peach.

(7 million liters). Yamazaki lies close to the old road linking Osaka and Kyoto, and it is easily reached, not only from those cities but from Tokyo, too. Three rivers meet here, so water is plentiful, transport links are good, and the region enjoys an ideal climate: hot and humid in the summer, cold in the winter.

This is the perfect example of the complex natures of some of Japan's distilleries. Over the years, it has been rebuilt and updated, and in 2005 billions of dollars were spent to install more stills to change production methods and update facilities. The distillery now boasts sixteen stills, all of different shapes and sizes, some coal-fired, others using steam, and with an array of angled lyne arms. By using a range of yeasts, casks of different sizes, and oak types previously used for a number of varying purposes, the production team has the resources to make scores of different spirit styles. Add other variables, such as a mix of condensers and worm tubs, fermentation times, length of spirit

YAMAZAKI SAMPLES
Some of the bottles that make up the distillery's impressive whisky library.

run, where the cuts are made, and the amount of peated barley used to make the wash, and you get a sense of the complexity of a distillery such as this one.

This state-of-the-art distillery sits in stark contrast to the tranquillity of the region and the traditional backdrop against which it operates. For all the calmness and confidence the distillery exudes, you suspect that, beneath the surface, there are plenty of people paddling hard to keep the malt moving forward. At a time when supply is struggling massively to keep up with worldwide demand, there might have been a temptation to take the foot off the gas in terms of quality, but this is not the case. The awards have continued to flood in, special releases such as the Mizunara Oak fly off the shelves, and in 2015 *The Whisky Bible* chose a Yamazaki limited edition sherry cask whisky as its World Whisky of the Year.

How Suntory will continue to meet expectations in the future remains to be seen, but a much younger drinker profile is discovering Yamazaki through the Hibiki Harmony blend and the Highball method of drinking it. Also, the promotion of its whiskies with Japanese and Eastern fusion foods suggests that the problem isn't going to go away any time soon.

If the quality of the whisky is operating at an impressively high level, so too are the visitor facilities. Suntory doesn't do things by halves, and visitors are spoiled. The tour is free and lasts for around an hour, culminating with a dram of Yamazaki. It is conducted in Japanese, but translations by headphones are available in English, Chinese, and French. There is a whisky library containing several thousand bottles, and a museum that displays artifacts, including disused stills and fermentation vessels, as well as Shinjiro Torii's original desk. For a small fee, you can gain entrance to the tasting counter, where more than 100 whiskies, including some distillery exclusives, are offered.

INTERVIEW

SHINJI FUKUYO

CHIEF BLENDER FOR SUNTORY'S
HAKUSHU AND YAMAZAKI DISTILLERIES

•

Great tasting expressions and
the pursuit of perfection

Shinji Fukuyo joined Suntory in 1984 and became chief blender in 2009. Ask him what his target is, and he'll tell you it's the pursuit of perfection.

"My job is to develop and blend various whiskies, including Yamazaki 12, Yamazaki 18, Hakushu 18, and Hibiki 21 year old, which have won multiple gold awards at global spirits competitions," he says. "I also develop more aged spirits, such as Yamazaki 50 year old, and Yamazaki 1984. As chief blender, I am also responsible for ensuring consistent quality across the entire Suntory whisky portfolio; developing new products, and improving the quality of unblended malt whiskies, as well as managing the team, and controlling the quality and quantity of the products in stock. Since developing its first whisky distillery, Suntory has refined its product quality dramatically. Every day, we strive to produce whisky that suits the wider palate, and the whisky connoisseur. We recognize that Suntory has become increasingly popular in recent years due to the high quality of our products. With this demand expected to increase in the future, we have implemented a number of measures to ensure the consistent delivery of high-quality products to market."

Shinji Fukuyo was born in Aichi Prefecture, in the Chubu region of Japan, in 1961, and graduated from the Nagoya University School of Agricultural Science (Agricultural Chemistry). He joined Suntory in 1984, originally working at the Hakushu Distillery. In 1992, he moved to the whisky blending department at Yamazaki Distillery. In 1996, he left Japan to study at Heriot-Watt University in Edinburgh, Scotland, and later he worked for Morrison Bowmore Distillers in Glasgow. He returned to Japan in 2002, became head blender in 2003, and chief blender in 2009. His career has spanned the period in which Japanese whisky has taken off, and he is adamant that it's due to the high quality.

"Japanese whisky is characterized by a complex and delicate taste," he says. "The main elements can be largely divided into nature and people. Considering the elements of nature, delicate spirits are created from clean, pure Japanese water, while the whisky develops a deeply complex maturity from the vastly changing seasons and warm climate. The details that Japanese people put into crafting their whiskies are closely monitored at every process, from producing unblended malt whisky to carefully

blending aged expressions, resulting in a consistent high quality. At Suntory, we have developed whiskies that suit the Japanese palate according to the uniquely Japanese 'whisky and water' culture."

Fukuyo believes that there are three main factors that contribute to the characteristics of Suntory whisky: the natural surroundings of the distilleries in Japan, the production of various types of whisky in one distillery, and the craftsmanship and skill set of the company's blenders.

"When I talk about nature, I specifically refer to water and climate," he says. "The pure water found in Japan helps us to create fine, delicate spirits. Each of the four seasons in Japan has a unique climate, where the change in temperature makes our whisky very complex and deep in flavor. For production, we have several types of wash backs, pot stills, and casks, so we can produce a plethora of whisky types. Most of the time in Scotland, one distillery produces only one whisky and exchanges its whiskies with other distilleries. In Japan, there are only a few distilleries, so we have to produce many types of expressions at one distillery. And the high skill sets of the blenders at Suntory are prevalent throughout the entire process of whisky making, from mashing, fermenting, distilling, and casking to storing, blending, and bottling."

For Fukuyo, the surge in interest in Japanese whisky is reward for years of hard work, innovation, and adherence to the highest quality standards. He is delighted that products such as the nonage statement whisky Hibiki Harmony are extending his country's reputation to a new generation. He hopes that more distilleries will help Japanese whisky to grow even further.

"For many years, I've worked to improve the quality of our products for the Japanese consumers, and now feel that those results are being recognized around the world," he says. "Hibiki Japanese Harmony was released to help satisfy the global thirst for Japanese whisky, now and in the future. It was very well received, and its popularity continues to grow. We are determined to continue innovating in the whisky world, developing great tasting expressions that are loved by all. I believe the increase in the number of distilleries in Japan can only be a good thing. I hope that, through friendly rivalry, we can produce high-quality whiskies that promote the reputation of Japanese whisky globally."

KARUIZAWA
DISTILLERY

LOCATION
KARUIZAWA CITY, NOGANO PREFECTURE, HONSHU

OWNER
KIRIN

FOUNDED
1955

CAPACITY
DEMOLISHED

RANGE
A RANGE OF RARE SINGLE CASK AND VINTAGE BOTTLINGS

VISITOR FACILITIES
NO FACILITIES

KARUIZAWA 1964 48 YEAR OLD
This is one of the oldest Japanese single malt whiskies in history. It matured for 48 years in sherry oak casks and only 143 bottles were produced.

The most astounding thing about Karuizawa Distillery is the way it has joined the likes of Scotland's Port Ellen or Brora in a small group of iconic closed distilleries in just a decade. Even by aged Japanese whisky standards, the malt produced here is special and can command tens of thousands of dollars on those rare occasions when it appears at auction.

The distillery was built in 1955 on an active volcano and was the highest distillery in Japan. It existed in a microclimate in which the high humidity ensured that water from the whisky evaporated, so the whisky maintained a high strength. An amazing concentration of flavors make this one of the tastiest whiskies ever produced. Big, bold, peaty, and fruity, Karuizawa is highly complex. For forty-five years, the distillery made traditional whisky using Golden Promise barley, some of it dried over peat fires, and matured mainly in sherry casks.

Perhaps if circumstances had been different, and owners Kirin had kept it open longer, it would still be producing today. It had started to win a following among whisky aficionados when it closed in 2000, and the growing interest in Japan's whiskies started going into orbit a few months later. Hindsight is a wonderful thing, and no one could have foreseen what was about to happen. Kirin sold the land to a property developer; the distillery was decommissioned and stopped producing spirit. Thankfully, the Number One Drinks Company, in association with Ichiro Akuto, rescued the remaining stocks, and those whiskies have since been sold for ever more eye-popping prices. Akuto has also created a whisky called Spirit of Asama, a small batch bottling made using selected casks of the final vintages of Karuizawa from 1999 and 2000.

There is another twist in this tale. There have been attempts to revive the distillery, even though the equipment has gone, and some of those associated with the original distillery have agreed to work with a Tokyo businessman to re-create the classic Karuizawa taste. According to whisky experts, a young entrepreneur was in talks to buy Karuizawa's land and buildings, but plans fell through. Undeterred, this unidentified potential investor is on the hunt for another location. It is said that, in the event that a deal is made, some of the key people from the former distillery have agreed to help him revive the spirit brand.

BELOW_KARUIZAWA CASKS
Casks lined up outside of Japan's smallest distillery.

HANYU
DISTILLERY

LOCATION
HANYU CITY, SAITAMA PREFECTURE, HONSHU

OWNER
ICHIRO AKUTO (OWNER OF STOCK)

FOUNDED
1941

CAPACITY
DEMOLISHED

RANGE
DOUBLE DISTILLERIES, CARD SERIES, ICHIRO'S MALT SELECTED RELEASES

VISITOR FACILITIES
NO FACILITIES

THE CARD SERIES
Each bottling has a different playing card, and the higher the card, the older the cask.

Hanyu and Karuizawa Distillery (see p.90) are linked to each other and no longer exist, but their influence on the success of Japanese whisky since the turn of the millennium has been important and disproportionate, because they have caught the attention of whisky lovers, collectors, and investors everywhere, and focused the world whisky spotlight on Japan.

Hanyu Distillery was established as an alcohol producer in 1946, in Hanyu city, northwest of Tokyo, but its roots go back much farther. The Akuto family started producing sake in 1626, and the nineteenth generation of the family set up the factory in 1941. It wasn't until 1980 that the company decided to produce a quality Scotch-style whisky. Production began with two stills, but it was a short-lived venture. Production was modest, the market wanted blended whisky instead of single malt, and by 2000, both the industry and this distillery had hit the buffers. Hanyu was sold to a new management uninterested in whisky. They sold off the stock and the distilling equipment.

That would have been the end except for two interventions: the first by northern sake maker Sasanokawa Shuzo, which took over the stock and production facilities and stored the casks. The second was by Ichiro Akuto, the grandson of the distillery's founder. He was able to form a new company, and rerack and bottle the stock with the support of Sasanokawa Shuzo.

Since then, the Hanyu stock has appeared in the market place in various bottlings, many under the name "Ichiro's Malt," and many through the European hub for Japanese whisky, La Maison du Whisky in Paris. However, the most sought-after Hanyu whisky is bottled as part of the playing card range. This was a brilliant piece of marketing on the part of Ichiro Akuto, with the casks released over a period of several years, each labeled with a different playing card. Higher numbers represent older casks, and each cask is easily identifiable to the whisky enthusiast, who is too often baffled by complicated vintages and cask numbers. The series ended in 2013 with two joker cards, making a total of fifty-four. The success of these, along with the sale of remaining Karuizawa stocks, gave Akuto the resources to build his own distillery, and through Chichibu distillery he has been able to keep the Akuto dynasty going.

MIYASHITA SHUZO
DISTILLERY

LOCATION
OKAYAMA, OKAYAMA PREFECTURE, HONSHU

OWNER
MIYASHITA SHUZO

FOUNDED
2015 FOR WHISKY PRODUCTION

CAPACITY
264 GALLONS (1,000 LITERS)

RANGE
N/A

VISITOR FACILITIES
NO FACILITIES

Miyashita Shuzo is one of the more intriguing players in the whisky industry. It is an established alcohol producer, but a whisky novice, which started to produce malt spirit in 2012 to mark its ninetieth anniversary. It is situated in the Okayama Prefecture in Western Honshu, above the island of Shikoku. It is primarily a sake producer, but its total output of 132,000 gallons (500,000 liters) is also made up of beer and shōchū.

The company's move to whisky has been an unconventional one and remains a work in progress. Research was carried out in Kentucky and Tennessee. The first batch of spirits was made using barley imported from Germany and England, and it was distilled on one of the company's shōchū stills. The company produced more spirit in 2013, which is maturing, and made its first whisky in 2015 as a three year old. The distillery is keeping its cards close to its chest about its future plans for whisky production, having previously given out mixed signals.

The initial run was just 264 gallons (1,000 liters), but exactly what the company is attempting to achieve is shrouded in mystery. The management has claimed to have a strong commitment to making whisky in the future and is said to have started buying in barley locally. Okayama is an established barley-producing region, so Miyashita is joining Chichibu in attempting to make a completely Japanese whisky.

Producing spirit on shōchū stills is merely a stop-gap move, and while blog website Nonjatta reports that the company has invested in proper German whisky stills, the management has said that its short-term plans are to increase production only to between around 530 and 1,600 gallons (2,000–6,000 liters) a year—still minuscule. Company president Buichiro Miyashita has expressed a desire to produce a soft, delicate whisky, but it would seem we're talking about a work in progress.

The company says, "Miyashita Sake Brewery is aspiring to become a comprehensive liquor manufacturer which produces all types of liquors, including shōchū, liqueurs, low-malt beer, spirits, and whisky as well as sake and beer. Currently, in addition to selling at the greater metropolitan areas, such as Tokyo and Osaka, we are also expanding our liquor exports to the United States, Europe, and Asian countries such as China."

MIYASHITA SHUZO SAKE
As well as producing sake, the new distillery is aiming to make whisky with homegrown barley. How much will be made in the future is unclear.

MARS SHINSHU
DISTILLERY

LOCATION
MIYADA-MURA, KAMIINAGUN, NAGANO PREFECTURE

OWNER
HOMBO SHUZO

FOUNDED
1984

CAPACITY
N/A

RANGE
KOMAGATAKE 5 YEAR OLD, SOME SINGLE CASKS

VISITOR FACILITIES
TOURS OF THE SMALL DISTILLERY AND THE NEIGHBORING BREWERY AND TASTINGS ONSITE

Of all the stories associated with Japanese whisky, that of Mars Shinshu Distillery is the most complex. It is a tale of false starts, location upheavals, and whisky style changes. The story of the distillery—or rather distilleries—stretches back to the original beginnings of Japanese whisky.

When owners Hombo started making whisky on a site at Yamanashi, in the Chubu region of Honshu, it was run by Kiichiro Iwai. Iwai had worked with whisky pioneer Masataka Taketsuru before he set off on his travels, and they had plans to build and open Japan's first malt whisky distillery. However, when Taketsuru returned, the company they had worked for had run into financial difficulties, and Taketsuru went to work with Shinjiro Torii at Yamazaki. Hombo obtained a whisky-making license in 1949 but didn't start producing whisky until 1960, and when it did it's believed that Iwai adopted Taketsuru's whisky-making blueprint. He made a heavy, peaty style of whisky, and, frankly, it wasn't popular. Production stopped in 1969, and the plant was used for making wine instead.

It took the better part of a decade before the company decided to try again. It needed a new location, so it moved to a site at Kagoshima, a long way south on the farthest tip of the southern island of Kyushu. Here, the climate was more subtropical and humid, but the company persevered with the heavy, smoky style of whisky. It seems that this wasn't a raging

HIGH ALTITUDE
Mars Shinshu lies at the foot of the Kiso mountains and is Japan's highest distillery, at an altitude of 2,618 feet (798 meters) above sea level.

success either, because by the mid-1980s the company had another rethink. Another new location was chosen, this time back up on Honshu, not far from Nagano. The new location was at altitude, and the owners flip-flopped its whisky style, eventually opting for a new distillation process and a lighter spirit. A decade later, hit by the same downturn that would finish off Hanyu and Karuizawa, production ceased.

Now the distillery is producing again and from 2015 began releasing whiskies, initially a blended malt mixing old Mars stock with Scottish single malt. In 2016 came the first release of a new single malt. The plan is to produce a range of whiskies using both peated and unpeated barley. The pot stills being used for the most recent venture have replaced the ones brought from the Yamanashi plant, but are still based on the design of the original Mars distillery creator Kiichiro Iwai, which in turn were based on the stills blueprint of Taketsuru. The high location means that in winter snow covers the distillery and temperatures can plunge to 5°F (-15°C), so maturation will be slow. In the meantime, they are making other spirits.

The distillery allows visitors, but it is in such a remote location that there are relatively few takers, and those who have visited produce mixed reports; some say the experience is outstanding. The mere fact that the distillery is back in operation, and attracting interest, is encouraging. Whisky expert Dave Broom, who has tasted the new spirit, says it is sweet, with pear notes, light peat, and a touch of sulfur in the mid-palate, which he expects to mature nicely.

MIYAGIKYO
DISTILLERY

LOCATION
SENDAI CITY, MIYAGI PREFECTURE, HONSHU

OWNER
NIKKA

FOUNDED
1969

CAPACITY
792,000 GALLONS (3,000,000 LITERS)

RANGE
MIYAGIKYO NAS 2015

VISITOR FACILITIES
GUIDED TOURS IN JAPANESE, UNGUIDED TOURS PERMITTED, TASTING FACILITIES, SPECIAL BOTTLINGS FOR SALE

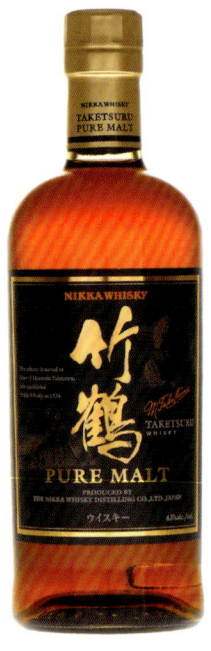

TAKETSURU PURE MALT
This unaged bottling is made up of a blend of malts. It is a fruity, elegant, and sophisticated whisky.

Miyagikyo is one of the two distilleries owned by Japan's second biggest whisky producer, Nikka. It lies in the north of Honshu close to the city of Sendai. The location was chosen by whisky pioneer Masataka Taketsuru after considerable research (three years, according to the company). The location is special. It's remote, but in a rich and verdant area, backdropped by mountains, with hot pools scattered around, and at the point where two sizable rivers meet. Legend has it that Taketsuru merely tasted the water before declaring it his chosen location, but there was much more to it than that. The plentiful supply of cool water, the clear air, and the high humidity levels no doubt all played a part. In winter, the distillery is enveloped in snow.

The distillery was established in 1969 in order to boost Nikka's whisky production when the industry was booming. The distillery, which was originally called Sendai, has been expanded twice since then: first in 1979, to accommodate the production of grain whisky, and again in 1989, to bring it up to the current capacity, which is estimated to be 792,000 gallons (3 million liters) of whisky a year. The distillery was renamed Miyagikyo in 2001 when Nikka was taken over by the Asahi Brewery company.

The distillery consists of eight large but conventional stills, and, unlike other distilleries in Japan, they are all of the same size and shape. That doesn't mean that there isn't room for diversity, however, and numerous different yeasts are used at the fermentation stage of the process. Most of the production is made with barley imported from England and Australia, which is mainly unpeated, although a heavily peated spirit is sometimes made. The most commonly produced spirit is rich and fruity, with an elegant and sophisticated aroma.

Maturation takes place in warehouses, where the whisky is stacked only two casks high, partly to take advantage of the humidity and partly due to the fact that the area is subject to earthquakes. There are more than twenty warehouses on site. That's the conventional part of the distillery. There are also two Coffey stills making three styles of whisky spirit, including one made using barley that is used for a twelve-year-old Coffey malt.

MIYAGIKYO DISTILLERY_ This distillery was built in a remote, rich, and verdant region of Japan, chosen for its clear air and fresh water.

TOP: THE STILLS_There are eight large conventional stills and two Coffey stills here.
BELOW: MATURATION_The whiskies produced at Miyagikyo are known for being softer than others.

WORTH THE JOURNEY_ The distillery offers an outstanding tour and the chance to sample rare Nikka whiskies.

COFFEY GRAIN
Made with whisky produced at Miyagikyo.

Using malt in a Coffey still would have happened in Scotland when Taketsuru was there, although the practice is frowned upon under Scotch Whisky Association rules today. The whisky produced this way at Miyagikyo is outstanding. It mixes bourbonlike polished oak with tropical fruits, dark chocolate, bitter coffee, and then nut-sprinkled vanilla ice cream.

Miyagikyo welcomes visitors and offers daily tours that lead you to a tasting room, where, historically, guests were invited to sample a number of Nikka expressions at their leisure. Whether that custom continues is uncertain, because in the fall of 2015, Nikka announced that to avoid running out of single malt whisky and facing closure, it would discontinue its portfolio of aged single malt whiskies and replace them with two new nonage statement whiskies. For the foreseeable future—and there have been rumors that "foreseeable" might mean semipermanently—there will be no more ten-year-old, twelve-year-old, or fifteen-year-old Miyagikyo. That bad news is offset somewhat by the fact that the new Miyagikyo is worthy of the Nikka name, and the company has come up with a whisky of outstanding quality. Whatever the stock issues, the popularity of Nikka and its whiskies goes from strength to strength.

SHIZUOKA
DISTILLERY

LOCATION
SHIZUOKA CITY, SHIZUOKA PREFECTURE, HONSHU

OWNER
GAIA FLOW

FOUNDED
SCHEDULED TO OPEN IN 2015, WITH FIRST WHISKY IN 2019

CAPACITY
PLANNED 52,830 GALLONS (200,000 LITERS)

RANGE
N/A

VISITOR FACILITIES
NO FACILITIES

Several new small distilleries are planning to produce whisky, but only two are in a position to release a single malt in the foreseeable future: Akkeshi and the Shizuoka Distillery, located close to the city of Shizuoka, on the Pacific coast in central Honshu. The area is mountainous; the coast here has been called "the Japanese Riviera." There is a plentiful supply of water from the Abe River, iconic Mount Fuji is close by, the site is convenient to Tokyo, and barley is grown locally.

The distillery is the brainchild of Taiko Nakamura, the chief executive of a whisky importer who had been planning it since 2012. He bought the equipment from the Karuizawa Distillery, although according to journalist Nicholas Coldicott and Nonjatta blog website editor Stefan Van Eycken, much of that equipment is unusable, having deteriorated since the distillery was closed at the turn of the millennium. The newer pot stills are being used, as well as the Porteus malt mill, and a hoops press machine.

"Nakamura says he's aiming to produce single malts and blended whisky, gin, brandy and liqueurs," says the 2016 *Malt Whisky Yearbook*. The production target for whisky is around 53,000 gallons (200,000 liters), which would leapfrog Eigashima (White Oak) on the production volume list. "The aim," says the boss, "is a bright, fruity, and delicate whisky whose 'beautiful aromas you can lose yourself in,' and if all goes to plan, we'll see the first release in 2019, just in time for the Japanese-held Rugby World Cup and the Tokyo Olympics."

THE ABE RIVER_ The Shizuoka Distillery is located in an area known as the Japanese Riviera, and the Abe River will supply the distillery with water.

WHITE OAK
DISTILLERY

LOCATION
AKASHI, HYŌGO PREFECTURE, HONSHU

OWNER
EIGASHIMA SHUZO

FOUNDED
1888

CAPACITY
13,210 GALLONS (50,000 LITERS)

RANGE
AKASHI NAS, SEVERAL SPECIAL RELEASES

VISITOR FACILITIES
TOURS AND A STORE

If ever there was a distillery that gives Japanese whisky a context, it's Eigashima Shuzo's White Oak. Here, whisky making would seem to be an afterthought, and although production is increasing gradually, it remains a junior partner to the company's main business interest: making the national rice wine, sake, as well as shōchū.

Founded by Eigashima Shuzo in 1888 close to Kobe on Honshu, in 1919 this became the first Japanese distillery to be granted a whisky license. Interest in whisky was there from the early days, and the website blog Nonjatta has a bottle that contained a liquid called "Holy" and was described on the label as "Old Scotch," but also states it was distilled at White Oak. It's a throwback to the days when all kinds of concoctions were being passed off as whisky and described as Scotch, but there is no record of what it was and how it tasted.

White Oak didn't start producing until the 1960s, and even then it did so infrequently, and it didn't release its first single malt until the company moved to new facilities in 1984. Whether it will step up to the plate now that demand for Japanese whisky is rocketing remains to be seen. Although there have been some moves toward increasing production and attempting to make whisky that is innovative, unusual, and different, the core business remains elsewhere. The distillery has separate still rooms for sake, shōchū, and whisky.

WHITE OAK AKASHI
White Oak Akashi is a blended whisky. It has been reserved in Japanese shōchū casks (American oak) for three years, aged in ex-bourbon casks, and finished in ex-sherry casks for two years.

AKASHI CASK_Akashi is the only whisky that is made by a Toji (grand-master in the art of sake making).

The company has been quick to react to market downturn, and so its whisky has had an on-off history ever since. In addition, nearly all the output has gone into blended whisky, including one known as White Oak. What single malt has been released, has been released young, although a fifteen year old was released in 2013. Recent reports have suggested that there is little stock at the distillery aged over eight years old.

The whisky is stored on-site and matured mainly in ex-bourbon casks, although there is some whisky maturing in wine, Cognac, shōchū, and virgin oak casks, as well as some casks made with a lesser known Japanese oak, konara. The distillery offers tours of all three of its production areas, and prospective visitors are advised to book in advance.

ABOVE_WHITE OAK DISTILLERY
This distillery was granted Japan's first whisky license in 1919 but it waited more than forty years before producing any whisky.

RIGHT_WHITE OAK PRESIDENT
Mikio Hiraishi is President of the White Oak Distillery, which has focused on producing blended whisky in recent years.

YOICHI
DISTILLERY

LOCATION
YOICHIMACHI, HOKKAIDO

OWNER
NIKKA

FOUNDED
1934

CAPACITY
528,300 GALLONS (2,000,000 LITERS)

RANGE
NAS 2015 AND A SERIES OF SPECIAL RELEASES

VISITOR FACILITIES
GUIDED AND UNGUIDED TOURS WITH A TASTING

Yoichi is located on the northern island of Hokkaido, 30 miles (50 kilometers) from Sapporo, and it is Japan's most isolated and northerly distillery. Yoichi itself is a fishing port, surrounded by mountains, and across the water is Russia. It's a long way from Tokyo, difficult to reach, and in winter the temperature plunges way below freezing.

This is where Masataka Taketsuru decided to establish his distillery when he first parted ways with Shinjiro Torii, and set up Dainipponkaju, which would later become the giant Nikka. It was a brave decision, but for Taketsuru the key elements for making great malt whisky were all in place here, and it has often been noted that the location and climate here have much in common with Scotland.

Originally called Hokkaido Distillery, the plant started distilling in the 1930s, using a still that doubled as a wash still and a spirits still. Output was modest—around 40,000 gallons (150,000 liters) a year—and from the outset Taketsuru sought to make the kind of spirit he had made at Yamazaki, and which had been a commercial flop—a heavy, oily, smoky whisky. At the head of his own business, however, Taketsuru thrived, but it wasn't until the 1980s that a single malt was released. The name of the distillery changed in 2001, when the company was taken over by Asahi Breweries, just as Japanese whisky was about to go stellar.

YOICHI DISTILLERY_Surrounded by mountains, the pretty location at Yoichimachi is difficult to reach.

Today, there are six squat, onion-shaped stills, each coal-fired, that are set up to make a robust and full-flavored spirit. Although there is peat locally and the distillery has its own malting kiln and pagoda roof, these are not used. The distillery imports its barley like nearly all Japanese distilleries.

The style that Yoichi is most associated with is a heavily peaty, robust one, and it continues to make a fair amount of it. It has often been compared to the kind of whisky produced on the Scottish island of Islay, but in his book *The World Atlas of Whisky*, Dave Broom makes the point that it has a touch of black olive and saltiness to it, and he looks not to Islay but to Kintyre on Scotland's Campbeltown peninsula.

For all the heavy peatiness of the house style, however, as with some other Japanese distilleries, the distillery produces a range of new-make styles—hundreds, perhaps even thousands of different spirit types. Over the years, Yoichi has put out many special releases that have surprised and delighted whisky aficionados through their diversity.

With its striking red roofs, stylish buildings, and quaint setting, Yoichi attracts a healthy number of visitors, in spite of its remoteness. Taketsuru and his wife Rita are buried here, and since the television drama series based on their lives was

ABOVE LEFT AND ABOVE_VARIED STILLS
Yoichi Distillery has six squat, onion-shaped stills, all of them coal-fired. These help to produce a robust and full-flavored spirit.

RIGHT_YOICHI'S SINGLE MALT
The range is becoming harder to find as Nikka phases out some of its age statement bottlings.

IN DEMAND_ Despite the remote location, Yoichi attracts a lot of visitors, particularly since the television series about Masataka and Rita Taketsuru.

screened on Japanese television in 2014 and 2015, the number of visitors to the distillery has quadrupled. This is good news for the distillery, but not so good for the stock of aged Nikka malt whiskies; guests can taste up to three at the end of their tour.

The distillery offers two types of tour: one guided in only Japanese, the other unguided, which allows visitors to wander round the distillery aided by a map. Both tours are free.

Not all the news has been positive. Nikka has become a victim of its own success and announced to a shocked whisky world that it was in danger of running out of stock altogether, was facing closure, and had to take radical action. That radical action was to replace all aged whiskies at both its distilleries with one nonage statement whisky for each distillery. In the case of Yoichi, this means we've lost the ten year old, the twelve year old, the fifteen year old, and the twenty year old.

INTERVIEW

TADASHI SAKUMA

NIKKA'S CHIEF BLENDER

•

True to tradition
and innovative at the same time

Tadashi Sakuma is Nikka's chief blender. He believes that Japan's distillers must continue to innovate and experiment to survive. When Japan's second biggest whisky company, Nikka, announced in 2015 that it was replacing its range of aged whiskies with two nonage statement whiskies, the industry's collective jaw dropped.

It seemed incongruous—here was a style of whisky so in demand that it was becoming hard to find practically any of it, and yet one of the top producers was seemingly "dumbing down" its offering. That judgment, however, turned out to be premature. Not only was Nikka not turning away from quality whisky, but it announced that it had no choice in any case, and if it hadn't reacted quickly, it would have run out of whisky altogether and gone out of business as a result.

In fact, the two nonage statement whiskies, one from each of the company's distilleries, have nestled in nicely among Japanese whisky fans, and they are both quality expressions. Nevertheless, it marked a difficult time for the company.

The man tasked with creating the nonage statement expressions is chief blender Tadashi Sakuma. He started his career at Nikka's Yoichi Distillery in 1982. In the following years, he learned about whisky in various jobs, including production, maturation, procurement of raw materials, and quality control.

Between 1995 and 2001, he was at the forefront of the initiative to export Japanese whisky by making his base in London and traveling throughout Europe as general manager of Nikka's European office. In April 2012, he was appointed chief blender and manager of the company's blending section.

Sakuma argues that there has never been any drop in the high-quality standards of Nikka, and that the new expressions are worthy additions to the Nikka canon. However, he explains that there was little choice anyway.

"To be honest, we did not anticipate this exceptional demand when we started exporting our whisky in the late nineties. The current craze would be partly because Japanese whiskies are a little bit difficult to outline and identify, and that stimulates the curiosity of whisky enthusiasts who try to find out the secret. This boom would also be the fruit of our effort to cultivate the markets together with our foreign partners.

"In addition to the recent Japanese whisky boom in foreign markets, Nikka experienced a kind of 'fever' in the domestic market caused by the TV drama retelling the story of [Nikka founders] Rita and Masataka. As the result, we decided to discontinue many expressions and reduce shipments. We cannot lump all the distillers together anymore. Distillers who make continuous efforts to keep standards high will do well and survive.

"It's been more than ninety years since whisky production in Japan began, and for most of that time the industry had developed in the domestic market. Only relatively recently have we seen the movement of globalization. As a result, the Japanese whisky industry is now exposed to competition in the world whisky market. We need to evolve more to survive. Although nonage statement whisky might be considered by some to be controversial, it frees me from the restrictions of aging, and allows me to use the whole range of unique whiskies that we have in stock."

Sakuma points out that he approached the nonage statement whiskies in exactly the same way as he would any other whisky—with no compromise on quality.

"Nikka has always been true to tradition," he insists, "but innovative at the same time. We are about quality and pioneering spirit. One of the best parts of being a producer is to surprise the world with products that no one has ever seen. Nikka has inherited tangible and intangible assets from our founder, including two distilleries with distinctive characters—the Coffey stills, blending skills, and so on. With these assets, we have tried countless combinations with regard to raw materials, fermentation, distillation, storage, maturing, and blending. That is the reason why we have a wide range of products to satisfy any connoisseur."

Sakuma claims that Nikka's aged whisky will remain a feature of bars for sometime, and that it's probable that as supplies run out, people will sell their collections. In the meantime, his company will be working on a new generation of whisky. For this reason, he is confident that Japanese whisky will continue to go from strength to strength, and he is relaxed about new distilleries entering the market. "It will be good to stimulate the market, and to provide whisky drinkers with a wider choice," he says. "At the same time, consumers will need to have considerable insight to choose a good one."

4
/
四
.

CHAPTER FOUR

•

TASTING NOTES

風味について

Every whisky featured in this chapter is accompanied by a flavor wheel that summarizes the main characteristics of each drink. The graphic is greatly simplified, and for broad guidance only; it makes no attempt to encompass all the subtleties and nuances of a fine whisky. A "fruit" band, for example, covers all red, orange, green, and yellow fruits; there are no bands for tastes, such as maltiness or nuttiness. These categories should not be taken literally: a band of peat in the wheel does not necessarily mean that the whisky in question contains peated barley; the reference is merely to an earthy underlying taste that is reminiscent of peat, even though it may, in fact, have been produced by sulfur from a sherry cask.

Japanese distilleries have been considerably more accommodating than most distillers when it comes to single-cask bottlings for specific events or outlets, and scores of releases nestle in just one or two Japanese whisky bars and have never made it overseas. Consequently, the following is merely a selection: a complete list would be impossible to compile.

The choices included here are bottles that were released in at least some international markets after the turn of the millennium and, with the exception perhaps of some of the Karuizawas, are likely to be obtainable somewhere. The choice is also restricted to whiskies that are good and worth tasting. The selection includes several discontinued bottles. But, of course, "discontinued" does not mean unobtainable: many whiskies that are no longer in production may be held in collections and will probably one day come up for auction. It may well be that some of these bottles are gathering dust on a shelf somewhere, waiting to be rediscovered.

SINGLE MALTS

CHICHIBU THE FIRST

Matured in ex-bourbon barrels released at just three years old, this was a statement of intent from Ichiro Akuto's new distillery. A limited edition, it is surprisingly rich and full, sweet, and easy drinking. There are vanilla notes and chewy fruits. With the addition of water, what seemed to be simplicity is replaced by a sophisticated mix of lemongrass, lemon, lime, and exotic spices.

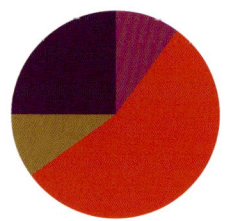

61.8% ABV

CHICHIBU PORT PIPE

Right from the start, Ichiro Akuto signaled his commitment to unconventionality, offering up this three year old and a whisky made with barley from Norfolk in England (see the following entry). This is clearly a work in progress, but a good one, with red fruits coming to the fore through the addition of water. However, there's some dustiness and youthful sappiness, too. It ends pleasantly enough and overall shows a great deal of promise.

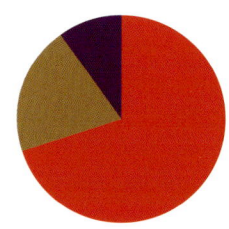

54.5% ABV

KEY: PEAT ●   FRUIT ●   WOOD ●   SPICE ●   SHERRY ●

CHICHIBU THE FLOOR MALTED 3 YEAR OLD

Chichibu is a tiny distillery, but Ichiro Akuto and his team provide a wide range of different whiskies, and they are not afraid to innovate. This remarkable work in progress is made from barley that was malted in Norfolk in eastern England. It reinforces the distillery's craft status—floor malting is rare and seldom carried out on a large scale. The result is rustic, and a little ragged, with cereal and sour fruits making an intriguing combination.

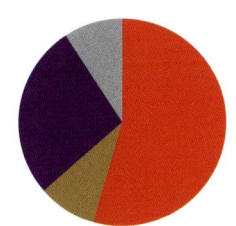

50.5% ABV

FUJI GOTEMBA 15 YEAR OLD

Distilled at the foot of Mount Fuji, this malt, and the closely related Fuji Sanroku, remain enigmatic because they are so rarely encountered, which is a pity. Fuji Gotemba has a strange nose, which is part malty wheat and part freshly baked bread. On the palate, this is a delicate, floral, sweet, and clean whisky, with honey, vanilla ice cream, and some sweet spice and oaky notes late on. The finish is rich and sweet.

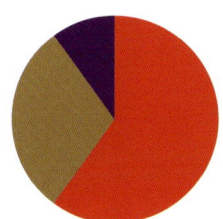

43% ABV

HAKUSHU 10 YEAR OLD

Described by owners Suntory as an attempt to make Japanese whisky for Japanese people, this is a beautifully made, scrupulously polite, and thoroughly enjoyable light drink. Hakushu can appear as a heavily peated malt, but not here. This is a crisp, "green" whisky, with apple, toffee apple, and pear dessert with a crumble topping and custard. There is some earthiness in the mix, but not a lot.

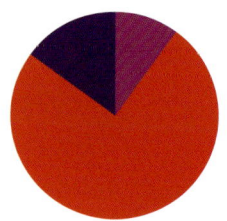

40% ABV

HAKUSHU 12 YEAR OLD

Suntory says that this is made to the same formula as the 10 Year Old (above), but the extra two years undeniably add a further dimension. It's just as refreshing as its younger stablemate, but there's a peaty smokiness here that gives it a greater depth. The green fruits remain, but there are chewy barley notes, hints of spearmint and licorice, and a touch of citrus. It is well worth seeking out.

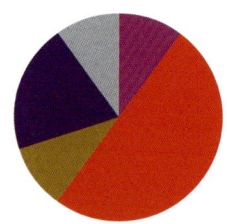

43% ABV

KEY: PEAT ●   FRUIT ●   WOOD ●   SPICE ●   SHERRY ●

HAKUSHU 18 YEAR OLD

This whisky picked up a slew of awards soon after it was launched; thereafter, demand exceeded supply, and it has been hard to get hold of ever since. I don't know how much variation there is between batches, but I have read notes by others that are some way from mine. In my experience, it starts sweet, with apple pear and distinctive, woody, sherried notes. However, the oakiness becomes too much and, by the end, the tannins are mouth-puckering.

43% ABV

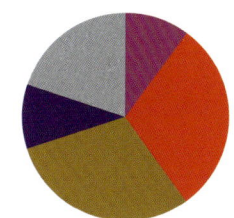

HAKUSHU 25 YEAR OLD

After the 18 Year Old (above), you might be forgiven for thinking that this one would be a step too far. It's not. In fact, it's great. Marcin Miller tells a story about the lengthy and unsuccessful trials that were carried out before a small quantity of "unusual" (that is, poor) whisky led to the creation of this winning formula. This is a big, sherry-trifle malt, with fruity jam, wood, and spice in the background. Green and overripe fruit can also be detected in the mix.

43% ABV

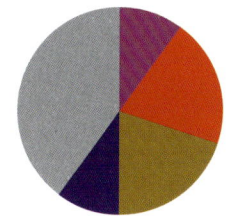

HAKUSHU 1989

If younger expressions of Hakushu are polite and pleasant, with hints of smoke, this is anything but. It's a beast that growls and grouches to impressive effect. Think about trying it neat, but then look at the strength and add water to release a complex and exciting procession of flavors, including stewed plums, toasted oak, lemon, and grapefruit. The sherry notes are dominant, but there is also some incenselike fragrance, making for a big, complex, and intriguing whisky.

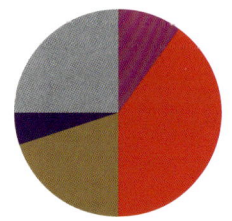

60% ABV

HANYU 1988 SINGLE CASK #9501

Hanyu stopped producing whisky at the turn of the millennium, but Ichiro Akuto, who owns Chichibu and is the grandson of the founder of Hanyu, bought the stock and has released it as part of his Ichiro's Malt range. This, however, was released by the Number One Drinks Company, which works closely with Ichiro Akuto. It is delicate and floral, with intense fruits, smoke, citrus, and vanilla. A touch of menthol and licorice is in the mix, and it has a long, sweet, and spicy finish.

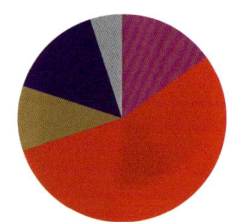

55.6% ABV

KEY: PEAT ● FRUIT ● WOOD ● SPICE ● SHERRY ●

HANYU 1991 SINGLE CASK

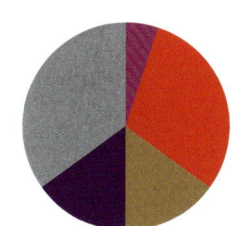

Entirely different from the 1988 single cask, this is another Number One Drinks Company product. It is a huge whisky, a heavy rock tour de force, Iron Maiden in a whisky glass; loud and proud, but aged, sophisticated, and with all parts working together as a mighty unit. After the briefest of introductions, it charges forward with everything turned up to maximum—sherried, with a lot of fruity jam notes, some dark cocoa, and plenty of oak and spice for good measure.

57.3% ABV

ICHIRO'S MALT CARD SERIES EIGHT OF HEARTS

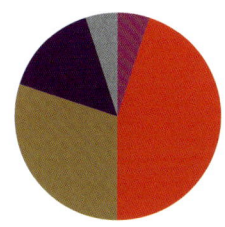

The Card Series showed that the new owner would do things differently from his predecessor. The playing cards refer to single casks of Hanyu single malt, part of 400 casks salvaged from the old distillery. Akuto released a whole deck of cards, including jokers, with the highest face values representing the oldest whiskies. This one is seventeen years old, and although the nose is dusty, the malt is fresh and zippy, with ginger, nutmeg, cinnamon, pepper, and some juicy berries late on.

56.8% ABV

ICHIRO'S MALT CARD SERIES FIVE OF SPADES

Ichiro Akuto's use of the Card Series made it easy for consumers to remember bottlings without having to remember dates, ages, and so on. The Five of Spades was distilled in the final year before Hanyu stopped production and the distillery was demolished. Little of the stock leaves Japan's shores, so grab the chance to try any of the range, if you get it. This one is rich in sherried trifle, and there are notes of strawberry flan and vanilla custard with nuts, oak, and pepper. Impressive.

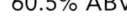

60.5% ABV

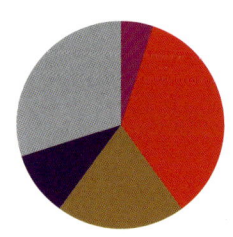

KARUIZAWA 17 YEAR OLD

This is the distillery that put Japan in the premier league when it came to collectable whisky. As Karuizawa has become rarer, the price of it has gone through the roof. Much of the remaining stock was bought by the partnership between Ichiro Akuto and the Number One Drinks Company, but this bottling is not part of that deal. This is a big and fruity number, with first sherbet notes and then cordial ones, balanced excellently by oak and spice.

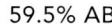

59.5% ABV

KEY: PEAT ●   FRUIT ●   WOOD ●   SPICE ●   SHERRY ●

KARUIZAWA 1967 SINGLE CASK #6426

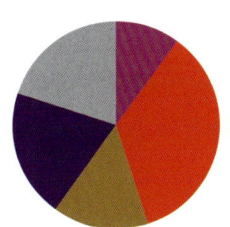

This whisky is forty-two years old. If you want it, first you'll have to find it, and then pay a premium. A bottle sold at auction in 2015 for €13,000 ($14,000 / £10,000), and prices have since been quoted upward of €30,000 ($32,000 / £23.000). It's rare to find a single malt whisky this old, and a Scottish equivalent might well have an ABV in the low forties. Unsurprisingly, this has a lot of wood upfront, but then there are some almost zesty, clean fruits, including grapefruit. There are touches of coffee, licorice, and prunes, too.

58.4% ABV

KARUIZAWA 1971 SINGLE CASK #6878

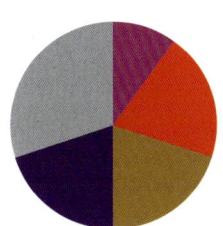

This has been described as one of the world's richest and most complex whiskies, and it is. However, it is also a high-octane, top-speed ride, and it takes some coming to grips with. That's due to a combination of slow maturation—thirty-seven years—and the full, rich, concentrated alcoholic strength. This is a joyful mix of fruit and nut, and rich fruitcake, and there's licorice, oak, polish, and dark chocolate in there somewhere as well.

64.1% ABV

SINGLE MALTS

KARUIZAWA 1976 SINGLE CASK #6719

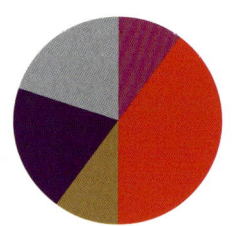

This is a special launch, released with a label bearing an image of a Noh performance, one of Japan's oldest art forms. It deserves attention, because it is exceptional—thirty-two years old, but still 63% proof—and it's because of the intensity of the spirit that the wood hasn't ruined it. There is incense, vanilla, and lemon creams early on, then a concentrated taste of various fruits. Its finish provides another twist, being gentle, soft, and well rounded.

63% ABV

KARUIZAWA 1985 SINGLE CASK #7017

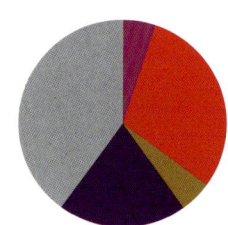

Those lucky enough to have tasted a number of Karuizawa whiskies will tell you that the individual bottlings all have highlights. None of them is subtle. This one is a big-hearted all-rounder that is well and truly in your face. With plum, prune juice, orange notes, intense oak, a lot of sherry notes, and a touch of aniseed and hickory, it all works well, but boy, is there a lot going on here.

60.8% ABV

KEY: PEAT ● FRUIT ● WOOD ● SPICE ● SHERRY ●

KARUIZAWA 1986 SINGLE CASK #7387

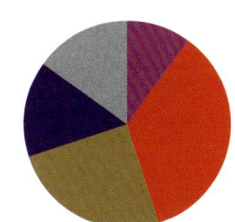

Think that Japanese whisky is just a recreational alternative to Scottish single malt? Here is powerful evidence to the contrary. This is plowing its own whisky furrow, big time. The distinctions are in the detail, and they're in abundance here. There's a damp, mushroomy note on the nose, but, on the palate, lemon and grapefruit are to the fore, and there are some distinctive orange and barley notes late on. It's like tasting fruits through a Japanese kaleidoscope.

60.7% ABV

MIYAGIKYO 10 YEAR OLD

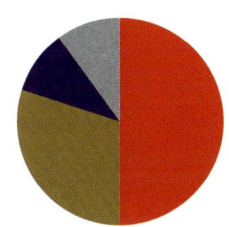

Miyagikyo is owned by Nikka and comes from a region chosen by the cofounder of Japanese whisky and creator of Nikka, Masataka Taketsuru, for its high humidity and pure air. Nikka itself compares the location to Scotland's Cairngorms. Parallels have also been made to the distillery set-up at Longmorn, where Taketsuru once studied. Certainly, this is a green and yellow fruit whisky, with vanilla and toffee notes, and some delicate spices. It wouldn't look out of place among the finest fruity Speysiders.

45% ABV

SINGLE MALTS 123

MIYAGIKYO 12 YEAR OLD

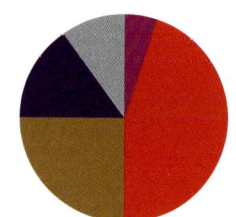

At the time of writing, Nikka was in the process of replacing its aged statement whiskies with two whiskies without an age on the bottle: one from Miyagikyo, the other from its second distillery, Yoichi. This is due to a world shortage of malt that Nikka says has threatened the future of the company. Shame, because it's fascinating going up through the gears as the age increases. This bottling has gooseberry, rhubarb, and cocoa on the nose, then sweet fruit, before razor-sharp, peppery spices cut through.

45% ABV

MIYAGIKYO 15 YEAR OLD

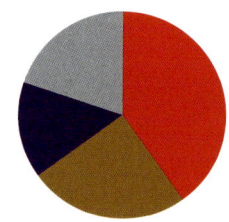

This is where Miyagikyo's malts finally come of age and really hit their stride—their extra oak and sherry justify comparisons with Longmorn, the great Speysider. This is a sweet, fresh, clean whisky. Rich and plummy, with canned peaches and pears, raisins, cocoa, vanilla, and a lot of sweetness, there is plenty going on here, all held together by a delightfully malty core.

45% ABV

KEY: PEAT ●   FRUIT ●   WOOD ●   SPICE ●   SHERRY ●

NIKKA MIYAGIKYO 1989 SINGLE CASK

While many Japanese whiskies are subtle, sophisticated, refined, and mysterious, this isn't one of them. This puts the boot in from the off and keeps on kicking. This is a big hitter of a sherried malt, with intense damp forest and some astringent savory notes. If it were a color it would be maroon; if it were a season, it would be fall.

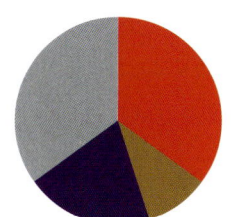

61% ABV

NIKKA YOICHI 1991 SINGLE CASK

This is from Yoichi, and it throws a curve ball by taking that distillery's trademark whisky characteristics of oil and smoke and turning them on their heads. Whisky doesn't come cleaner, sweeter, or fruitier than this. The pie chart shows the emphasis on fruit, but it can't reflect the deep bowl of flavors—candy, vanilla, banana, and toffee on the nose, and a taste of sweet, fruity soda, and black currant Starburst on the palate. There is some spice in there late on.

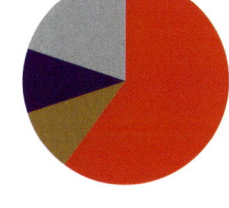

58% ABV

SINGLE MALTS   125

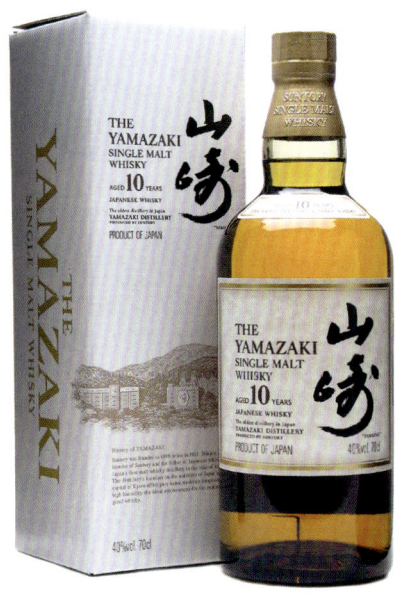

YAMAZAKI 10 YEAR OLD

This is widely regarded as the most accessible of all Japanese whiskies, and it has a sweetness that derives from being matured mainly in white oak casks. It's a light, easy-drinking product that has a lot going on and is a fruity delight. It's clean and sweet, with soft banana, fluffy apples, melon, some sweet spices, and, toward the finish, some vanilla and toffee. For an entry-level whisky, it produces a virtuoso performance.

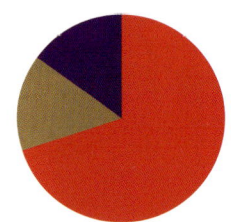

———
40% ABV

YAMAZAKI 12 YEAR OLD

This is as juicy as whisky gets, a great, big, luscious malt that coats itself over your mouth and doesn't want to move. Imagine mixing three fruit smoothies of different flavors and adding alcohol, and you're getting there. There's plenty more to enjoy here, too: polished wood and pine on the nose, for instance, and a long, delightful, wispy, dancing finish.

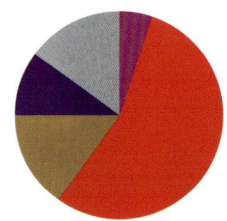

———
43% ABV

KEY: PEAT ●   FRUIT ●   WOOD ●   SPICE ●   SHERRY ●

YAMAZAKI 18 YEAR OLD

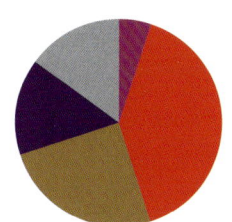

This is one of the world's most iconic eighteen-year-old whiskies; indeed, it's one of the most iconic, period. It's also difficult to find, and its price has shot up due to supply shortage. Not surprising, really, because it's a real star. Something of an all-rounder, too: sweet, with a mélange of fruits, including mango, kiwi, and tropical fruits, all wrapped in spice and wood. There is a distinctive fungal note late on, and an intriguing damp forest and wood finish.

43% ABV

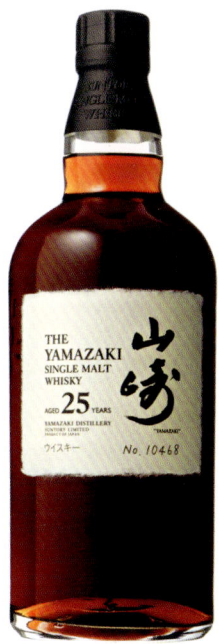

YAMAZAKI 25 YEAR OLD

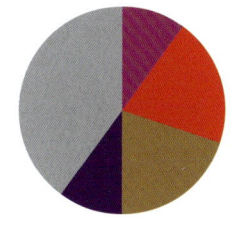

When this could still be found without difficulty, it supported those who maintain that Japanese whisky merely emulates what happens in Scotland. It's a big, classy, sherried whisky that could easily pass as a twenty-five-year-old Speysider, known for its tanning woody notes, and intense red and blackberry sherry hit. Those two characteristics seem to have buried its Japanese personality, making it the whisky equivalent of an outstanding tribute band: great, but ultimately, undeniably unoriginal.

43% ABV

YAMAZAKI 1984

Released in 2009 to mark the twenty-fifth anniversary of Yamazaki making single malts, this is a fine creation, a lovingly assembled new malt that is daringly different, and it is strikingly unlike anything else in the range. There are subtle spices and wood notes, an incense feel, and a rich, dark chocolate and cherry finish. It is undoubtedly a sweet, stylish whisky with a big taste.

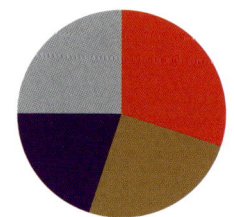

———
48% ABV

YAMAZAKI 1993

A couple of 1993 Yamazaki casks have made it overseas in recent years. French retailer and importer La Maison du Whisky had a big, sherried one that was reputedly excellent. But this is something else again. If you happen to find it, you'll no doubt check the bottle at least twice, because it really is an oddball—a big, oily, peaty, and fishy malt on one side, and a flip-flop floral, buttery, hickory, and citrus palate on the other. Amazing.

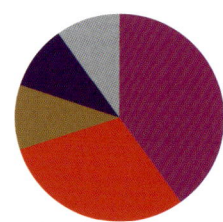

———
62% ABV

KEY: PEAT ●   FRUIT ●   WOOD ●   SPICE ●   SHERRY ●

YAMAZAKI BOURBON BARREL

Suntory has been showing off in recent years. Whisky making in Japan is complex, and often involves several malt styles produced under the same roof. Different yeasts and stills are used to make new spirit, as well as a number of different casks, creating intricate malts. So Suntory has been releasing styles of whisky representing just one aspect of its flag bearer, the twelve year old. This one majors in the sweet—toffee, and banana split, with a lot of vanilla ice cream.

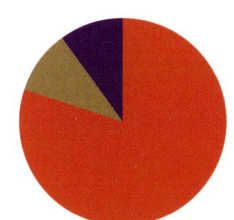

48.2% ABV

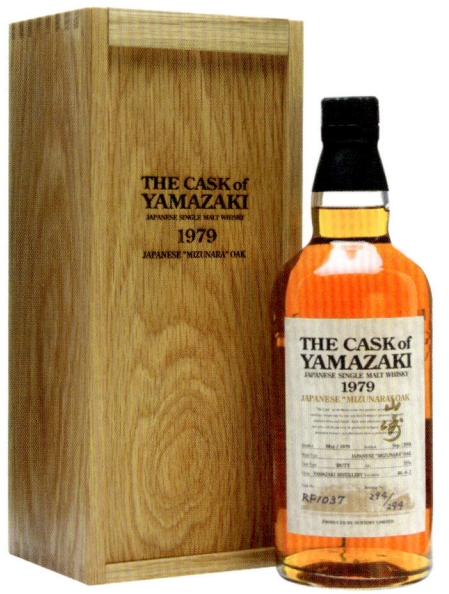

YAMAZAKI 1979 MIZUNARA OAK CASK

Mizunara oak is indigenous to Japan and is thought to be responsible for the delicate, spicy, incense-like flavor that normally characterizes the nation's single malts. However, there is nothing subtle here. This has a big, peppery, earthy, and woody flavor, and the balance is all over the place. Heavy smokers might like it, or people who burn their steak, and then eat it with hot chili sauce. It's not a fair reflection of Japanese style, and there are better examples of mizunara oak.

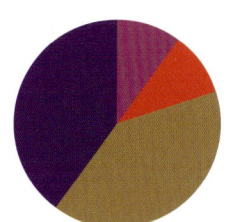

55% ABV

YOICHI 10 YEAR OLD

Yoichi is not only Japan's most northerly distillery, it's way up north. It snows a lot, Russia is just across the sea, and it is difficult to reach. However, Nikka makes excellent, weighty, peaty, and oily whisky here. That's not the whole story, however. In fact, the usual house style is held in check, and canned fruits, some saltiness, and some distinctive sherry notes all make appearances. A great entry-level whisky. Try it while you can.

45% ABV

YOICHI 12 YEAR OLD

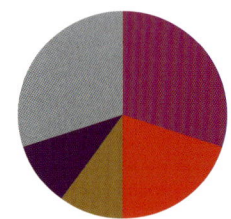

One of the hardest feats to pull off is combining sherry and peat so that the resulting whisky works. It's the oral equivalent of a complicated trapeze act: filled with risk, but when it succeeds, it has you purring with pleasure. And that's what happens in this malt, with peat and sherry batting out front, and apple, vanilla, and dried fruits providing backup. It's knife-edge stuff, but it holds together into a fruity, peaty conclusion. Wonderful.

45% ABV

KEY: PEAT ●   FRUIT ●   WOOD ●   SPICE ●   SHERRY ●

YOICHI 15 YEAR OLD

There are many Japanese whiskies that can bear favorable comparison with anything else on the planet, and this is one of them. It's extraordinary how much is going on here, how much is crammed in on the taste buds, and how different this is from anything else. The nose is wispy, understated, and floral, and, on the palate, sherry and smoke open the door up front, but in behind them march salt and pepper, hickory, clove, toffee, stewed apricots, and pear. That's some combo, and this is some whisky.

45% ABV

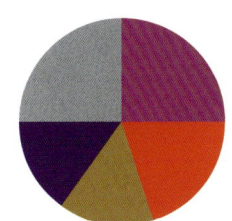

YOICHI 20 YEAR OLD

I have two separate tasting notes for this fabulous malt. The earlier is positive but restrained. The later starts with the assertion: "This is one of the world's greatest whiskies." Perhaps I have been seduced by Japanese whisky. Certainly, this takes some getting used to: oily, nutty, peaty, with big, earthy notes, as well as dark chocolate molasses, barbecued fish, and sea spray. It's an absolute treat, one of the greatest whiskies you're ever likely to taste.

52% ABV

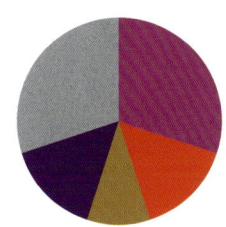

SINGLE MALTS

JAPANESE BLENDED AND BLENDED MALT WHISKY

HIBIKI 12 YEAR OLD

The Hibiki range is all the proof you will ever need that Japanese whisky has an identity all of its own. This whisky is special because it steps away from its Hibiki siblings and recalls one of Suntory's traditional cornerstones. The company has successfully sold plum liqueur finished in American oak. Here, this whisky is finished in plum liqueur casks, so that it is a fresh summer cordial of a drink, with zesty fruit, vanilla, and a dollop of sweet spices. Impressive.

BLENDED WHISKY

43% ABV

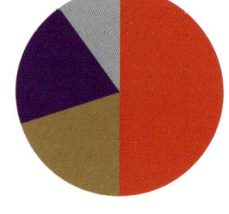

HIBIKI 17 YEAR OLD

This is one of Japan's most famous whiskies, having won a bucketful of awards, and rightly so: Hibiki is Japanese for "harmony," and this is harmonious without ever being a compromise of flavors. It's rich, with a lot of fruitiness and spice, but graceful and rounded at the same time. There is a lot going on, with exotic fruits, cherry, melon, unripe banana, red berries, and vanilla in the mix. Big, full, and rounded, this is a heavyweight champion.

BLENDED WHISKY

43% ABV

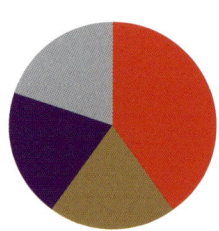

KEY: PEAT ●   FRUIT ●   WOOD ●   SPICE ●   SHERRY ●

HIBIKI 21 YEAR OLD

This was the rightful winner of *Whisky Magazine*'s World's Best Whisky award in 2015. The delicate aromatic spices come from mizunara oak, the berry and orange compote notes come from sherry oak, and the smoothness and body come from the grain whisky. Every one of the flavors here — and there are many of them — is wrapped up in polished church bench. Truly top drawer.

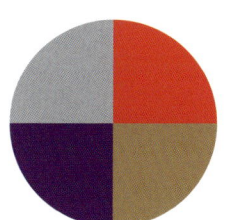

BLENDED WHISKY

———

43% ABV

HOKUTO 12 YEAR OLD

Some mystery surrounds this one. Whisky expert Jim Murray categorizes it as "an unspecified malt," but the makers call it "pure malt," so we can probably conclude it's made up of malt from more than one distillery. It comes from Suntory, so that means it's from Yamazaki and Hakushu. Whatever, it's unusual but captivating. There are dusty wood shavings and stewed fruit on the nose, prune, petal water, and sherbet on the palate, and pepper and oak at the finish.

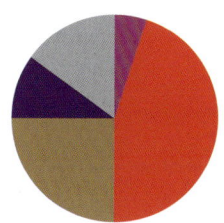

———

40% ABV

NIKKA TAKETSURU PURE MALT 12 YEAR OLD

Japan does vatted malts as well as any country in the world, and Nikka's extensive Pure Malts are a perfect vehicle to introduce novices to the country's mature whisky-making style, because despite shortages and pressure on prices, these whiskies have often stayed affordable. This one is a delight, with molasses, and soft toffee, but mainly with dark chocolate, chili pepper, and, in the finish, some sweet pepper.

VATTED/PURE/BLENDED MALT

40% ABV

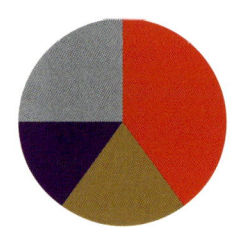

NIKKA TAKETSURU PURE MALT 21 YEAR OLD

This should be the best of the bunch, and it is, by some distance. The nose is distinctively Japanese, with incense and mushroom, and on the palate there is an earthy and rustic undercarpet that may be due to peat or sulfur sherry, then licorice, vanilla, and berry fruits. Spice and some tanny bitterness from the wood serve to give the whole an excellent shape. This is an outstanding whisky.

VATTED/PURE/BLENDED MALT

43% ABV

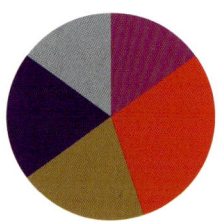

KEY: PEAT ●   FRUIT ●   WOOD ●   SPICE ●   SHERRY ●

NIKKA PURE MALT BLACK

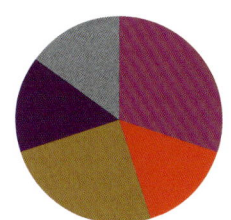

To paraphrase Spinal Tap, whose happy ending was, of course, that they were big in Japan, this whisky is as black as black can get. It has an intense savory nose, with horse chestnut, damp leaves, and molasses. The palate is decidedly moody, an oral peaty fog with dark cherry, throat lozenges, canned peaches, and orange fruits appearing from time to time. The finish is surprisingly delicate after all the foregoing moodiness, with sweet fruit and savory spice.

———

43% ABV

NIKKA PURE MALT RED

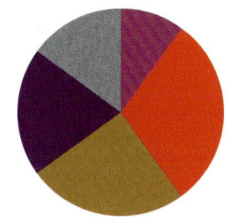

This is lighter and brighter than its Black sibling (above). It has two distinctive sides, and it flip-flops between them. One aspect has vanilla, cocoa-rich dark chocolate, exotic fruits, and toasted oak; the other is heavy, like a full-flavored German sausage doused in olive oil. The two sides don't seem like they should necessarily work together, but this is a Simon and Garfunkel of a whisky that brings two dissonant parts to one harmonious conclusion.

———

43% ABV

NIKKA PURE MALT WHITE

Tasting these pure malts was so much fun. Sometimes you look at a sample, and your heart sinks; other times, it soars. And sometimes, as here, you know you're doing the best job in the world. This one is a big, sweet, dollop of peat, rich and oily, with barbecued trout and sea coast running through its heart. That heart is a sophisticated one, too, and delicate incense spice, and some delightful oak notes, take it to a place all of its own.

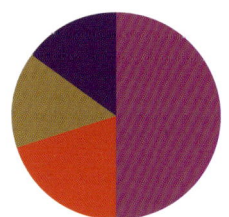

43% ABV

NIKKA RARE OLD SUPER

This is an oddball that appeared from nowhere and then disappeared again. Be warned—the marketing blurb on the label misleadingly describes this whisky as a smooth blend. It's anything but, and all the better for it. It buzzes with oaky notes, and on the palate it is feisty and assertive, prodding the mouth with peat, coating it with sherry fruits, and sprinkling spice with abandon.

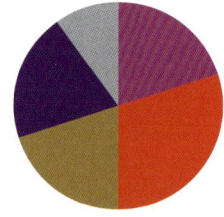

BLENDED WHISKY

45% ABV

KEY: PEAT ●   FRUIT ●   WOOD ●   SPICE ●   SHERRY ●

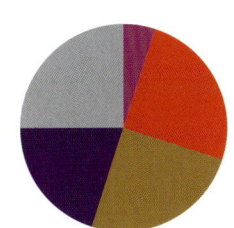

NIKKA WHISKY FROM THE BARREL

Blended whisky is a mix of different malts and grain. The amount of malt can massively affect the overall taste, and when the content is jacked up, you can end with something like this: a wonderful, full-tasting whisky that stands up well on its own without mixing. There is a big wave of sherry and orange marmalade, toasted oak, delicate spice, and some citrus and tropical fruits before a toasted and dusty oak conclusion. Very seductive.

BLENDED WHISKY

51.4% ABV

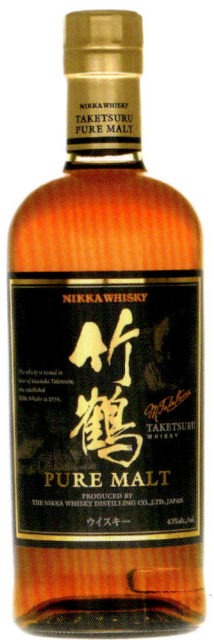

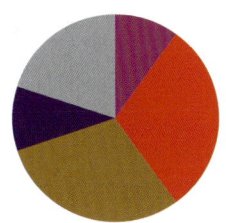

NIKKA TAKETSURU PURE MALT

Released in 2015 and 2016 to replace the age statement whiskies that Nikka is withdrawing from the market, this vatted malt is labeled as "pure," a term that could not be applied to it if it were Scottish. Containing malt from Yoichi and Miyagikyo, this whisky is good, if perhaps a little tame. It has nice, earthy, almost mushroomy notes, sherried undertones, wispy smoke, and some plum and apricot. It's sweet, rounded, rich, and well ordered.

43% ABV

5 / 五.

CHAPTER FIVE

•

THE RISE OF JAPANESE WHISKY

日本ウィスキーの台頭

As we have seen, Japan has distilleries with complex whisky-making capabilities, scores of bars and restaurants, and a sophisticated hospitality culture. Couple with that the fact that Japan is inquisitive about drinks worldwide and has imported an impressive range of Scotch and Irish whiskies, bourbons, rums, and brandies, and the result is a vibrant and diverse drinking culture.

Japan's whisky makers have taken a Scottish blueprint and evolved it to suit the Japanese palate, through innovation, experimentation, and investment in the finest ingredients. So it might appear churlish, Western-centric even, to dedicate a chapter to a group of Europeans, and to credit them with kick-starting the revolution that swept all before it between 2001 and 2015. The truth is, however, that Japan looked to Scotland for inspiration, and until the end of the twentieth century put all its resources into easy-drinking and quaffable blended whisky. When it did turn its attention to single malt, few people in Japan took notice. The late, great whisky writer Michael Jackson told a story about being detained on the Canadian border, because customs said Canada already had whisky writers: "At the risk of sounding bigheaded, I told them, did they not think that people might think Canadian whisky was very good if I told them it was, rather than a Canadian whisky writer?"

So when the likes of Jackson, Jim Murray, and Dave Broom sang the praises of Japanese single malt, people listened, then explored. Japan's whisky makers had slowly and surely put together the fuel needed to start the fire, but a group of Westerners struck the match and then fanned the flames. Here, then, are the views of those who were witness to the revolution, and who played key roles in bringing Japanese whisky to the Western drinking palate.

EYEWITNESS: MARCIN MILLER

When you ask Marcin Miller how he came to play such a fundamental role in the development of Japanese whisky, he'll tell you it was due to good timing.

And it was, but timing can be influenced by a range of different factors. The way Miller tells it, he was blessed with a degree of good fortune. To the objective observer, however, it would appear that he's benefited from the same kind of luck the professional angler has when he catches a record-size fish. It is the same kind of luck that comes from lengthy preparation, intense observation, the best equipment, and being in the right place at the right time. Miller landed his fish for a very good reason.

Miller is, in whisky terms, a lot of things. He is the founding editor and editorial publisher of *Whisky Magazine*, which he launched with a business partner in the late 1990s, successfully riding what was, at the time, a small but growing wave of interest in all things whisky, and, in particular, single malt whisky. He is also a cofounder of Whisky Live, *Whisky Magazine's* live festival, and had a part in choosing Tokyo as the city to launch it in. He was involved with launching The Best of The Best, an event in which the highest-scoring whiskies in *Whisky Magazine* were taken to be judged by leading whisky writers, distillers, and retailers across the world before the best-scoring one was crowned Best of the Best. In 2001, the first time it was held, that honor went to a Japanese whisky, causing a sensation in the world of spirits.

Miller is a founder and codirector of the Number One Drinks Company, which was formed in 2006, just as Ichiro Akuto, owner of the remaining stock from closed distillery Hanyu, was launching the Malt Card Series, which the Number One Drinks Company exported. It was Miller who stepped in to buy all the remaining stock of Karuizawa when it became available.

WHAT ARE YOU DRINKING?

YOICHI 10 YEAR OLD:
You never forget your first Japanese whisky.

KARUIZAWA 1981 #103:
One of the early single casks bottled by Number One, magnificently broad-shouldered with late peat.

HIBIKI 17 YEAR OLD:
A perfectly balanced example of the blender's art.

ICHIRO'S MALT CARD SERIES ACE OF DIAMONDS:
I have fond memories of this whisky.

CHICHIBU ON THE WAY:
A fantastic indication of what the future holds.

MARCIN MILLER
Miller has been a key player in the growth of the Japanese whisky industry.

Karuizawa can sell for tens of thousands of dollars now, and is among the most sought-after whiskies in the world.

Finally, Miller built a relationship with Ichiro Akuto, who used money raised from sales through the Number One Drinks Company to build his own distillery, Chichibu. Its whisky is now distributed by the Number One Drinks Company, and it barely touches the shelf, such is the demand for it.

"If only we'd known," Miller says whimsically, when thinking back to how things have changed. But he did know, didn't he? Or at least he had a good idea. "No, timing really is always crucial," he says. "The founding of Number One Drinks in 2006 pretty much coincided with Ichiro's first Card Series releases, single casks from the Hanyu Distillery built by his grandfather. Ichiro rescued the last casks when the distillery closed in 2000, prior to it being destroyed in 2004. It had long been a dream for Ichiro to build his own distillery, and in 2007 he achieved that with the construction of Chichibu Distillery, in the same town in which his family has been brewing sake since 1624. With Karuizawa, I was somewhat underwhelmed by the standard products, but utterly impressed by the cask samples my business partner David Croll and I had been fortunate enough to taste. When on a visit to the distillery, it became apparent they hadn't been distilling for some years, I thought it was time to aim high, and offered to buy the entire inventory."

As you do. So Miller has had a front seat at every stage of the Japanese whisky story. Amazingly, though, he hadn't tasted Japanese whisky when he first got on the plane for Tokyo.

"I'm pretty sure I hadn't," he said. "I arrived in a state of ignorance, and left beguiled. When *Whisky Magazine* launched in the late 1990s, we wanted to have a Japanese-language version of the magazine, and to hold the inaugural Whisky Live tasting event in Tokyo. Japan was always seen as a key market for whisky, and I was intrigued by the similarities and differences between the familiar and the unfamiliar. I think Whisky Live Tokyo was, in essence, a dry run, as it were, for the first London event. Having said that, the Japanese version grew to be my joint favorite iteration, along with Paris. On subsequent occasions, I traveled with Jim Murray and the late Michael Jackson who, together with the generous hospitality of Suntory and Nikka, gave me an education. Since then, Dave Broom has been a regular (if occasionally demanding) mentor, as well as a delightful travel companion."

It's hard to imagine just how little was known about Japanese whisky at the turn of the millennium, and how

ABOVE_KARUIZAWA WHISKY
Some bottles of this whisky have attracted thousands of dollars at auction (see p.121).

RIGHT_WHISKY LIVE JAPAN
These tasting and seminar events are now held across the world, but the first was in Tokyo.

A GREAT NIGHT OUT

I love going out in Tokyo, Kyoto, Osaka, and beyond, guided by whisky-loving locals. There are hundreds of wonderful, crazy bars that can accommodate half a dozen folk, and all have their own quirks. Shot Bar Zoetrope is one; black-and-white Fatty Arbuckle movies on a loop, brilliant music, and all the Japanese whisky you could hope for, washed down with a Minoh beer or two.

ignorant even enthusiastic whisky drinkers were about it. In fact, worse than that—they had a decidedly negative view of it, although they had almost certainly never tried it.

"Most people's opinions of Japanese whisky—mine included—until the early 2000s were borne entirely from ignorance," Miller says. "People who hadn't tried Japanese whisky were very happy to venture an opinion. Having said that, younger people tend to be less set in their ways and, by extension, more experimental. I like to think of whisky blogger Dave Alcock's comment: 'There are fans of Japanese whisky, and those who have yet to taste any...,' or words to that effect."

Miller says that the rapid growth of interest in Japanese whisky can be traced in a series of milestones between 2000 and 2016: "The increased coverage of Japanese whisky has played a part. The success of Nikka first, and subsequently Suntory in the *Whisky Magazine* Best of the Best tastings; the Malt Maniac awards; *Jim Murray's Whisky Bible;* the increased consumer interest in whisky as a broader category; and the birth and development of social media have all been important. Jim Murray has consulted with Nikka over the years, and that will have helped raise its profile. I'd agree that Japanese confidence in its whisky has increased greatly over the last ten to fifteen years, leading to an ever-stronger identity."

As for the future, Miller says that once more it is up in the air. The stock issue is well documented, but he says that a combination of the difficulty creating new distilleries in Japan, along with the evolution of new world distilleries and the inquisitive nature of dedicated whisky fans, could mean that the tide could start to go out for Japan.

"To be granted a distilling license, you have to have built the distillery and have all the equipment in place ready to press the green button before approval will be granted. Obviously, there is risk attached to this, which may have put a lot of people off. Also, is Japan a country of entrepreneurs? As it stands, I don't think Japan will see the level of craft distilling that, for example, the United States has enjoyed over the last few years. As for the future, that's an interesting one. With a shortage of mature stock, will lovers of Japanese whisky wait or look elsewhere? Single malt enthusiasts are by nature promiscuous in their drinking habits so they may well look elsewhere. On the other hand, there may be other spirits being distilled in Japan which the domestic population might take to its heart; I know of a small rum distillery being built, and there is talk of Japanese gin, too."

EYEWITNESS: CHRIS BUNTING

If you're looking for a fine example of a blog that punches above its weight, then take a look at Japanese whisky website Nonjatta. It is an effervescent, personal, and professional take on Japanese whisky, produced as a labor of love by a small group of enthusiastic amateurs whose passion is evident at every click. It is thorough, authoritative, and has the confidence to wander off-piste, look at whisky and the industry across the world, and to write about other Japanese drinks when it feels like it. And that's how it should be. Nonjatta was the brainchild of Chris Bunting, a journalist whose chance discovery of Japanese whisky led to his passion for Japan's diverse and exciting drinking culture, not just of whisky, but of all drinks.

"I found myself in Japan in 2005 because my wife had been offered a job at a Japanese university. Until that point, I was living a fairly hectic life working for various national newspapers in the United Kingdom. Then I suddenly found myself in semirural Japan with a very young child to look after. My love affair with Japanese whisky started about that time on a visit to a local supermarket. My wife was at an overseas conference, and I was shopping with my son. I saw a Japanese single malt on the shelf. I thought 'I can't stand a bottle of wine on my own—that would be a bit sad—but a dram of something a bit exotic after the little one goes to sleep won't do me any harm.' I tried it that evening—it was a Hakushu single malt from Suntory—and it was absolutely fantastic. I started my blog—Nonjatta—a few days later, and started exploring Japanese whisky. I quite quickly got a lot of readers, and my drink writing and Japanese whisky quaffing developed from there."

Bunting started exploring all kinds of Japanese drinks from that point, but while the West's whisky lovers were embarking on a journey of discovery elsewhere, and Japan's whisky star was rising apace, the opposite was true in Japan itself.

WHAT ARE YOU DRINKING?

This is what I would like to be drinking in the United Kingdom, but many of the bottles are too rare or expensive to get.

YOICHI 15-YEAR-OLD SINGLE MALT (NIKKA):
A classic Yoichi with stewed fruit, marmalade, and coffee notes.

HAKUSHU 12-YEAR-OLD SINGLE MALT (SUNTORY):
I loved the balance between sweetness and pepperiness.

HAKUSHU (NO AGE STATEMENT; SUNTORY):
I loved the Hakushu 12, but this one is now easier to get in the UK. It captures the light, sweet, and herb-inflected tastes that are characteristic of their whiskies.

YAMAZAKI 1984 SINGLE MALT WHISKY (SUNTORY):
This one is the most memorable Japanese single malt I have tasted, with a unique influence from the mizunara oak casks, and a wonderfully balanced mix of butter, nuts, and slight hints of pine, with a cereal and vanilla baseline.

TOP_THE FIRST JAPANESE WHISKY
Suntory Whisky Shirofuda (white label) was the first Japanese whisky, launched in 1929.

ABOVE_JUSO TORYS BAR, OSAKA
This iconic bar is one of the last Torys bars remaining in Japan. Fortunately, it reopened after burning down in March 2014.

"For most of the period from 2001, the story was of a decline in the popularity of Japanese whisky—at least as a domestic mass-market product," Bunting says. "Whisky consumption in Japan fell year-on-year from before the start of the new millennium until 2009. It only started to recover after a Suntory advertising campaign succeeded in doing what whisky producers had been trying and failing to do for years: sell whisky to fashionable and female, post-bubble, young people.

"Whisky had been THE drink of the post-World War II economic boom years. It started off as an unobtainable symbol of sophistication, the drink of the Western occupiers and the prewar elite. But in the 1960s and 1970s, it became the quintessential drink of the Japanese salaryman, and of the economic miracle he (and it almost always was a 'he') had helped create. By the early 2000s, whisky was deeply unfashionable precisely because of this close association."

Bunting points out that, just as whisky as a mass-market product was reaching its nadir, the rest of the world was waking up to the quality of Japanese product. Japanese whisky scored some game-changing victories in international competitions in the early 2000s, and the advocacy of experts, such as Michael Jackson, was pivotal. The global appreciation of Japan's best whisky acted as a counterpoint to the travails in its domestic market during this period.

"Let's be clear: the international 'popularity' is still just a drop in the ocean compared to domestic sales," Bunting continues. "Unlike, say, the Scottish, Irish, or Canadian whisky industries, which have always been strongly export-orientated, Japanese whisky is still predominantly made for drinkers in Japan. What happened between 2000 and 2015 was, the world suddenly realized that the continuing rarity of Japanese whisky abroad was a great shame, because it is very good indeed."

Bunting, who has since returned to the United Kingdom, says that there have been some really big changes in the world of Japanese drinking culture in recent years. "They include an interest in shōchū, awamori, and sake, much more drinking at home rather than in bars, a decline in the importance of the salaryman generation, and a rise in the centrality of young female drinkers to alcohol makers' strategies," he says.

"The last of these is undoubtedly central to the thinking behind the Highball campaign, and the first may be part of a more general theme since the 1980s: less swilling of rubbish alcohol with fancy branding, and a greater appreciation of genuinely good alcohol. This is not that surprising. Japan has changed from a thrusting, if slightly gauche, industrial powerhouse to a postindustrial economy with a highly sophisticated media and consumer economy. You would expect its consumers to know what is good, and much of Japan's whisky is—like its shōchū, awamori, and sake—very good."

The acceptance of Japanese whisky in Japan itself did not come about spontaneously. Older drinkers, in particular, took the view that Scottish whisky was good and Japanese whisky was bad. "My father-in-law still basically feels that a good Scotch is the real thing," says Bunting. "And that is because brands, such as Johnnie Walker, which were priced artificially high throughout the 1960s and 1970s, because of Japan's swinging import tariffs, were the epitome of foreign sophistication when he was a young man. Young people now have no preconceptions, are much more likely to have read Japan's sophisticated media coverage of alcohol, and are just generally much more self-confident about the quality of Japanese products across all industries."

Bunting's interest in Japanese drinks eventually led to the publication of *Drinking Japan: A Guide to Japan's Best Drinks and Drinking Establishments* (2011). It captures wonderfully the unique nature of Japan's drinking culture, exploring myriad tiny bars hidden away in office buildings and back streets.

"Some time after I launched Nonjatta, I got talking to Tuttle, an English-language publisher in Japan, and we realized nobody had written a comprehensive guide to Japanese alcohol culture. By that time, I was convinced that it was very special indeed, mixing a very long tradition of native alcohols including sake, shōchū, and awarmori with superb new traditions developed since Japan's late-nineteenth century modernization.

"In whisky making—but also to some extent in wine and beer making—Japanese producers had shown they could produce alcohols that were at least the equal of their rivals in more established centers. On top of that, Japan had and has a phenomenal bar culture. We sometimes talk about big cities never sleeping, but in Japan they really do never sleep. I discovered that in some marathon sessions forced on me in research for the book. Tucked away in all these high-rise entertainment districts, in places such as Tokyo, Osaka, and Kyoto—but also in cities all over Japan—they have an outstanding selection of excellent drinking establishments offering experiences you just can't get anywhere else."

Bunting says that the main Japanese whisky producers are now successfully targeting the younger, trendier drinker

ABOVE_ATSUSHI HORIGAMI
Owner of the hugely popular Shot Bar Zoetrope, Atsushi Horigami, in front of a selection of the 250 whiskies available here.

RIGHT_THE HOME OF JAPANESE WHISKY
Shot Bar Zoetrope is named after the circular mechanism used in the early days of filmmaking.

A GREAT NIGHT OUT

For me, the first destination on arriving in Tokyo would definitely be Atsushi Horigami's Shot Bar Zoetrope in Shinjuku. This is the home of Japanese whisky in that city. Unlike the Suntory or Nikka-tied bars, it sells everything. Horigami-san is incredibly knowledgeable, and gives an education on every visit. The bar itself is just cool, and fun to drink in.

in Japan, and they are in the process of providing a serious quantity of quality whisky for export. He feels that the current trend could be seen to be boring, because the "almost-never-at-home salaryman is being replaced by a more sophisticated, but also slightly less thirsty, younger consumer."

However, this has brought about some positive changes. "One is the shift in focus from a 1970s male drinking culture, where there was a lot of focus on hostess bars. These were not quite as sleazy as Westerners might sometimes have imagined—hostesses usually just poured the drinks and humored their increasingly drunk companions. However, their decline has shifted the focus to the bar and what it is serving. We now have bars in Japan that have a range of quality alcohol that is unrivaled anywhere in the world."

And the future? "One vague prediction I would hazard is that at some point in the short-to-medium future we are going to see a quantity and quality of Japanese whisky that will finally establish itself as a significant export product. Those whiskies are being matured now by highly sophisticated companies that are capable of seeing a major commercial opportunity, and have clearly demonstrated their ability to make world-class whiskies."

EYEWITNESS: STEFAN VAN EYCKEN

If you're a lover of Japanese whisky and you talk to enthusiast Stefan Van Eycken for any length of time, you'll struggle not to feel a pang of envy. Stefan is now editor of the leading Japanese blog Nonjatta, knows masses about his subject, and has accumulated an armory of anecdotes and experiences. More than that, however, he has tasted some of the finest and rarest Japanese whiskies and has experienced malts that were once ignored and are now gone forever. He has lived in Japan since the turn of the millennium and has visited Japan's distilleries many times. He has done it through a great deal of hard work, enthusiasm, and love. But, as he readily admits, there was a degree of being in the right place at the right time.

"When I moved here in 2000, I assumed my days of 'whisky immersion' were over . . . a bit like a surfer who found himself in the Sahara," he says. "Nothing could have been farther from the truth, of course, but at the turn of the century 'Japanese whisky' wasn't a category that many people got excited about, least of all in Japan. I can't recall exactly when I discovered Japanese whisky, but I do remember that the first Japanese distillery I visited was Karuizawa. I fell in love with it—the whiskies and the place—and I went back regularly. Gradually, I realized that there was more to whisky than just Scotland. I was exhilarated by the quality of the domestic whisky I was coming across in Japan, but also more than a little baffled at the cold shoulder it was getting in other parts of the world."

That statement is jaw-dropping, given that Karuizawa Distillery is now gone, and is posthumously building the kind of legendary status reserved for the likes of closed distilleries Port Ellen and Brora in Scotland, and attracting prices that run into thousands of dollars. It's hard to accept that someone just popped into the distillery on a whim, but it's even more amazing than that.

WHAT ARE YOU DRINKING?

Tricky, but in no particular order:

KARUIZAWA 1964:
The pick of the bunch as far as I'm concerned, and I've been privileged to try loads of Karuizawas, spanning the entire history of production.

NIKKA 40 YEAR OLD:
A fabulous blend.

YAMAZAKI 1986 OWNER'S CASK:
Bottled in 2007 for Bar Barns in Nagoya (matured in Japanese oak).

CHICHIBU NEWBORN 2009 HEAVILY PEATED:
Bottled for Whisky Talk Fukuoka 2013.

KAWASAKI 1980 SINGLE CASK GRAIN:
I bottled this for my own "Ghost series."

STEFAN VAN EYCKEN
Sitting with a glass of the Yamazaki 18 Year Old at Suntory headquarters, appropriately surrounded by furniture made from old Yamazaki barrels.

"Having followed the Karuizawa situation from way before the boom, I can say that hardly anyone in Japan was interested in Karuizawa whiskies when they were in plentiful supply," says Stefan. "At one point, you could even mail order a bottle of your preferred vintage directly from the distillery, which the staff would tap from the cask, stick a label on, and send to you. It wasn't until people abroad were starting to drop the sort of sums of money on them previously reserved for old Macallans, that whisky fans in Japan started to get out their wallets. The irony is that—at that point—it was already too late for whisky fans in Japan to follow suit, as the stock had been bought up by Number One Drinks, and largely split between the three foreign distributors involved."

Stefan says that, unbelievable as it might seem now, single cask bottlings of Japanese whisky that would sell out in a matter of seconds now were on the shelves for months and years. He recalls buying some of the earlier Ichiro's Card Series releases: "Their labels were literally falling off, because they had been on the shelves of liquor shops for so long. Until five years ago, you could pick up a single cask Hakushu or Yamazaki any day of the week. Even a major electronics store, with branches all over the country, had more than a dozen different single casks on sale for years. Now people would camp in front of the store if they knew a single cask bottling was coming out," he says.

So what changed? Stefan says that there is more than a grain of truth in the theory that it took attention from experts in the West to get Japanese whisky drinkers interested. "An analogy with the art world springs to mind, in which very often an artist or artwork needs to be validated abroad before being able to find traction and momentum back home," he says. "It's clear that 'validation abroad' played a crucial role in this change of heart in Japan."

Stefan attributes this change to three landmark moments. "The first one happened abroad," he says. "In 2001, a ten-year-old Yoichi single cask won *Whisky Magazine*'s Best of the Best. It undoubtedly helped in putting Japan on many 'serious' whisky drinkers' maps. The second one was the founding of Number One Drinks Company in 2006. They played a crucial role in supplying foreign markets with Japanese whiskies of a caliber that was difficult to find, even in Japan. The third key moment was a domestic one, in 2009, when Suntory started pushing highballs as an alternative to beer. That was the start of what is now known as the 'Highball boom.' For the first time since the peak of whisky drinking in Japan (1981),

Suntory managed to reverse the sharply declining trend in consumption."

Suntory picked up the baton with aplomb, and has done a remarkable job in turning the fortunes of Japanese whisky in its domestic market. So successful was it that, at one point, to meet the demand in Japan, the company was recalling stock from the United Kingdom. Japan has a tradition of adapting quickly, and there can be no doubt that Suntory and Nikka will work hard to address the stock and price issues to ensure a future for Japanese whisky. Stefan is convinced that they will succeed, but with the caveat that they need to face up to some issues ahead.

"I do think the Japanese whisky industry will have to solve the price/quality issue, which has gotten out of hand," he says. "If now, you have to pay €150 ($160/£117) for a three-year-old whisky or €400 ($447/£311) for a nonage statement 'special limited edition,' what will people have to pay for a ten-year-old single cask farther down the line? No matter how good, it's still liquid at the end of the day, and there is other liquid of comparable quality out there elsewhere. Obviously, producers will charge what the market will bear, and there are enough people now willing to part with their hard-earned cash to get their mitts on a bottle that 'everybody wants,' but there's a limit to how far people are willing to go."

And the future generally? "I have given up trying to predict the future of Japanese whisky." However, it's worth checking on Nonjatta regularly; if anyone's going to provide a steer, it's Stefan and his friends.

YAZAMAKI 1986 OWNER'S CASK
A rare, special release of whisky matured in mizunara oak.

A GREAT NIGHT OUT

I like bars such as Bar Cask Strength, Wodka Tonic (see p.160), Ne Plus Ultra, and White Label, where you can drink legendary old bottles of Scotch at unbeatable prices . . . ld Samaroli or Sestante bottlings, old OBs, etc. I had a dram of 1956 Highland Park at one of the aforementioned bars just a few days ago, for the price of a large takeout pizza. That being said, I also have a soft spot for bars where you can try a lot of recent bottlings—places like Jay's Bar, Malt Bar South Park, and Bar Nadurra—because there's nothing more heartbreaking than trying a whisky and really falling in love with it, but knowing you will never be able to enjoy it in peace and quiet at home, or in the company of good friends. So, I spend a lot of time going to bars where there's lots of whisky fresh off the bottling line, because in the current climate, with literally thousands of releases coming at you every year, one cannot just buy blind and hope every purchase will turn out to be a bull's-eye.

THE IMPORTANCE OF NONJATTA

JAPANESE WHISKY WEBSITE
Nonjatta can be found on: www.nonjatta.com

Few whisky blogs command as much respect as Japanese whisky website Nonjatta. There's a good reason for that: providing new and exciting information from the Japanese whisky industry is like panning for gold. It requires a big investment in time and effort, with only the occasional nugget as a reward, and no guarantee even of that.

Japan has few whisky distilleries, and unlike in the West, where marketing is considered essential to successful branding, Japan's whisky producers do not court whisky writers and bloggers to anywhere near the same degree. Add in the language issue, and you need a dedicated team of enthusiasts prepared to sign up for the long haul—which is exactly what Nonjatta is all about.

It was founded by British journalist Chris Bunting (see p.144) shortly after he arrived in Japan in 2007. After an initial flurry of online activity, however, Chris was forced to focus on his paid employment, and his posts became less frequent. Meanwhile, Stefan Van Eycken had set up the Tokyo Whisky hub to post to the international whisky community. Eventually, Stefan agreed to post on the Nonjatta site, and when Chris moved back to the United Kingdom in 2011, Stefan took the helm. Since then, the plan was to make the site a community one, but while one or two people have contributed from time to time, the vast burden of the work falls on Stefan and Osaka-based webmaster Niko Neefs. Stefan says it's hard work.

"But we get a lot of encouragement from our readers, so whenever we wonder why we keep pouring our time and energy into this without any remuneration or fringe benefits whatsoever (which people find hard to believe, but it's true), we read through some of our fan mail, and find that there is a real need for information about what's happening on the Japanese whisky scene reported from the ground."

EYEWITNESS: NICHOLAS COLDICOTT

While many put the overwhelming responsibility for the revival of the Japanese whisky industry down to the attentions of the West, international travel and hospitality writer Nicholas Coldicott isn't one of them.

Coldicott is an English-born journalist who has lived in Tokyo since 1998, and he is one of Asia's most respected drinks writers. He also has a sharp pen and a self-deprecatory sense of humor. He has played a key role in shining a light on Japan's astounding food and drink offerings, writing for a range of outlets, most recently *The Japan Times*. He has not only been a key witness to the rebirth of Japanese whisky, but has also played an important part in it, not that you'd ever know from talking to him. Ask him about writers covering the Japanese whisky scene, and he's eager to deflect attention away from himself.

"I moved to Japan in 1998, and stumbled into food and drink media," he says. "I realized that many people in Japan pursue their interests to a point of obsession, and that's pretty great when it's applied to cocktails, sake, and whisky. But when it comes to influence, I'd say Michael Jackson had a minor impact on how Japanese people saw their whisky, and I have had substantially less. But lots of people were writing in Japanese, and in English there was Michael Jackson, Ulf Buxrud, Chris Bunting, and Dave Broom. Plenty for me to plagiarize."

Coldicott says that the idea that there was a change in attitude within Japan toward Japanese whisky in the early part of the millennium is a false one. Japanese whisky was recognized in the West in 2001, he says, but little changed in Japan, and there was a lengthy "phony war" period.

"I think people talk about 2001 because it was the first time a Japanese whisky won a major international award, but for years after that there was barely a twinkle of interest," he says.

WHAT ARE YOU DRINKING?

I'm drinking whatever's left in the cupboard. Some of it has to be sipped sparingly, because I can't buy it anymore, like the Yoichi 15 Year Old. And some falls into the category "should've auctioned it, but too late now," like an old Karuizawa, and a few Hanyu malts I opened before I knew how silly the prices would get. I can still find Yamazaki 12 Year Old every now and again, and I'll never get bored with that.

NICHOLAS COLDICOTT
The respected whisky journalist analyzes the nose of a whisky.

TOP: ROCKFISH BAR_ The Rockfish bar, in Tokyo's Ginza district, is located two floors below Bar High Five (see p.162) and serves a great highball.
ABOVE: SUNTORY ADVERTISEMENT_ Since their successful Highball campaign Suntory whisky has been consumed by younger drinkers.

"In 2008, you could stroll into a liquor store and find a selection of Ichiro's Malt Card Series bottles for ¥10,000–15,000 ($88–133) each, and they weren't selling fast. I should have bought the lot. So it was more a slow trickle and then a tidal wave. There were a lot of people promoting Japanese whisky before it became fashionable. Atsushi Horigami was running the Zoetrope bar, the Number One Drinks people were giving away bottles of whisky from the Karuizawa distillery, and Ichiro Akuto was releasing his Card Series bottles, and all that helped people with an interest in whisky see the quality of the local product."

It may have been that it would have stayed like that, he says, with enthusiasts in the West raving about special whiskies that were not available in Japan, while whisky continued to decline in Japan itself. He attributed the turnaround almost entirely to Suntory, and its decision to market the highball to a younger whisky drinking audience and to women.

"When Suntory launched its Highball campaign, everything changed," he says. "People were drinking whisky sodas instead of beer. Women's lifestyle mags started talking about whisky. It's hard to overstate how much that campaign changed things. After that, every time someone gave an award to a Japanese whisky, more people in Japan noticed, and more journalists wrote about it."

The final cherry on the cake, however, came when old-school British writer Jim Murray chose a Japanese whisky as his Whisky of the Year in 2014. The reaction leaves Coldicott a little bemused. "I can't explain why, but none of those awards had anything like the impact of Jim Murray naming a Yamazaki his whisky of the year," he says. "It wasn't seen as one guy picking his favorite release of the year, but as a foreign expert anointing Japan the whisky capital of the world."

While all that was going on at home, Suntory has increasingly been looking globally for its future. It already owned Morrison Bowmore and its three distilleries in Scotland, and then it grew into one of the biggest liquor companies in the world by forming Suntory-Beam, and it secured lucrative trade routes to Africa and Asia. It's hard to see it as purely a Japanese liquor company anymore, and one of the big unanswered questions for the future is whether it will challenge Diageo and Pernod-Ricard globally, and beat them by focusing on unique selling points, such as distinctive Japanese whiskies, or compete with them by joining them and matching Scotch whisky by emulating them. Coldicott isn't sure.

ABOVE_SUNTORY HIGHBALL
The Suntory Highball is now a well-known drink, thanks to Suntory's advertising campaigns over the years.

RIGHT_ICHIRO'S MALT CARD SERIES
This series of whiskies is now one of the most collectable. A set of all fifty-four whiskies in the series sold for HK$3,797,500 ($489,703) in 2015.

A GREAT NIGHT OUT

I would visit the Ginza district, starting with a highball in Rockfish, then a whisky cocktail or two in one of the big cocktail bars (Star Bar, High Five, Orchard, Dice, and Mimitsuka are top of my list), and then maybe a dram at the tiny Campbelltoun Loch after I realize I've missed my train home.

"Suntory seems equally committed to nonage statement releases as Scotland is," he says. "I don't imagine age statements ever making a comeback seriously. In terms of copying Scotch, of course Japanese whisky is rooted in Scottish traditions, but I think these days it's more that all whisky makers face similar challenges, so wherever the ideas come from, the good ones will spread. And the lines are blurred anyway, when you've got Japanese companies owning Scotch distilleries."

For the future, Nick Coldicott is optimistic. "Clearly, there's not enough of the good stuff to go around. I'm guessing age statements won't ever make a big comeback," he says.

"Pessimists might point to the vast gulf between the hype and the supply, and worry that Japanese whisky is a boom that's going to go bust. I think the fundamental quality of most distillers here is so high that people will still be keen when the older stuff is back on shelves. With a bit of luck, the new distilleries will be half as good as Chichibu, and that might help tide some of us over, and in the meantime I'll drink Taketsuru 17 Year Old."

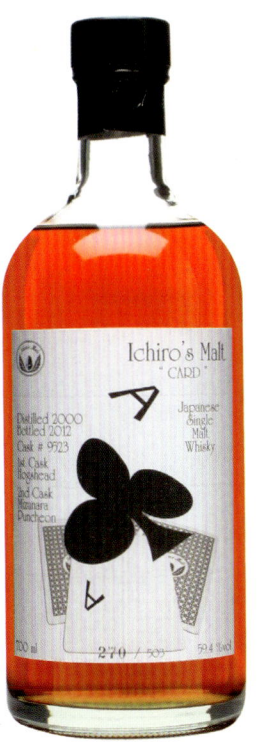

6 / 六 .

CHAPTER SIX

•

JAPANESE WHISKY BARS

日本のウィスキー・バー

In his excellent book, *Drinking Japan,* Chris Bunting contends that Japan is the best place on the planet to drink alcohol. In Scotland, you'll find great places to drink Scotch whisky; in Ireland, there are brilliant Irish whiskey bars; and in Kentucky, superb bourbons. In Japan, you will find a great choice not only of Japanese drinks, but also of other international drinks. Japan has become a melting pot for the world's best spirits.

Others argue, too, that nowhere matches Tokyo for cocktails, and that the theater that goes with providing innovative drinks made with the finest ingredients is without equal. The sheer variety of bars, pubs, restaurants, and other uniquely Japanese venues makes for a vibrant, dynamic, neon-lit mind cluster, and the cities provide a framework for a hedonistic hybrid of social venues. Throw in the blurring of social lines (bars in office buildings, pubs below clothes stores, etc.), and you can wonder where to begin.

If you like a road map, you'll want to pre-plan a trip to the key whisky bars, but Tokyo offers three good reasons why that might not be the best idea: one, the spontaneity of stumbling over a strange, fascinating space is half the fun; two, the combination of a thousand distractions and time wasted trying to find your destinations means you may miss half of them; and three, because no matter how many times you head to Japan, you'll never know it as a whole. So why try? Why not do what Japan does best, and go with the flow?

Japan's nightlife is a traveling carnival: a mass of noise and light, with any number of big and small rides all designed to separate you from your money in the nicest possible way. Japan wants you to have fun and to come back often. In the following pages, we look at the key areas of the major cities for a good night out. It's not exhaustive, but it does provide a guide to some of the iconic whisky venues. Enjoy!

TOKYO
MINATO DISTRICT

The Minato District is a sizable and affluent downtown region of Tokyo, and there's a little bit of Jekyll and Hyde about it. The name means "port," and part of this region does back onto the harbor area, but it stretches well into the city, too, because over the years land has been reclaimed. The Tokyo Tower lies bang in the center of it.

During the day, this is a smart and wealthy business district, and it's populated by office staff heading toward its impressive skyscrapers. By night, the area is a throwback to the great Japanese salarymen days, when businessmen would pour into the bars for long drinking evenings. Nowadays, besuited and smartly dressed professionals still head for the bars. Many of the venues are high up in the office buildings themselves.

The variety offered in this part of the city is truly astounding. From the office bars to the glitzy restaurants, to a floating shopping center in what was the notorious sprawl of the entertainment district of Roppongi, there is something here for everyone. Roppongi has been a meeting point for Tokyo for centuries, and after World War II, it attracted American military personnel, drawn by a range of entertainment and recreation venues aimed at Westerners. In time, Japanese tourists also started to visit these establishments. The area features numerous bars, nightclubs, strip clubs, restaurants, hostess clubs, cabarets, and numerous other forms of entertainment. Roppongi, once known for its gang connections and lurid stories of spiked drinks and bag snatching, is now building a reputation for organized events, such as art festivals, darts, and billiard tournaments, robot exhibitions, and beauty pageants.

RAINBOW BRIDGE_ This iconic landmark connects the island of Odaiba to Shibaura Pier in Minato.

RIGHT AND BELOW_HELMSDALE BAR
The owner here is obsessive about Scotch whisky, but the bar also offers Irish and world whiskeys, too.

The area tends to be favored by business people, students, and off-duty U.S. military personnel, with the emphasis on the younger crowd.

Among the best known bars to head for are:

WODKA TONIC
Open every day of the year, and happy to stay open for as long as you want to stay drinking, this is a dark and intimate venue where tuxedo-shirted bar staff will chip ice to suit your glass with flair and style. The bar is well known for its excellent selection of whiskies.

➡ *Tamura Building B1F, 2-25-11 Nishiazabu, Minato-ku, +81 (3) 3400-5474, wodkatonic.tokyo*

CASK STRENGTH
This bar has won an Icon of Whisky Award from *Whisky Magazine,* and it's not hard to see why. Not the cheapest bar in Tokyo, but, if you're a whisky geek, the huge array of rare bottles will keep you fascinated for hours.

➡ *Main Stage Roppongi Building (Basement), 3-9-11 Roppongi, Minato-ku, +81 (3) 6432-9772, cask-s.com*

HELMSDALE BAR
With tartan carpets, antlers on the wall, and a huge choice of Scottish single malts, this is a shrine to Scotland run by a man who knows more about Scotland than many Scots do. Scottish malts dominate, but you'll also discover about thirty Japanese expressions.

➡ *Minami-Aoyama Mori Building 2F, 7-13-12 Minami-Aoyama, Minato-ku, +81 (3) 3486-4220, www.helmsdale-fc.com*

BAR SOCIETY

This is the official outlet for the Scotch Malt Whisky Society, and here you'll find more than fifty bottles of the Society's special, single cask, cask-strength bottles. You'll also be able to experience an amazing view over Tokyo, although you'll pay the price for it. The bar is on the twenty-fifth floor of the Park Hotel. Japanese whisky is available here, as well as some stylish whisky cocktails.

➤ *Park Hotel Tokyo, Shiodome Media Tower 1-7-1 Higashi-Shimbashi, Minato-ku, +81 (3) 6252-1111, en.parkhoteltokyo.com*

NIKKA BLENDER'S BAR

Home to all the whiskies of Nikka, including rare and single cask bottlings, although how long that will remain the case no one knows, given that Nikka has scrapped its age statement range. You enter the quaint bar by way of a staircase in front of Nikka's impressive Aoyama building.

➤ *B1, 5-4-31 Minami-Aoyama, Minato-ku, +81 (3) 3498-3338, www.nikka.com/eng*

BELOW_BAR SOCIETY
Not only are single malts offered here, but also a wide range of cocktails.

TOKYO
GINZA DISTRICT

Ginza is widely regarded as one of the most stylish and luxurious shopping malls in the world and attracts thousands of tourists to its highly fashionable, cutting-edge stores. It mixes big-name flagship department stores, some of the most famous brand name outlets, stylish boutiques, and high-end coffee shops with some of the city's smartest and most chic restaurants.

Most stores in the Ginza District are open every day of the week, and the best time to visit is at weekends after 12p.m. from April to September, when the central Chuo Dori Street is closed to automobiles and becomes a large pedestrian zone.

The region is also known for its theater district, and when the stores close for the night, a vibrant night life unfurls, with everything available, from British theme pubs and American diners to karaoke and traditional kabuki. A number of theaters present traditional Japanese performing arts, which are well worth trying to soak up some culture. Otherwise, you can drink and dance into the early hours at a huge variety of venues.

These include:

BAR HIGH FIVE

A small and intimate basement bar, with killer cocktails and more than 200 whiskies. There's no menu, but tell the bar staff your tastes, and trust them to rustle something up. The bar is typical of the Ginza District. It has now moved from the fourth floor of the Polestar building to the basement, doubling its size.

➡ Efflore Ginza 5 Building BF, 5-4-15 Ginza Chuo-ku, www.barhighfive.com, +81 (3) 3571-5815

TOP_GINZA DISTRICT
The streets of Ginza are full of stylish shops as well as pubs, bars, and restaurants.

ABOVE_GINZA STATION
The gateway to the Ginza District is one of the busiest Metro stations in Tokyo.

STAR BAR

This is a pretty serious bar, with staff wearing bow ties and suspenders, and the service is immaculate and intense. Legendary Tokyo mixologist Hisashi Kishi oversees proceedings. Wonderful snacks.

➤ Sankosha Bild B1F 1-5-13 Ginza, Chūō-ku, www.starbar.jp/english, +81 (3) 3535-8005

HIBIYA BAR WHISKY-S

This is where Suntory's Mike Miyamoto brings his guests, and the extensive whisky list in English and some tapas-style meals make this a stylish place to visit.

➤ B1 Kaneko Biru, 3-3-9 Ginza, Chūō-ku, www.hibiya-bar.com, +81 (3) 5159-8008

BAR LUPIN

This has a strong Japanese literature theme, with photographs of Japan's most celebrated writers along the walls. The bar is steeped in history and was a favorite hangout for many famous Japanese writers. The bar has a modest but high-quality selection of whiskies and bourbons.

➤ B1F, 5-5-11 Ginza, Chūō-ku, www.lupin.co.jp, +81 (3) 3571-0750

BAR EVITA

Named after Eva Perón, this bar is inspired by Argentina. It offers a full range of Argentine cocktails, bitters, and seasonal foods, with a romantic musical background of Argentine tango. The bar boasts an extensive range of world whiskies. Note the website is only in Japanese.

➤ Fuji Building 9F, 8-4-24 Ginza, Chūō-ku, www.bar-evita.jp, +81 (3) 3574-5571

TOP LEFT AND ABOVE LEFT_HIBIYA BAR WHISKY-S
This bar opened in 2014 and boasts an impressive whisky list that is available in English. It is particularly good for varieties of Hakushu.

LEFT_BAR LUPIN
Established in 1928, Bar Lupin has hosted writers such as Kyoka Izumi and Kan Kikuchi. The walls are decorated with photographs of famed customers.

NEXT PAGE_GINZA BY NIGHT
Colorful bar menus and price lists adorn the streets of the Ginza District.

TOKYO
SHINJUKU DISTRICT

Shinjuku is one of Tokyo's twenty-three city wards, but the name commonly refers to just the large entertainment, business, and shopping area around Shinjuku Station.

Shinjuku is something of a transport hub within Tokyo, and it includes the world's busiest railroad station, which is a meeting point for several different railroads and subway lines. Buses—both local city and long distance—also stop here. Shinjuku also sits at the heart of some of Tokyo's most vibrant businesses, with the skyscraper district just to the west of the railroad station. Some of Tokyo's best hotels are also located in this region.

Northeast of the station is the large and notorious red light district. It's a shopper's paradise, too, with department stores, malls, and Tokyo's famous electronic stores all clustered around the station. Even by Tokyo's busy standards, this is a hustling, bustling area, but it's also a mass of contradictions. Step to one side, and you can take sanctuary beneath the cherry blossoms of Shinjuku Gyoen, one of Tokyo's favorite parks.

At night, Shinjuku becomes the contemporary heart of Tokyo, a city within a city, and an area that never seems to slow down. It offers the visitor everything from fine dining to rowdy pubs, from sex and sleaze to one of the world's most vibrant gay entertainment districts.

ABOVE_SHINJUKU
Expect a hustling, bustling night out in this lively and diverse entertainment center.

RIGHT_DUBLINERS
This popular pub is part of a national chain. There are four in the Shinjuku region alone and around thirty-six throughout Japan.

The Kabukicho section of Shinjuku should be approached with caution. It contains all of the things one might expect to find in a red-light district anywhere in the world. You may be hassled here and ripped off if you're unwary. However, with a little caution, it is safe enough to walk through, even at night.

Golden Gai is a block of bars just east of Kabukicho that preserves the Tokyo of the 1960s. Many of these bars are tiny, and several can be trashy and sleazy. Unsurprisingly, they attract a wide range of characters.

Shinjuku Ni-chome is an enclave of mostly tiny bars catering for Tokyo's gay scene, but there are more spacious cruise bars, dance clubs, bookstores, cafes, and saunas. It is in this area that you'll find some of the most highly respected whisky bars, including the highly acclaimed and much-loved Shot Bar Zoetrope (see below). It is also a great area to meander through, dipping into different bars as you go.

Whisky fans should seek out the following bars:

SHOT BAR ZOETROPE

This could well lay claim to being the world's greatest bar. All visitors rate it among their favorites, and with good reason. It's the brainchild of former video games designer Atsushi Horigami, who has combined his two passions: whisky and classic old movies. You can sip wonderful drams while chilling to classic Buster Keaton and Laurel and Hardy comedies.

➤ *Gaia Building #4 3F, 7-10-14 Nishi-Shinjuku, Shinjuku-ku*
  +81 (3) 3363-0162, homepage2.nifty.com/zoetrope

BAR ARGYLL

Not cheap, small, and a little geeky, but also friendly and with a stylish wood interior. The good range of whiskies includes some interesting bottlings.

➤ *Daiichi Hōtoku Building 3F, 1-4-17 Nishi-Shinjuku, Shinjuku-ku*
  +81 (3) 3344-3442

DUBLINERS

Another chain outlet. An Irish theme pub, with other outlets in Ikebukuro, Shibuya, Akasaka, Toranomon, and Shinagawa. As you might expect, this is the place to go for Irish whiskey, but there are other bottlings, too. Shinjuku address:

➤ *Shinjuku Lion Beer Hall 2F, 3-28-9 Shinjuku, Shinjuku-ku*
  +81 (3) 3352-6606, www.dubliners.jp/en

THE HUB

These faux-British pubs are popular with the younger crowd, who go to them to meet and flirt, with tourists and locals mixing seamlessly. By Tokyo standards, the whisky choice isn't the best, but the venue is fun if nothing else.

- *Ginza Corridor 1F, 7-10-8 Ginza, Chūō-ku,*
  +81 (3) 3289-8733, www.pub-hub.com

BAR PLASTIC MODEL

Strangely named and with an odd concept, this bar has been described as a 1970s and 1980s retro themed bar, but there is more to it than that. You can browse through a large seven-inch Japanese singles collection while enjoying a larger-than-average whisky selection.

- *G2 Street 1F, 1-1-10 Kabukichō, Shinjuku-ku,*
  +81 (3) 5273-8441, www.plastic-model.net

TOKYO LOOSE

Late-night bar/club with remarkably cheap drinks during Happy Hour. Toshima is the large computer district. It is also multicultural, with about one in twelve residents from China, Korea, or the Philippines.

- *2B, 2-37-3 Kabukichō, Shinjuku-ku*
  +81 (3) 3207-5677, www.tokyoloose.com

The district is noted for business and evening entertainment, particularly the Ikebukuro area. Its attractions include a large sake market. There is a wide range of bars here, including:

QUERCUS BAR

This is one of Chichibu's Ichiro Akuto's favorite bars, and it is reasonably priced and friendly. Not surprisingly, there is a bias toward Chichibu, but you'll find some rare Karuizawa bottlings here, too. Each year the bar releases its own single cask offering, normally from Scotland.

- *Ōkuma Building B1, 1-32-5 Higashi-Ikebukuro, Toshima-ku,*
  +81 (3) 3986-8025, quercusbar.com

THE ITTEN BAR

A lot of style, subdued lighting, cool jazz, and a tank with large fish in it, this is the ideal venue for a sophisticated night out. As you'd expect in such a cool environment, there is a good choice of whisky to chill out with.

- *Golden Plaza Building 8F, 1-17-13 Minami-Ikebukuro, Toshima-ku,*
  +81 (3) 3981-0018, www.itten-bar.com

ABOVE_NEON SIGNS OF SHINJUKU
At the end of this street is the Mode Gakuen Cocoon Tower, which houses three schools and is the seventeenth-tallest building in Tokyo.

PAPER MOON

A deliberately dated and somewhat scatterbrained bar with an emphasis on cool, late-night drinking and snazzy jazz. The bar space is tiny, but there is a healthy choice of whisky and an even better selection of cocktails.

➡ *Umemoto Building 4F, 3-29-3 Nishi-Ikebukuro, Toshima-ku, +81 (3) 3985-0240*

KENNY'S BAR

Ikebukuro has built up a strong reputation for jazz bars and clubs. It's not a hip region, but has a laid-back, retro feel. At Kenny's Bar, you'll find Mingus and Coltrane posters on the walls, and it's an extremely friendly place to enjoy a dram or two.

➡ *Palace Garden Milano Building 1F, 2-63-6 Ikebukuro, Toshima-ku, +81 (3) 5391-1073, www.kennys.jp*

BELOW_YAKITORI ALLEY
This vibrant alley spans a railway track and is made up of unique food stalls that hark back to a simpler time. It is best known for its grilled meat and beer.

NEXT PAGE_KABUKICHO CROWDS
This is Tokyo's red-light district and a wide variety of entertainment venues can be found here, including theaters and restaurants.

TOKYO
SHIBUYA DISTRICT

Shibuya is another of Tokyo's twenty-three city wards, but the name often refers to just the popular shopping and entertainment area found around Shibuya Station. It is a major center for youth fashion and culture, and it is from here that much of Japan's fashion and entertainment trends originate. It is one of Tokyo's most colorful and busiest districts, packed with shopping, dining, and nightclubs serving swarms of visitors. You'll find more than a dozen major department store branches in this region, and all types of shoppers are catered to.

If all this sounds formal and upmarket, it shouldn't: Shibuya is also both fun and cutting edge, with skate shops and streetwear boutiques ensuring that the district reflects all the latest fashions. As with other areas of Tokyo, it is possible to escape from the hustle and bustle of modern city life. The Harajuku District and natural attraction Yoyogi Park are within its bounds, and visitors can journey to nearby Meiji Shrine, a verdant escape from the neighborhood's frenzy.

Much of Shibuya's nightlife is centered on Dogen-zaka, a street also known as Love Hotel Hill for the numerous short-time inns that accommodate affectionate couples looking for privacy. However, this is the region to come to if you're a music lover, with some of Tokyo's best music and dance clubs, playing every style of music from trance to techno and rock to reggae.

ABOVE_BAR CAOL ILA
The bar has one of the biggest collections of the iconic Islay malt anywhere in the world.

BAR CAOL ILA

The Japanese are noted for pursuing their passions to extremes, and here is a case in point. The bar is named after the iconic Islay Distillery—and here you will find more than seventy expressions of its whisky, possibly the largest bar collection of Caol Ila in the world and certainly in Japan. The bar offers food to go with the whisky, such as what sounds like a mixed smoked breakfast dish with Caol Ila 12 Year Old. There are seventy other bottles, too, so don't be put off if peaty whisky isn't for you.

➡ MST Dogen-zaka 3F, 1-13-3 Dogen-zaka, Shibuya-ku, +81 (3) 5428-6184, www.caolila.tokyo

SPINCOASTER MUSIC BAR

Fantastic reviews suggest that this is a must for music fans, and the bar includes a great selection of vinyl records and high-resolution audio tracks. It's small, friendly, and offers guests the chance to select the music. It has been described by one happy visitor as "surreal." Stocks some rare Japanese whiskies, including the World Whisky Awards whisky of the year: Hibiki.

➡ 2-26-2 Yoyogi, 1-C 2nd Kuwano Building, Shibuya-ku, +81 (3) 6300-9211, bar.spincoaster.com

BAR BLACK SHEEP

Another cozy and friendly bar, with reasonably priced drinks, and it has a chatty owner who speaks fluent English. There is no menu, so you just ask for what you want, and trust the establishment. Loads of fun.

➡ Wakatsuki Building 2F, 2-29-13 Dogen-zaka, Shibuya-ku, +81 (3) 3496-7330

BELOW_SPINCOASTER MUSIC BAR
As well as whisky, this bar offers customers a large selection of vinyl records.

BELOW RIGHT_COLORFUL SHIBUYA
Shibuya is a district that is youthful, fashionable, and cutting edge.

TOKYO
THE REST

Japan's love of whisky means that the chances are you'll stumble across interesting bottles wherever you travel. However, one word of warning: The world has focused on the high end of Japanese whisky, and it would be easy to conclude from a book like this that all Japanese whisky is wonderful. It is not. You may spot many unusual bottles and be tempted to invest in a glass. Be warned: There are plenty of Japanese whiskies that are at best ordinary and, at worst, dreadful. With that said, you can always trust your host to point you in the direction of something from a local distiller—if you can communicate in Japanese, that is, as there is no guarantee that local people will speak languages other than their own.

In addition to the districts we've mentioned, which are renowned for their nightlife, there are others that are also worth seeking out.

They include:

NERIMA-KU, TOKYO
Malt House Islay: With 1,800 bottles of whisky, this is a serious whisky bar, but it is not as formal as some of its competitors elsewhere. The owner of the bar regularly bottles his own whiskies made up of whiskies from—you guessed it—Islay.

➤ Kijimi Building 2F, 5-22-16 Toyotama Kita, Nerima-ku,
+81 (3) 5984-4408, homepage2.nifty.com/islay

MEGURO-KU, TOKYO
Speyside Way: A reasonably spacious venue, with a comfortable publike feel, and some great Japanese craft beers. Unsurprisingly, the big attraction is the vast range of whisky, close to 1,000 bottles in all, mainly from Scotland with a healthy selection of Japanese malts. Some delicious food to eat alongside them, too.

➤ Mikasa Building 5F, 1-26-9 Jiyugaoka, Meguro-ku,
+81 (3) 3723-7807, www.speysideway.co.jp

TOP_CHIYODA-KU DISTRICT, TOKYO
Home to the small and excellent Campbelltoun Loch Bar.

ABOVE_MALT HOUSE ISLAY
This well-stocked whisky bar is a two-miniute walk from Nerima station.

SHINGAWA-KU, TOKYO

The Mash Tun: This is an intimate little whisky bar located on the second floor in a backstreet near Meguro station. It is laid back and friendly, has about 250 different malts, and the passionate owner avoids any of his bottles going "stale" by holding cut-price tastings of bottles that have sat on the shelf for a lengthy time and are getting low.

➤ Mikasa Building B 2F, 2-14-3 Kami-Osaki, Shinagawa-ku, +81 (3) 3449-3649, www.themashtun.com

CHIYODA-KU, TOKYO

Campbelltoun Loch: In the basement of the Matsui Building, this establishment is small, even by Tokyo bar standards. In fact, it can probably accommodate ten people, tops, but the choice of whisky is great. The bulk of it is from Scotland.

➤ Matsui Building (Basement), 1-6-8 Yurakucho, Chiyoda-ku, +81 (3) 3501-5305

BELOW AND BELOW RIGHT_THE MASH TUN
This small bar stocks around 250 malts, which are rotated regularly to keep them fresh. As well as Japanese whisky, it also stocks Scotch, and drinkers are sometimes welcomed by the sound of bagpipes.

OSAKA

Osaka has a lively nightlife and falls into one of two categories for the foreign visitor: gaijin bars/pubs or nightclubs. Gaijin means "foreigner," and indicates that the bar regularly has foreign clientele, and so it should be able to handle customers who don't speak Japanese. These are also places where some Japanese locals come to meet and chat with foreigners, so you would have a better chance of finding English-speaking Japanese people here.

There are dozens of bars and clubs, many of which specialize in specific interests, such as sports or rock music. On the whisky front, Osaka has a huge bias toward Suntory, and Suntory City is here, which reflects the fact that the company's headquarters is located in the Dojima District of the city. The best whisky bars include:

BAR AUGUSTA TARLOGIE

It's conveniently located in the Umeda District of Osaka and it opens at 5 p.m., which is early by Japanese standards, making this the perfect starting place for a bar crawl through the city. The bar is small but well stocked. The majority of the whiskies are Scottish, and the owner/bartender Kiyomitsu Shinano really knows this field inside-out. No wonder the bar functions as the Osaka branch of the Scotch Malt Whisky Society's Japan chapter. There's also an interesting selection of Japanese whiskies available.

➧ Arakawa Building 1F, 2-3 Turuno-cho, Kita-ku, Osaka, +81 (6) 6376-3455, www.bar-augusta.com

NAMBA OSAKA
Among the bright lights and billboards of Osaka, the Gilco Man has become something of an icon.

BAR K

At the heart of one of Osaka's most lively areas, Bar K is hidden away down a staircase. It's a calm, easy-going venue with great drinks and first-class service. It's noted for its outstanding cocktails, and there are some of the rarest Japanese whiskies you will probably ever come across.

- Koyo Building B1F, 1-3-3- Sonezakishinchi, Kita-ku, Osaka, +81 (6) 6343-1167, www.bar-k.jp

TAKA BAR

Behind the bar, it's pretty much an all-Suntory affair here. There are a lot of rare owners' casks and cask-strength bottlings, and the aural backdrop comes courtesy of an extensive range of classical music, so you can enjoy your whisky while listening to a favorite piece.

- Under Tree Building 1F, 1-7-30 Sonezakishinchi, Kita-ku, Osaka, +81 (6) 6344-1311

BAR ROCK ROCK

Osaka is a big, brash, partying city with its roots in loud rock music. There are plenty of bars where Iron Maiden, Deep Purple, and Mötley Crüe provide the music, and whisky is consumed in quantity for fun. This bar is where many of the visiting acts unwind after a show—and it's rockin'!

- Shinsaibashi Atrium Building 3F, 1-8-1 Nishi-Shinsaibashi, Chūō-ku, Osaka, +81 (6) 6244-6969, www.rockrock.co.jp

HIGHBALL BAR UMEDA 1923

Named after the year in which the Japanese whisky story is supposed to have started, the Highball Bar was part of the campaign to bring younger drinkers to whisky. New drinkers found old-style whisky bars intimidating, so Suntory created specialty bars that offered premium-quality highball cocktails to attract a young crowd. There is a wide choice of cocktails, and a selection of food that goes well with highballs, such as mixtures of white miso, Yamazaki whisky, and sea urchin miso, served with narazuke pickles and cucumber sticks. Decorated to reflect a "nostalgic modern" theme, this Highball Bar is popular.

- Umesendo Building 1F, 2-1-3 Shibata, Kita-ku, Osaka, +81 (6) 6375-2300

TOP_BAR K
This place is known for its impeccable cocktails as well as its whiskies.

ABOVE_HIDDEN GEMS
Bars and restaurants line the side streets of the Namba region in Osaka.

ABOVE_KYOTO BY NIGHT
This city is one of the oldest in Japan and is known as the thousand-year capital, but these days it is set up for tourism and entertainment.

KYOTO

Kyoto city has a lot of good bars and clubs, as well as restaurants that stay open late into the night. Kiyamachi is the street where the young tend to gather, and it has a number of good bars. If you want something more sedate, you can also find bars that have a relaxed atmosphere, where you can go in just to enjoy a cocktail or sit and talk with friends and family. Kyoto also has many karaoke bars, where your group can hire private rooms at reasonable prices. Whisky is, as always, easy to find.

Here are some bars to look out for:

K6
Larger than many Japanese whisky bars and elegant without being pretentious, K6 is a an L-shaped bar with a lengthy counter. It has a pleasant atmosphere and more than 600 whiskies, including some genuine diamond drinks.

- *Vals Building 2F, Higashi-iru, Nijo-dori Kiyamachi, Nakagyo-ku, Kyoto, +81 (75) 255-5009, ksix.jp*

BAR CORDON NOIR
This whisky bar has it all: intimate and cozy atmosphere, friendly knowledgeable staff, reasonable prices, and a whisky list to die for—more than 600 including some long-lost Scotch malts and some very old and rare Japanese ones at highly competitive prices. The bar only seats about 35 people so get in early.

- *Matsushimaya Building 3F, 121 Ishiyacho, Nakagyo-ku, Kyoto, +81 (75) 212-3288, ameblo.jp/bar-cordon-noir*

FUKUOKA

Fukuoka is not as well known as many other Japanese cities but it is still sizable. With some 2.5 million people, it is the capital city of the Fukuoka Prefecture and is the most populated city on the island of Kyushu. It is sited on the island's north coast. Fukuoka has a huge variety of venues. There are izakaya (Japanese pubs) on virtually every corner, and these offer a wide array of alcoholic beverages and foods. Because Fukuoka is famed for its shōchū, try a glass with some sashimi (raw fish). If clubbing is more your thing, Fukuoka will have something to suit you. There's an extraordinary variety of music, ranging from hip-hop to trance via regular pop.

Whisky enthusiasts simply have to visit:

BAR KITCHEN TENJIN

There's no food, but the venue boasts 1,500 bottles of rare Japanese and Scotch whisky, as well as an assortment of premium and vintage bourbons. The somewhat intimidating selection includes bottles from independent bottlers, single cask bottlings, owners' casks, bottlings from the Scotch Malt Whisky Society, vintage official bottlings, and any number of rare Japanese offerings, including an extensive number of Hanyu and Karuizawa expressions, and all of the Ichiro Card Series. It goes without saying that this makes the venue something of a whisky lover's paradise.

➤ *Grand Park Tenjin 107, 1-8-26 Maizuru, Chūō-ku, Fukuoka-shi, Fukuoka, +81 (92) 791-5189*

TOP_FUKUOKA
This is a great destination for a wide range of quality music, as well as Japanese pubs.

ABOVE_BAR KITCHEN TENJIN
A kitchen with no food, but more than enough whisky to compensate.

SAPPORO

Home city of Japan's most famous beer of the same name, Sapporo is the largest city on the northern Japanese island of Hokkaido. It is the capital of Hokkaido Prefecture, a long way north. As a result it has a climate not unlike that of Scotland, so, unsurprisingly, there is a hardcore whisky scene here. You'll find plenty of it in the Susukino, Japan's largest entertainment district in the north of Sapporo. This is the area to go to for the region's best bars and restaurants, but you'll also find the red-light district here, stores of all kinds, and karaoke bars. If you want to try Sapporo's famous ramen—a noodle dish—you'll find scores of places serving it in Ramen Yokocho.

There are plenty of whisky bars, including a series of Suntory bars, but head especially to:

THE BOW BAR

As the name might suggest, this bar specializes in Scotch single malt whisky. Most of it is less than twenty years old, but there's an important twist: these are whiskies that were released in the 1960s, 1970s, and 1980s, so while the liquid might be under twenty years old, it may have been originally distilled as long ago as the late 1940s, giving drinkers a unique chance to discover how whisky used to taste.

➤ *Hoshi Building, 7-5 Minami 4, Nishi 2, Chūō-ku, Sapporo, +81 (11) 532-1212, www.thebowbar-sapporo/English.html*

NIKKA BAR

Named after the whisky maker who owns the nearby Yoichi Distillery, this bar stocks a diverse range of Nikka expressions.

➤ *Dai-3 Green Building 2F, Minami 4 Jo, Nishi 3 cho-me, Chūō-ku, Sapporo, +81 (11) 518-3344, nikkabar.jp*

TOP_NIKKA BAR
The place to go for all of the excellent whiskies from Nikka: while stocks last.

ABOVE_BOW BAR
This is good place to relax and sample some of the oldest spirits you're likely to come across.

The list in this section is, of course, not exhaustive, and in Japan the world of bars and restaurants is constantly evolving. You'll find it impossible to explore everything. It is best, therefore, to make sure you visit the bars that appeal to you most of all, and then go with the flow and see where it leads you.

7
/
七
.

CHAPTER SEVEN

•

BARS AROUND THE WORLD

世界のウィスキー・バー

Few cultures lend themselves more readily to the theater of food and drink than Japanese culture does.

The bright, fresh, and simple nature of Japanese imagery and wording is the perfect signpost to a culinary culture based on precise, beautifully executed, fresh and wholesome food and drink.

Japanese restaurants are now both numerous and widespread all over the world, from the "fast food" feel-good chains such as Yo! Sushi and the surprisingly diverse street food ramen outlets to the exquisite and precise culinary master classes at the top restaurants, many of which are open-plan and on premises within some of the world's finest hotels.

Japan has proved to be remarkably adept at being flexible, and pan-Asian and pan-European outlets in cosmopolitan cities, such as Sydney, New York, and London, are relatively commonplace. In other words, the world no longer has to beat a path to Japan's door; Japan has (perhaps belatedly) come to the world.

However, while Japanese food is readily obtainable, it is less common to find a dedicated Japanese whisky bar. Such places exist, of course, and they are often stocked with extensive whisky ranges that stretch back several years or have been donated from private collections. But they may take some finding.

They vary greatly, from dedicated bars with expensive furnishings, to a no-frills, down-to-earth Highland bar in the shadow of one of Scotland's most iconic whisky hotels. This chapter includes bars that are stylish and elegant, and ones that are designed to reflect the chaotic, bustling, and ever-so-slightly sleazy street bars of Tokyo, from which they draw their inspiration.

BAR JACKALOPE
LOS ANGELES, USA

Bar Jackalope, at the back of the Seven Grand bar in downtown Los Angeles, is at once a laid-back, fun, atmospheric, and unpretentious venue, and a serious drinking outlet where things are done properly. The bar tries to re-create the intimate atmosphere of the many small bars in Japan. It's a place to sip whisky quietly. It serves only whisky, and only by the glass, with no cocktails except the Japanese Highball. It says it has as many entry-level whiskies under $10 as it has rarities over $100. With Japanese whisky, this bar carries every release legally offered to it, whereas, for every other whisky category, the bar offers only one bottle per line. Bar Jackalope is currently battling to keep prices real, as demand for Japanese whisky grows. Seven Grand, next door, is a fallback for food and craft beer.

WHAT SETS THE BAR APART? "We have a 'spirit guide' on staff," says general manager Andrew Abraham. "The entire Bar Jackalope group also meets weekly for training sessions and puts in a substantial amount of work learning about all things whisky. We often travel to learn first-hand. Besides touring Japan, we have been to Ireland, Scotland, Kentucky, Tennessee, and Canada, as well as to many microdistillers throughout the U.S." In 2012, with House Spirits Distillery in Oregon, the team even made their own malt and rye whiskey, which is currently maturing.

WHAT DO THEY RECOMMEND? Andrew says: "Start with Hibiki. I think the 12 is the way to go, since the cherry-wine finish makes it stand out from the 2015 release, Harmony, which is heavier on the sherry side. An all-round balanced and great Japanese whisky, and perfect to start with.

"Then have the Yoichi 15. The ever-so-slight touch of peat will show the range in Japanese whisky, while never straying from what I think the Japanese palate looks for in flavors. Finish with Hakushu 12, but have fun with it, and try it as a Highball: one part whisky to three parts very bubbly club soda. Slap a sprig of mint to garnish."

BAR JACKALOPE · SEVEN GRAND, 515 WEST 7TH STREET #2, LOS ANGELES, CA 90017, USA
+1 (213) 614-0736 | WWW.SEVENGRANDBARS.COM

WHAT'S ON THE BAR?

Bar Jackalope's Japanese whisky selection is almost a "greatest hits" of great Suntory and Nikka expressions, some of them rare, though it also offers unusual selections from Mars Shinshu.

Yamazaki 12 Year Old
Yamazaki 18 Year Old
Yamazaki 25 Year Old
Hakushu 12 Year Old
Hakushu 18 Year Old
Hakushu Heavily Peated
Hibiki Harmony
Hibiki 12 Year Old
Hibiki 17 Year Old
Hibiki 21 Year Old
Nikka Taketsuru Pure Malt NAS
Nikka Taketsuru Pure Malt
  12 Year Old
Nikka Taketsuru Pure Malt
  17 Year Old
Nikka Taketsuru Pure Malt
  21 Year Old
Yoichi 15 Year Old
Miyagikyo 12 Year Old
Nikka Coffey Grain
Mars Iwai
Mars Iwai Tradition

BAR JACKALOPE
Described as a whisky library and tasting room, and noted for its friendly and helpful staff.

YUSHO
CHICAGO, USA

The bar at Yusho is situated directly adjacent to the Japanese Binchotan Grill, and often the line between bar and kitchen is intentionally blurred. Bar guests are seated overlooking both stations, and are invited to participate in discussion with bartenders and grill chefs alike over the preparation of craft cocktails and seasonally inspired dishes. The beverage program at Yusho is designed to support the unique flavors coming from the kitchen each night. The bringing together of each element of the program—craft cocktails, carefully selected sake and wine offerings, unexpected Japanese beer selections, and Japanese whisky—provides us with an array of tools to highlight the food flavors and ensure a revealing dining experience. In terms of the whisky selection, they feel a deep responsibility to appropriately represent the unparalleled technique and craftsmanship employed in the spirit's production.

WHAT SETS THE BAR APART? "Our whisky choice is outstanding, and includes some rare and exciting whiskies," says Yusho general manager and beverage coordinator, Timothy Koenig. "I oversee Yusho's selection of Japanese whisky. Regular staff training is conducted with a focus on empowering staff members with knowledge to create dynamic experiences at each table." Koenig is dedicated to studying and spotlighting every Japanese beverage, including whisky, sake, craft beer, and shōchū. He has received both sake professional and advanced sake professional certification from the Sake Education Council in Tokyo.

WHAT DO THEY RECOMMEND? "Nikka Yoichi Single Malt 12-Year: This bottling is a wonderful representative of Yoichi's signature robust-yet-refined style. The undeniable smokiness is balanced by notes of honey, crisp apple, and dark chocolate. The 12-year-old single malt is a rarity, both because Nikka has recently halted age statement bottlings for overseas markets, and in that its 15-year-old counterpart was the only Yoichi single malt released in the United States."

YUSHO · 2853 N. KEDZIE AVENUE, CHICAGO, IL 60618, USA
+1 (773) 904-8558 | WWW.YUSHO-CHICAGO.COM

WHAT'S ON THE BAR?

There is an emphasis on Nikka expressions at Yusho, whiskies that are more in demand than ever after Nikka discontinued many of them. Ichiro Akuto's whiskies are also well represented.

Yoichi 12 Year Old
Yoichi 15 Year Old
Yoichi NAS
Miyagikyo 12 Year Old
Miyagikyo 15 Year Old
Miyagikyo NAS
Nikka Coffey Grain
Nikka Taketsuru Pure Malt NAS
Nikka Taketsuru Pure Malt
   17 Year Old
Nikka Taketsuru Pure Malt
   21 Year Old
Nikka Whisky From The Barrel
Nikka All Malt
Chichibu The Floor Malted
   3 Year Old
Chichibu On The Way
Ichiro's Malt Hanyu 15 Year Old
Ichiro's Malt Whisky Talk
   12 Year Old
Ichiro's Malt Mizunara Wood
   Reserve
Ichiro's Malt Double Distilleries
Ichiro's Malt Wine Wood Reserve
White Oak Akashi Blended Grain
White Oak Akashi Single Malt
Mars Komagatake The Revival 2011
Mars Iwai Tradition

YUSHO
A vibrant party venue offering craft beer, cocktails, sake, shōchū, and some rare and special whisky.

NEXT PAGE
Just one of the tasty dishes on offer.

190   BARS AROUND THE WORLD

WHAT'S ON THE BAR?

With Japanese whisky so scarce, Zuma says its whisky list is very fluid and it buys in what it can, when it can.

White Oak Akashi Blended Malt
Chichibu Chibidaru 2009
Chichibu The Peated 2010
Ichiro's Malt Card Series The Joker
Hanyu 2000 Zuma Roka Single
   Cask #919
Karuizawa 1970 Single Cask
   #6177
Karuizawa 1982 Bourbon Cask
   29 Year Old
Nikka Coffey Grain
Nikka Whisky From The Barrel
Nikka Pure Malt Black
Nikka Pure Malt Red
Nikka Pure Malt White
Yoichi NAS
Hibiki 17 Year Old
Hibiki 21 Year Old
Hakushu 12 Year Old
Hakushu 18 Year Old
Hakushu Distiller's Reserve
Suntory Rolling Stones 50 Year Old
Yamazaki 12 Year Old
Yamazaki 18 Year Old
Yamazaki Distiller's Reserve
Togouchi 18 Year Old
Yamazaki Sherry Cask

ZUMA
Inspired by the informal dining style of izakaya, Zuma serves dishes that are designed to share.

Zuma is an internationally acclaimed, upmarket, contemporary restaurant serving award-winning modern Japanese cuisine. It specializes in authentic and sophisticated dishes designed to share, and is inspired by the informal dining style of izakaya (after-hours bars). The three kitchens present a range of eating options, all characterized by bold flavors and simple presentation, highlighting quality ingredients. Japanese whisky is now core to Zuma's snack and food offerings. "Ten years ago, Japanese whisky was rare and relatively unexplored, but now it is booming," says bar development manager Simon Freeth. "It also features extensively on Zuma's cocktail menu, and has become one of the key characters in all the restaurant's menus. The bar staff have made it a point of principle to educate customers on its strengths."

WHAT SETS THE BAR APART? There are several Zumas across the world, but this one has been chosen because Japanese whisky dominates the back bar; this is both a cause and a sign of the drink's growing popularity in Manhattan. Zuma New York has one of the most decorated head chefs in North America, and the restaurant offers an authentic but not traditional take on Japanese culture, style, and flavors, where whisky may be integrated into the menu. It combines the buzz of central New York with a style of food rarely found outside Japan. Behind the bar you'll find treasures such as Vintage Hanyu.

WHAT DO THEY RECOMMEND? Simon says: "Suntory Yamazaki 12 Year Old single malt: a great introduction to Japanese whisky: sweet, delicate, and very easy to drink neat!

"Nikka From The Barrel is a great, versatile, Japanese whisky— bold, strong, and great as a sour or with fleshy fruits.

"And finally, Hanyu Vintage 2000: Zuma bought a bottle from the last cask of a vintage 2000 Hanyu. It's very special."

ZUMA · 261 MADISON AVENUE, NEW YORK, NY 10016, USA
+1 (212) 544-9862 | WWW.ZUMARESTAURANT.COM

THE FLATIRON ROOM
NEW YORK, USA

Visiting The Flatiron Room is like stepping back in time. It's a classical, theatrical venue that exudes warmth and sophistication. It stocks more than 1,000 whiskies, and serves simple but well-made food, including cheese boards, flatbreads, steaks, and ribs. The atmosphere is relaxed and appealing, and the backdrop of live jazz adds to the grandeur of the venue. The bar has gone out of its way to seek new and unusual Japanese whiskies, because the demand is broad, across a market ranging from experienced drinkers to a new wave of inquisitive imbibers who have heard about the award-winning whiskies that have beaten the best Scotches and bourbons.

WHAT SETS THE BAR APART? Owner Tommy Tardie says that The Flatiron Room has positioned itself as the flagship bar for all things whisky. "We have tried to create a whole new form of luxurious hospitality," he says. "The whisky industry has embraced what we are doing, and it is regularly the center for launch events and promotions."

In addition to the award-winning food, and huge whisky choice, The Flatiron Room offers a whiskey school and has a private room dedicated to whiskey tasting and education. The Flatiron Room goes to considerable lengths to refresh its Japanese whisky offering.

WHAT DO THEY RECOMMEND? Tommy says: "Yamazaki 12 Year Old. When most people think of Japanese whisky, they typically think of Yamazaki. This 12 Year Old is superb—light, fresh, lots of character, and layers upon layers on the finish.

"Then go for Nikka Coffey Grain—with a mash that's dominated by corn, it's a great way to introduce a Japanese to bourbon drinkers.

"And finally, Hakushu 12—fresh and light, yet with an unmistakable zip of peat that runs straight through this whisky. A nice alternative to a softer, and sometimes smoother, Islay malt."

THE FLATIRON ROOM · 37 WEST 26TH STREET, NEW YORK, NY 10010, USA
+1 (212) 725-3860 | WWW.THEFLATIRONROOM.COM

WHAT'S ON THE BAR?

Then Flatiron Room has a healthy stock of whiskies from the two main producers, and it is adding exciting new whiskies as they become available.

Hakushu 12 Year Old
Hakushu 18 Year Old
Hibiki Harmony
Hibiki 12 Year Old
Hibiki 17 Year Old
Hibiki 21 Year Old
Chichibu The Floor Malted
   3 Year Old
Ichiro's Malt & Grain
Nikka Taketsuru Pure Malt
   12 Year Old
Nikka Taketsuru Pure Malt
   17 Year Old
Nikka Taketsuru Pure Malt
   21 Year Old
Nikka Coffey Grain
Chichibu The First
Mars Iwai
Mars Iwai Tradition
Yamazaki 12 Year Old
Yamazaki 18 Year Old
Yamazaki Sherry Cask
Yoichi 15 Year Old

FLATIRON ROOM
Elegant Italian style wallpaper, chandeliers, and rolling ladders are targeted at discerning whisky drinkers.

THE FLATIRON ROOM

COPPER AND OAK
NEW YORK, USA

Lovers of the finest spirits may well be familiar with the Brandy Library on N. Moore St. Copper and Oak is from the same management, but twists a concept into something new. This is a very intimate whisky shrine, and it really is small, fun, and quirky. When full, a sign lights up, and the door is locked. When people leave, the sign welcomes new punters. The space itself is aptly named: the walls are made of deconstructed bourbon barrels, and the caps from old copper whiskey bottles act as knobs on the bathroom sink. It's a tiny space, packed with 600 bottles lining the walls all around the customers, and is casual, and dressed-down. The owners have traded the soft jazz of the Brandy Library for a bit more upbeat 1980s rock. It doesn't accept reservations. In contrast to the Brandy Library's comfy couches, its one bar top is lined with tall stools, leaving the opposite bar top for standing. Food is snacky.

WHAT SETS THE BAR APART? You don't get more intimate than this—it is like a tiny library crossed with a cathedral dedicated to the worship of fine spirits. Owner Flavian Desoblin says the staff's experience counts for a lot. "All spirit sommeliers working at Copper and Oak are also part of the Brandy Library team, two of the three for more than ten years," he says. "They have all visited Japanese whisky distilleries, and are well versed in most aspects of Japanese drinking culture."

WHAT DO THEY RECOMMEND? "Start with Chichibu The First because, although it is very young, it gives an indication that the future of Japanese whisky is safe in Ichiro Akuto's hands.
   "Then go for Ichiro's Malt Mizunara Wood to experience the uniquely Japanese scented and spiced notes from the Japanese oak.
   "And finally, you have to try a Karuizawa before it's all gone or locked away in private collections."

COPPER AND OAK · 157 ALLEN STREET, NEW YORK, NY 10002, USA
+1 (212) 460-5546 | WWW.COPPERANDOAK.COM

WHAT'S ON THE BAR?

In addition to an extensive Suntory and Nikka list including rarities, a small number of the highlights include:

White Oak Akashi NAS
Chichibu Chibidaru
Chichibu Newborn 2009 Heavily
   Peated
Chichibu Port Pipe
Chichibu The First
Chichibu The Floor Malted
   3 Year Old
Ichiro's Malt Hanyu 1990
Ichiro's Malt Whisky Talk
Ichiro's Malt Hanyu 2000–2010
   The Final Vintage
Ichiro's Malt Hanyu 23 Year Old
Ichiro's Malt Mizunara Wood
   Reserve
Isawa Blended Whisky
Mars Iwai
Mars Iwai Tradition
Karuizawa Memories
   of Karuizawa 16 Year Old
Karuizawa 1981
Karuizawa 1981 Noh Series
   31 Year Old
Karuizawa 1984–2012
   International Bar Show
Karuizawa Asama
Karuizawa Multivintage
Kawasaki 1981/Bot. 2009

COPPER AND OAK
A tiny, elegant, gem of a bar and a tribute to the copper and oak used in whisky production.

SAKAMAI
NEW YORK, USA

SakaMai is something of an oasis nestling among the legions of Lower East Side dive bars known for their hustle and bustle, and overflowing with cheap beer and food. It describes itself as a Japanese "gastro lounge," and the dimly lit space is an upscale Americanized twist on izakaya—the Japanese after-hours bars where food is served to accompany the drinks. It is designed to offer a Japanese spin and whisky sake expertise in a nightlife-loving neighborhood. With an extensive list of Japanese-style snacks and sushi rolls, the venue offers a kind of high-quality Japanese tapas.

WHAT SETS THE BAR APART? Co-owner Natalie Graham says that the carefully constructed combination of talented and highly trained staff with a delicate balance of Japanese culture and downtown New York bar gives SakaMai something you will find nowhere else. "The team includes a sake sommelier, an award-winning mixologist, and an executive chef who hails from a lineage of Japanese sushi experts," she says. "Visitors can enjoy a few glasses of boutique Japanese liquor while snacking on everything from braised veal cheek to black cod with miso." The bar boasts of one of the best selections of Japanese beverages in North America, with a large selection of sake, shōchū, Japanese beer, and whiskies.

WHAT DO THEY RECOMMEND?
Natalie says three above all: "Firstly, Hibiki 12 Year Old, which is a round, full, and luscious blended whisky, well-balanced, and with many layers.

"Secondly, Hakushu 18 Year Old is an excellent example of a Scotch-style Japanese single malt whisky with an artfully done, light, smoky peatiness.

"And finally, Ichiro's malt 'On The Way,' which is a strong and incredibly deep and complex whisky made by blending batches of whisky aged three, five, and seven years old."

WHAT'S ON THE BAR?

SakaMai hasn't got the most extensive whisky list, but its selections represent a carefully balanced collection of all the different characteristics that Japan is famous for.

Hakushu 12 Year Old
Hakushu 18 Year Old
Hibiki Harmony
Hibiki 12 Year Old
Nikka Coffey Grain
Nikka Taketsuru Pure Malt 12 Year Old
Nikka Taketsuru Pure Malt 17 Year Old
Yamazaki 12 Year Old
Yamazaki 18 Year Old
Yoichi 15 Year Old
White Oak Akashi NAS
Chichibu On The Way
Chichibu The Peated

SAKAMAI · 157 LUDLOW STREET, NEW YORK, NY 10002, USA
+44 (646) 590-0684 | WWW.SAKAMAI.COM

SAKAMAI
Izakaya-style food with an extensive drinks range and a distinct New York twist.

SAKAMAI 197

198 BARS AROUND THE WORLD

DR. JEKYLL'S PUB
OSLO, NORWAY

WHAT'S ON THE BAR?

Wow, Dr. Jekyll's might be something of a rowdy bar, but it has some extraordinarily rare Japanese whiskies, even by Japanese standards.

Karuizawa Martins Selection Vintage 1973
Karuizawa 19 Year Old 10th Whisky Live
Karuizawa 1988 Vintage
Karuizawa 1967 42 Year Old
Ichiro's Malt Card Series Ace of Diamonds
Ichiro's Malt Card Series Four of Diamonds, Cask #9030
Ichiro's Malt Hanyu 23 Year Old
Karuizawa Kohaku 1995 Vintage 10 Year Old
Hanyu Noh Whisky 21 Year Old Cask #9306
Yoichi The Scotch Malt Whisky Society 23 Year Old
Hanyu 1988 "Nice Butt" Cask #9307
Karuizawa Noh Series 14 Year Old
Karuizawa Noh 29 Bourbon
Karuizawa Noh 31 Sherry
Karuizawa Spirit of Asama
Chichibu The Floor Malted 3 Year Old
Chichibu Port Pipe
Nikka From The Barrel
Togouchi 12 Year Old
Togouchi 18 Year Old

This is the most rough-and-ready bar in this selection, and not all the reviews of it are favorable. It's a spacious bar on a smelly side street, and it gets very busy. It has an Irish theme, but looks like an Australian drinking warehouse. It is proof that Japanese whisky doesn't have to be tasted in exclusive bars and lounges, and it has an amazing whisky list. "Dr. Jekyll's has seen a change in clientele for Japanese whisky," says manager Peter-André Dahl. "We attract real connoisseurs who want to taste the special releases, and they are now joined by a general public which has opened its eyes to the great quality of many Japanese whiskies."

WHAT SETS THE BAR APART? Dr. Jekyll's is a no-frills pub first and foremost, but it has a whisky club with more than 800 members. It holds tastings every three weeks. Whisky is also given a higher profile than in many pubs. "We employ a specialist whisky manager, and we are proud of our passionate and educated staff who put an emphasis on whisky," says Peter-André. The Japanese offering is quite amazing, and the pub even has its own whisky range, Dr. Jekyll's Expressions, which include a Karuizawa Noh edition 14 Year Old, and a cask-strength, Japanese-style Bordeaux barrel whisky.

WHAT DO THEY RECOMMEND? Peter-André says: "Nikka From The Barrel is a great starter for anyone who wants to try out whisky from Japan for the first time. The Yamazaki Anniversary Bottling 84 introduces drinkers to mizunara, the Japanese oak. It gives the whisky complexity, and different aromas and flavors. An outstanding bottling. And finally, Karuizawa 1967 vintage. The complex aromas between the tannins, smoke, and full-bodied mouth feel are not something you will taste every day!"

DR. JEKYLL'S
First and foremost a busy pub, with an 800-member-strong whisky club and some very rare Japanese whiskies.

DR. JEKYLL'S PUB · KLINGENBERGGATA 4, 0161 OSLO, NORWAY
+47 22 41 30 44 | WWW.JEKYLLS.NO

THE HIGHLANDER INN
SPEYSIDE, SCOTLAND

Nestling in the heart of the Speyside bens and glens that make up Scotland's Malt Whisky Trail, and at first sight a typical regional pub, The Highlander Inn isn't perhaps where you'd expect to find an extensive range of specialty Japanese whisky or, indeed, one of the spirit's most respected ambassadors. The Highlander is in the small village of Craigellachie, opposite the stylish Craigellachie Hotel. You'll find all the best of a Scottish inn: an impressive range of draft beers and single malt whiskies, affordable accommodation, and good, hearty food. But this pub rises above the norm, not just because of its excellent whisky range, but also because it was an early champion of fine Japanese whisky, and now simply excels in it.

WHAT SETS THE BAR APART? This pub has been listed as one of the world's best whisky bars for years. That's because for years it was run by Duncan Elphick, a whisky connoisseur who defected from the Craigellachie across the road, taking Japanese whisky expert Tatsuya Minagawa with him. Tatsuya built up the Japanese offering during his first spell at the pub between 2005 and 2012, and then in 2015 he took over the business. The result is a whisky venue like no other—a Highland inn with the kind of Japanese whisky range you'd expect to find in the better bars of Singapore, Tokyo, or Taipei. Tatsuya is justly proud of Japanese whisky, and was promoting it well before everybody wanted a piece of the action. He performs an impressive balancing act in the heart of Scotch whisky country, but argues that most people are open-minded, love whisky, and accept that Japan can give at least some fine Scottish single malts a run for their money.

WHAT DO THEY RECOMMEND? Give him the time, and Tatsuya will introduce you to scores of great whiskies. But he goes for the following: "Hibiki 17 Year Old, because it's a Japanese classic. Yamazaki 18 Year Old is a multi-award winning whisky with great complexity; and Chichibu Single Bourbon Barrel, which is young, but has a lot of flavor, and will be great stuff in a few years' time."

THE HIGHLANDER INN · CRAIGELLLACHIE, SPEYSIDE, BANFFSHIRE, AB38 9SR, SCOTLAND, UK
+44 1340 881 446 | WWW.WHISKYINN.COM

WHAT'S ON THE BAR?

In addition to extensive Suntory and Nikka bottlings, selected highlights include:

Chichibu Single Cask Bourbon Barrel 3 Year Old
Chichibu Peated Bottled 2015
Hakushu Single Cask Osaka 3rd Anniversary
Ichiro's Malt Hanyu 23 Year Old
Hanyu Single Cask Whisky Talk Fukuoka 2011
Ichiro's Malt Card Series The Joker
Ichiro's Malt & Grain
Ichiro's Malt Double Distilleries Pure Malt
Ichiro's Malt Wine Wood Reserve
Hibiki 17 Year Old
Mars Malt Gallery American White Oak
Mars Komagatake Single Cask 25 Year Old
Yamazaki 18 Year Old
Yamazaki Single Cask Whisky Live Tokyo 2012

THE HIGHLANDER INN
Seemingly a typical Scottish pub in the heart of Scotch whisky territory—but home to Japanese whisky enthusiast and expert Tatsuya Minagawa.

202 BARS AROUND THE WORLD

SEXY FISH
LONDON, ENGLAND

WHAT'S ON THE BAR?

In addition to large collections of Hanyus and Karuizawas as well as Suntory and Nikka whiskies, others include:

Chichibu Chibidaru
Chichibu Port Pipe
Ichiro's Malt Mizunara Wood Reserve
Ichiro's Malt Double Distilleries Pure Malt
Ichiro's Malt Wine Wood Reserve
Fuji Gotemba Single Grain Blender's Choice
Kirin 18 Year Old
Mars The Revival 2011 Komagatake
Mars The Lucky Cat
Mars Maltage Komagatake Pure Malt 10 Year Old
Mars Maltage Komagatake 10 Year Old Wine Cask Finish
Mars Komagatake 2012 Sherry Cask #146
Nikka Whisky From The Barrel
Rainbow Whisky
Wakatsuru Shuzo Sun Shine 20 Year Old
Yamazakura 15 Year Old Pure Malt
Yamazaki 18 Year Old
Kawasaki 1976 33 Year Old Ichiro's Choice Grain
Kawasaki 1982 Whisky Live Tokyo 29 Year Old 2011 Single Grain

SEXY FISH
A stunning room with Frank Gehry fish lamps and art by Damien Hirst and Michael Roberts.

Sexy Fish is in the heart of London's Mayfair. It is split-level, with a private room on the lower ground floor, and the restaurant and terrace on the ground floor. The food takes its inspiration from the seas of Asia, with a focus on Japan. It's a stunning room. The decor in the restaurant is a mix of onyx marble floors, dark oak-clad walls and pillars, with leather banquettes and chairs. The ceilings are adorned with customized coral-patterned linen panels from artist Michael Roberts. Frank Gehry's fish lamps hang above the bar, and there is a flowing water wall behind it. A 13-foot (4-meter) glossy black silicone mosaic crocodile crawls across the wall of the dining room. Damien Hirst has created three site-specific artworks for the restaurant: a pair of bronze mermaids, positioned on either end of the bar; and a 15-foot (4.5 meter) bronze panel of a mermaid alongside a shark. Counter seats at the stone bar look straight into the kitchen.

WHAT SETS THE BAR APART? There are more than 170 Japanese whiskies, from seventeen distilleries. The collection has been put together by Xavier Landais, Caprice Holdings' executive bars manager. "I have been working with independent distilleries directly, as well as renowned producers, such as Suntory and Nikka, for more than four years," he says. "It's been a kind of addiction, and so the collection just grew and grew, and now we are so proud to have the largest collection in Europe." Along with whisky expert Jerome Allaguillemette, the bar team spends a minimum of an hour a day searching for new additions, and replenishing the collection.

WHAT DO THEY RECOMMEND? Nikka From The Barrel: "An incredible entry whisky, affordable and full of character."
   Yamazaki 18 Year Old: "A silky dram. Oily and complex, fruity and zesty. Not cheap but never disappoints."
   Karuizawa 30 Year Old #5347 Sherry Cask, Geisha: "Thick, rich, sweet, with an everlasting finish. Not much left so each dram is a privilege."

SEXY FISH · BERKELEY SQUARE, LONDON W1J 6BR, UK
+ 44 20 3764 2000 | WWW.SEXYFISH.COM

SHŌCHŪ LOUNGE
LONDON, ENGLAND

WHAT'S ON THE BAR?

The bar's mix of more than forty years brings together some favorites from Suntory and Nikka with some genuine rarities.

Yamazaki 12 Year Old
Yamazaki 18 Year Old
Yamazaki 25 Year Old
Hakushu 12 Year Old
Hakushu 18 Year Old
Nikka Taketsuru Pure Malt
  12 Year Old
Yoichi NAS
Yoichi 12 Year Old
Miyagikyo NAS
Miyagikyo 12 Year Old
Karuizawa Sherry Cask 30 Year Old
Karuizawa Bourbon Cask
  29 Year Old
Karuizawa 1981
Hanyu 2000 Zuma Roka Single
  Cask #919
Mars Komagatake The Revival 2011
Togouchi 8 Year Old
Togouchi 12 Year Old
Ichiro's Malt Wine Wood Reserve
Chichibu Port Pipe
Chichibu The Peated
Chichibu Chibidaru
Chichibu On The Way
White Oak Akashi NAS

SHŌCHŪ LOUNGE
Wild and wacky murals, low seductive lighting, and an extensive Japanese drinks list make this bar under iconic restaurant Roka well worth a visit.

Enter Roka and you're in a clean and smart contemporary Japanese restaurant. It exudes class, style, and sophistication. Food with a worldwide reputation for quality is served with hushed efficiency. The staff are attentive and professional. The finest meat, seafood, and vegetables are lovingly prepared by top chefs. Then go downstairs to the Shōchū Lounge and wow, you're suddenly in a different world. This is an atmospheric, sexy, denlike bar bordering on decadent, and with garish Japanese murals and a youthful vibe that is in stark contrast to Roka. The environment is fun, but the whisky is serious.

WHAT SETS THE BAR APART? Walk down the stairs and into the Shōchū and that question is well and truly answered. Few bars anywhere have been so skillfully designed to contrast with the restaurant upstairs. Manager James Shearer says: "This venue offers two very Japanese gastronomic experiences. The Shōchū one is an aural and visual assault to the senses, with an excellent range of Japanese whiskies as well as shōchū, sake, well-crafted cocktails, and food. The bar prides itself on creating unique atmosphere, and puts great emphasis on its attention to detail."

WHAT DO THEY RECOMMEND? James says: "For something different and more exclusive, two whiskies: the Hanyu 2000 Cask 57.6%, which was bought and bottled exclusively for Roka and Zuma. It has intense flavors, and is woody, with toffee and spices. It benefits from a small amount of water.

"The Karuizawa 1981, 63.4%, is dark, and has notes from the sherry cask, dark berries, licorice, and spices. There are very few bottles of this left, so when it's gone, it's gone. Definitely one to try once in your lifetime! Also Suntory's Yamazaki 18 Year Old, 43%, has a well-deserved reputation, is always in demand, and is a top-class whisky.

"Finally, Nikka's Yoichi 2015 nonage statement 43%. Nikka has excelled at entry-level whiskies. This one is great: soft peat notes characteristic of Yoichi, great on its own or versatile in cocktails."

ROKA · 37 CHARLOTTE STREET, LONDON W1T 1RR, UK
+44 207 580 6464 | WWW.ROKARESTAURANT.COM

TONKOTSU
LONDON, ENGLAND

Tonkotsu is a spacious and modern bar and ramen restaurant, with clean, fresh precise fittings, and stylish bar seats and circular bench seats. The long, zinc-topped bar sits at the front of the restaurant, which serves some of London's best ramen made with fresh noodles and long-simmered broths. Head past the bar for dinner in a cozy booth, or sit at the bar for a few whiskies, snacks, and a chat with the bar team who'll recommend whiskies to go with your food.

WHAT SETS THE BAR APART? There are more than sixty whiskies here, most of which are Japanese, and there is an impressive selection from both Nikka and Suntory, including some rare bottles. Paul John from Goa, India, is also on the shelf, along with a few whiskies from the Taiwanese Kavalan. Group bar managers David Wrigley and Martina Fortunato have been building the list over several years. They host regular whisky tastings, and are able to match a whisky with most dishes on the menu.

"It's useful to think about terroir as you would a wine," says Dave. "Whiskies from coastal regions tend to bring with them vigorous, salty elements. They therefore pair very well with fish and sushi in particular. I often look to pick out distinct tastes and aromas from a whisky, and think how those elements work with food. A whisky that's particularly nutty I will try to pair with something earthy like mushrooms. If a whisky has a strong orchard fruit character, I'll match it with pork."

WHAT DO THEY RECOMMEND? "For an expression of what Japanese whisky is all about, the Hibiki 17 is a great choice," says Dave. "There are mizunara characteristics, coconut and sandalwood, with some pine resin and oak.

"Ichiro's Malt Double Distillery has whisky from the Hanyu distillery. Vanilla, coconut, and generally bourbonlike characteristics are initially apparent, followed by some wonderful wood and spice notes. For something a bit different, the Nikka Coffey Malt is perfect. Clean citrus fruit, dense spice and rich oak."

TONKOTSU · 382 MARE STREET, LONDON E8 1HR, UK
+1 0208 533 1840 | WWW.TONKOTSU.CO.UK

WHAT'S ON THE BAR?

Tonkotsu's collection of Japanese whisky mixes a core range of classic whiskies with some impressive rare and oddball malts.

White Oak Akashi NAS
Ichiro's Malt Wine Wood Reserve
Chichibu Chibidaru
Hakushu 18 Year Old
Hibiki 17 Year Old
Ichiro's Malt Double Distilleries
   Pure Malt
Ichiro's Malt & Grain
Karuizawa Spirit of Asama
Mars Maltage Cosmo
Miyagikyo 15 Year Old
Nikka Coffey Grain
Nikka Coffey Malt
Nikka Super Revival
Mars Komagatake The Revival 2011
Togouchi 18 Year Old
Nikka Taketsuru Pure Malt
   17 Year Old
Yamazaki Bourbon Barrel
Yamazaki Puncheon 2013
Yamazaki 18 Year Old

TONKOTSU
The staff here go to some lengths to pair their food with their whiskies.

LE SHERRY BUTT
PARIS, FRANCE

WHAT'S ON THE BAR?

Japanese whisky is a key aspect of The Sherry Butt's appeal in a region of Paris with a high number of bars.

Chichibu The First
Chichibu Port Pipe
Chichibu Chibidaru
Nikka Coffey Grain
Nikka Coffey Malt
Hakushu 12 Year Old
Hakushu 18 Year Old
Hanyu 1990 "The Wave"
   Cask #9305
Ichiro's Malt Card Series Eight
   of Clubs 1988
Hibiki 12 Year Old
Hibiki 17 Year Old
Hibiki 21 Year Old
Karuizawa Spirit of Asama
Miyagikyo 10 Year Old
Miyagikyo 12 Year Old
Nikka Whisky From The Barrel
Nikka Taketsuru Pure Malt
   21 Year Old
Yamazaki 12 Year Old
Yamazaki 18 Year Old
Yamazaki 1979 Mizunara Oak Cask
Yoichi 10 Year Old
Yoichi 12 Year Old
Yoichi 15 Year Old

LE SHERRY BUTT
This bar offers a fantastic whisky range while maintaining a cozy, comfortable, rustic-style café bar atmosphere.

Le Sherry Butt is located in a little side street in the Marais district and is described as a middle point between the busy cocktail bars of Saint-Germain and the hip bars of Bastille. It was opened in 2014 by two people with a long track record in the Parisian cocktail scene, and initially that was where it was placed. But the owners had around 60 bottles of quality whisky at the outset, and that has grown to more than 100, with Japanese whisky taking pride of place. As a result, whisky is as much a feature now as cocktails are. The bar consists of two sizable rooms, and there is a distinctly rustic feel, with exposed brick walls and a large blackboard with the recipes for the bar's seasonal cocktails. Many of the ingredients are homemade. The atmosphere is relaxed and intimate, and comfortable leather couches adorn both rooms. Food is simple finger food.

WHAT SETS THE BAR APART? The mix of quality world whiskies and outstanding cocktails. Part of what Le Sherry Butt is about is introducing whisky to cocktail drinkers. "We offer a seasonal menu with twelve cocktails on the list, plus an array of whisky flights, which consist of four different drams served in Glencairn glasses on an oak board," says owner and founder Amaury. "This gives us the chance to attract whisky lovers and cocktail aficionados on a same level, plus the usual cocktail bar crowd. I always recommend our customers start with a cocktail and then move on with some serious spirits if they're game. At the moment, and although it's becoming rarer and rarer, we do offer around ten to fifteen Japanese whiskies on our menu. Our refrigerated glass cabinets, and our use of crystal-clear ice pretty much sets us apart on the bar scene in Paris."

WHAT DO THEY RECOMMEND? "If I had to pick three, it would be Hanyu 1990 The Wave, because it is one of my favorites of all time; Karuizawa 1969, probably because it is the rarest we still have. And Yoichi 10, because it's simply delicious, and they've stopped doing it for the years to come."

LE SHERRY BUTT · 20 RUE BEAUTREILLIS,
4ᴱ ARRONDISSEMENT, PARIS, FRANCE
+ 33 9 83 38 47 80 | WWW.SHERRYBUTTPARIS.COM

LE GAMIN DE BASTILLE
PARIS, FRANCE

Le Gamin de Bastille looks like the kind of café bar you find thousands of in France—a typical coffee and newspaper stopping point. It sits in a row of other bars and stores, and according to its owners, Ihab and Imene Mikhael, they're operating in a lively and touristy area and on their street alone there are forty bars. Le Gamin was just one of them until the Mikhaels set out to change it. Now, as Madame Mikhael puts it "*C'est un peu la caverne d'Ali Baba*" (Its a little like Ali Baba's cave"). In fact, there is something slightly eastern about the interior, the furniture rustic, and the bar ramshackle in the best possible way.

WHAT SETS THE BAR APART The extensive whisky and rum range, the crêperie, and the joie de vivre of the owner. "One day my husband wanted to drink a whisky and went to a number of bars, but each time he found practically the same bottles and no choice," recalls Madame Mikhael. "He wanted a choice of spirits, and so he began to grow our range of whisky, rum, gin. At the beginning, our aim was to get to forty different whiskies, then sixty, eighty, 120. Today we have almost 200 from across the whole world."

WHAT DO THEY RECOMMEND? "Yamazaki 18 Year Old won many medals between 2007 and 2013, and is made up of whisky from a sherry butt and a Japanese mizunara cask," says Imene. "It is a whisky that does not leave you disappointed."

Nikka Yoichi 1991: "This 23-year-old single cask is one of the rarest Japanese whiskies, with the release limited to just 423 bottles worldwide, a good reason for enthusiasts to be torn apart in their wish to have a bottle."

Karuizawa, various vintages. "These days this whisky heads the list of the most sought-after malts. After production stopped in 2000 and the distillery was dismantled in 2011, prices have gone up and up. We have four different vintages: 1981, 1982, 1983, and 1984, two from bourbon casks and two sherry butts. An exceptional rarity."

LE GAMIN DE BASTILLE · 34, RUE DE LAPPE 75011, BASTILLE, 11ᴱ ARRONDISSEMENT, PARIS, FRANCE
+ 33 1 40 21 01 82 | LEGAMINBASTILLE.FR

WHAT'S ON THE BAR?

On the face of it Le Gamin is just another quaint and pleasant, but unexceptional, café bar. That is, until you notice the Japanese whisky list.

Hakushu 12 Year Old
Hakushu 18 Year Old
Hibiki 12 Year Old
Hibiki 17 Year Old
Hiibiki 21 Year Old
Karuizawa (various vintages)
Miyagikyo 10 Year Old
Miyagikyo 15 Year Old
Nikka Pure Malt Black
Nikka Whisky From The Barrel
Nikka Coffey Grain
Nikka Taketsuru Pure Malt
  12 Year Old
Nikka Taketsuru Pure Malt
  17 Year Old
Nikka Taketsuru Pure Malt
  21 Year Old
Yamazaki 12 Year Old
Yamazaki 18 Year Old
Yamazaki Bourbon Barrel
Yoichi 20 Year Old

LE GAMIN
This place can be described as a little like Aladdin's cave.

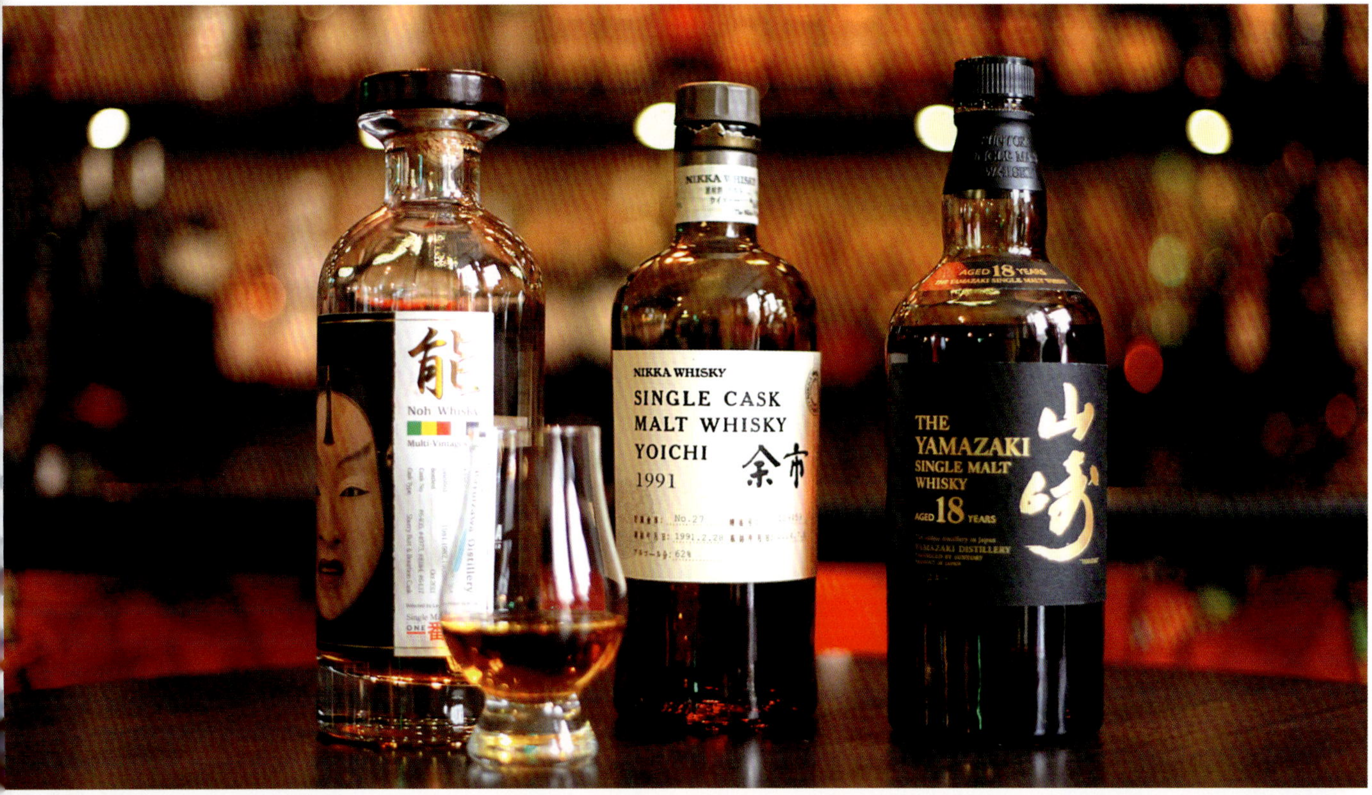
能
Noh Whisky
NIKKA WHISKY
SINGLE CASK
MALT WHISKY
YOICHI
1991
余市
AGED 18 YEARS
THE YAMAZAKI
SINGLE MALT
WHISKY
AGED 18 YEARS
山崎

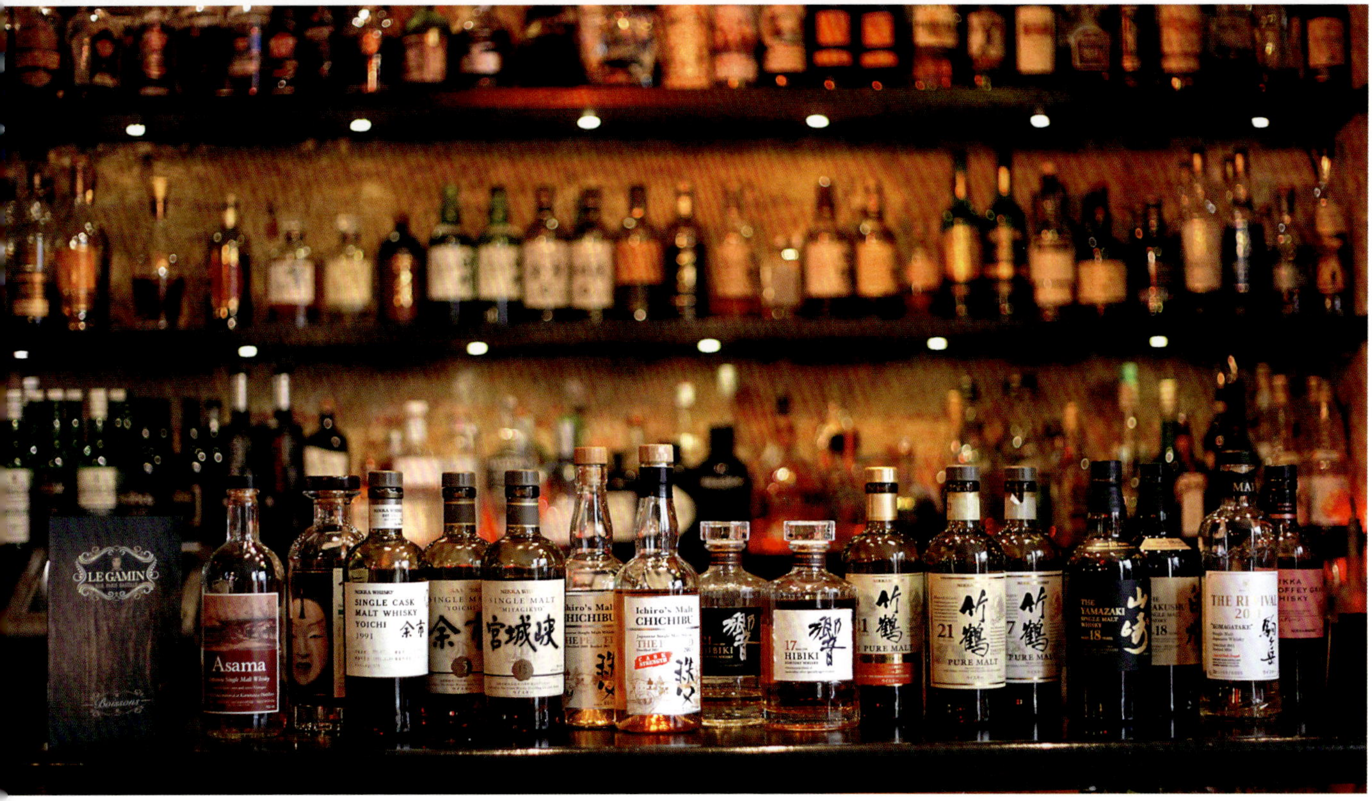
LE GAMIN
Asama
SINGLE CASK
MALT WHISKY
YOICHI
余市
宮城峡
CHICHIBU
17
HIBIKI
響
竹鶴
21
PURE MALT
THE YAMAZAKI
18

WHAT'S ON THE BAR?

Sushi & Soul has around 200 Japanese whiskies, including an extensive collection of single-cask bottlings, and some very rare whiskies, particularly from Nikka's two distilleries.

Chichibu Chibidaru 2009 cask #286
Ichiro's Malt Double Distilleries
    Pure Malt
Ichiro's Malt Mizunara
    Wood Reserve
Ichiro's Malt Hanyu 2000–2010
    The Final Vintage
Nikka Gold & Gold Samurai
Nikka Pure Malt Black 8 Year Old
Nikka Rare Old Super
Nikka Malt 70th Anniversary
    12 Year Old
Nikka Super Genshu
Nikka Hokkaido 12 Year Old
Suntory 1991 Furudaru Shiage
Suntory Kakubin
Suntory 1981 Kioke Shiomi
Suntory 2000 Millennium
Suntory Reserve Whisky Silky
Suntory Royal Whisky
Nikka Tsuru 17 Year Old

SUSHI & SOUL
This bar offers between forty and fifty whisky seminars each year, attracting new whisky drinkers.

In the heart of Munich, this restaurant is large by Japanese standards, with space for 180 covers. The interior is a timeless mix of classic design elements. At its center is a long izakaya-style table which seats around thirty people, flanked by traditional Western tables for smaller groups and couples, as well as by Japanese tatami—floor matting on which diners sit in front of a small fireplace. The sushi bar is at one end of the long table; diners here can watch the chefs preparing the food. In addition to sushi, the restaurant offers an array of hot and cold Japanese dishes, from yakitori skewers for starters to sweet *matcha* mousse for dessert.

WHAT SETS THE BAR APART? Besides Japan-themed cocktails and long drinks, it offers an ever-growing selection of Japanese whisky.

"For about a decade we were buying far more of it than we sold," says owner Chris Herbst. "Now, with more than 200 different bottlings, we have the world's largest collection of Japanese whisky. We especially focus on rare single-cask bottlings of Hanyu, Karuizawa, Yoichi, and Miyagikyo."

Sushi & Soul also plays a leading role in whisky education.

"Every year we offer around forty to fifty whisky seminars that provide the opportunity to try out-of-stock bottlings. Even though most of our customers prefer whisky as a digestif, more and more enthusiasts are discovering exciting combinations with our food."

WHAT DO THEY RECOMMEND? "Our current favorite is Chichibu first-fill bourbon barrel single cask 2008/2014. Also we have a bottling which we shared with Bar Zoetrope in Shinjuku, Tokyo. Despite its 61.6% strength, this whisky does not have a sporty taste, but is dominated by the strong and fruity aroma of yellow plum, peach, and pear, and a strong flavor of vanilla pudding and candied fruit.

We are also big fans of the Nikka distilleries Yoichi and Miyagikyu. On our regular visits to Japan, we bring back bottlings that you probably would not be able to find anywhere else in Europe."

SUSHI & SOUL · GLOCKENBACHVIERTEL, KLENZESTRASSE 71,
80469 MUNICH, GERMANY
+49 (0) 89 201 09 92 | WWW.SUSHI-SOUL.DE

DOM WHISKY
WARSAW, POLAND

There are three Dom Whisky, which translates to "House of Whisky," bars in Poland—in Jastrzębia Góra, Wroclaw, and Warsaw—each of them with slightly different whisky collections. "They represent the only places in Poland devoted entirely to whisky, with one of the three stocking more than 1,700 bottles," says a bar spokesman. "Whisky House is built on the model of the Scottish distilleries, and ambassadors are dressed in Scottish kilts. In summer, there is live music. We also organize whisky tastings held on our premises." Since 2000, the staff have regularly traveled to distilleries all over the world, including in Japan, and have developed Dom Whisky to capture the atmosphere and tradition of the whisky industry.

WHAT SETS THE BAR APART? Dom Whisky may try to emulate the great distilleries of the world, but there is something distinctly Polish about this place, and drinking whisky here is a unique experience in its own right. All three bars within the group have whisky ambassadors who are trained professionals. Staff travel to whisky festivals in Paris, London, and Limburg, and attend master classes at each of them. They travel to Scotland and Ireland to visit distilleries each year, and they hold their own whisky festival, inviting top professionals from across the world to speak at them.

WHAT DO THEY RECOMMEND? "Go for Hibiki 12—one of the first Japanese blends to get world attention and appreciation. Full of fruit aromas and complexity. Plum liqueur casks maturation is a great characteristic, too (because Polish folks like Choya so much).

"Also Nikka Coffey Malt—from fresh and clean, to robust and spicy, a full range of flavors, and a great malt to start the adventure with Japanese whisky.

"And finally, Yamazaki 18 Year Old—rich, woody, fruity, sherried, aromatic, a wonderfully balanced legend form the oldest Japanese distillery. We are the only place to stock it in Poland . . . and one of the few in central Europe."

COCKTAIL BAR MAX & DOM WHISKY · UL. KRUCZA 16/22, 00-526 WARSAW, POLAND
+48 691 71 00 00 | WWW.DOMWHISKY.PL

WHAT'S ON THE BAR?

There are three Dom Whisky outlets, each with its own whisky list. In addition to most Suntory and Nikka whiskies, the Warsaw bar boasts a range of rare whiskies, including:

Wakatsuru Shuzo Sun Shine 20 Year Old
Suntory Whisky Excellence
Nikka Gold & Gold Samurai
Nikka Pure Malt White
Nikka Pure Malt Black
Nikka Pure Malt Red
Hibiki 12 Year Old
Isawa Blended Whisky
Isawa Single Malt 10 Year Old
Isawa Malt Vintage 1983
Ichiro's Malt Mizunara Wood Reserve
Miyagikyo Single Cask 1990
Miyagikyo 15 Year Old
Nikka All Malt
Nikka Pure Malt Black 8 Year Old
Nikka Coffey Malt
Nikka Coffey Grain
Nikka Rare Old Super
White Oak Tokinoka Blended Malt
Yamazaki 18 Year Old

DOM WHISKY
One of three Dom outlets in Poland, each with its own whisky list, and dedicated and enthusiastic whisky fans as staff.

AULD ALLIANCE
SINGAPORE

The Auld Alliance serves a huge selection of Japanese whisky, along with some of the rarest bottlings from all over the world. Director Emmanuel Dron believes that you will not find a larger or more varied collection of Japanese whisky outside Tokyo. They're not above opening their very rarest bottles, and when they do, they post a picture on Facebook. "As soon as people see them, they just react and travel to drink the special bottles we've just opened, because they are worried it will be finished fast. Every month people fly from Hong Kong, Taiwan, and more specifically from Japan, sometimes taking the morning flight, then coming directly to the bar, and leaving the morning after or even that same night. This is quite crazy, and it really happens every month. We are one of the last bars in the world to open crazy rare bottles and serve them just by the glass."

WHAT SETS THE BAR APART? The rarity of the whisky is pretty special, as is the range of choice, but the Auld Alliance also prides itself on its staff. Emmanuel Dron has worked in the whisky industry for more than twenty years, including thirteen years at La Maison du Whisky in Paris. "We are all very passionate," he says. "I travel a lot, and always take one of the team with me for the experience. My team is lucky because they have tried most of the best whiskies ever."

WHAT DO THEY RECOMMEND? First, Emmanuel suggests "Nikka Taketsuru 35 Year Old. Only 1,000 bottles were produced a year, and it is very difficult to find. It was not sold in Europe. It was such a refined Japanese whisky, with still some beautiful red fruit flavors. It reminds me of a great old-style Longmorn from the 1960s. I have tried a few batches, and have always loved it."

Second, he goes for Mars 25 Year Old: "I knew this bottle well, even before it started winning awards. I liked the finesse on the wood, and the elegance and acidity of the fruit."

And finally, Yamazaki 1990 Sherry Butt "The Cask of Yamazaki": "Always very clean, with no sulfur notes. A bit extreme, but I loved it."

AULD ALLIANCE · 9 BRAS BASAH ROAD,
RENDEZVOUS HOTEL, SINGAPORE 189559
+65 6337 2201 | WWW.THEAULDALLIANCE.SG

WHAT'S ON THE BAR?

Auld Alliance in Singapore has one of the most extensive Japanese whisky lists in the world with more than 220 whiskies, including an extensive range of Hanyu and Karuizawa bottlings. The range includes:

White Oak Akashi Single Malt
Chichibu Port Pipe
Ichiro's Malt Card Series
   (more than 20)
Hibiki 12, 17, 21, 30 Year Old
Hibiki Deep Harmony
Hibiki Mellow Harmony
Karuizawa Cask Strength
   1st, 2nd, 3rd Releases
Karuizawa 2000 12 Year Old
   Dragon Label
Karuizawa Noh Series 14 Year Old
Karuizawa Single Cask (selection)
Mars Iwai Tradition Wine
   Cask Finish
Mars Komagatake Single
   Cask 25 Year Old
Miyagikyo 10, 12, 15 Year Old
Miyagikyo Single Cask (selection)
Nikka Taketsuru 35 Year Old
Nikka 40 Year Old
Yoichi 10, 12, 15, 20 Year Old

AULD ALLIANCE
Located on the second floor of the Rendezvous Hotel, the bar now has space for about sixty people.

BINCHO AT HUA BEE
SINGAPORE

Inspired by the small grilling stalls in Osaka known as yakitori-ya, Bincho is pretty well hidden away from the bustle of the city center, so it's a cozy and intimate place to enjoy whisky. Located in a seventy-year-old traditional kopitiam (coffee shop), the small dining area offers omakase meals of yakitori and other tasty treats. There is an old-school mee pok stall, with evergreen marble tables, rickety old wooden chairs, and an open-style yakitori bar. The bar combines traditional Singapore with a more modern one, but it's the bar behind that stocks the really best stuff. In a setting that looks like a stylish nuclear bunker, they have an impressive array of Japanese whiskies.

WHAT SETS THE BAR APART? Bincho is almost clubby, its intimate and welcoming space populated by whisky enthusiasts, as well as lovers of all things Japanese. The combination with a traditional Singapore environment makes for a very special and different dining experience. Joe Chan, head barman and mixologist, says: "Despite its size, one of the bigger collections of Japanese labels (more than forty) in Singapore." Aside from the whiskies, the bar also specializes in other beverages, such as sakes, Japanese craft beers, and shōchū, alongside Japanese-style cocktails made with fresh, seasonal fruits.

WHAT DO THEY RECOMMEND? Joe says: "Usuikyou 1983 Vintage. Very rare and only sold domestically in Japan—full-bodied, with a high level of peatiness for those who enjoy malts like Laphroaig. Nikka Coffey Malt—distilled from a Coffey still pot, which keeps the flavor of the whisky. This whisky is slightly on the sweeter and less peaty side, and is hence perfect for people who want to try whisky for the first time!

"Ichiro Ace of Clubs—the last four cards of the 52 Cards Series before the joker! It was sold out instantly upon its release, but the bar is fortunate to have one."

BINCHO · THE MEE POK STALL AT HUA BEE,
78 MOH GUAN TERRACE, SINGAPORE 162078
+65 6438 4567 | WWW.BINCHO.COM.SG

WHAT'S ON THE BAR?

Bincho has a wonderful mix of Japanese whiskies and one or two genuinely rare ones, such as Ichiro's Malt Hanyu from Whisky Live 2011, and Sun Shine 20 Year Old.

White Oak Akashi NAS
Chichibu Port Pipe
Ichiro's Malt Card Series Ace
 of Clubs 2000
Ichiro's Malt Hanyu 2011 Tokyo
 Whisky Live
Ichiro's Malt Card Series Six
 of Hearts
Mars Iwai Tradition Wine
 Cask Finish
Kirin 18 Year Old
Wakatsuru Shuzo Sun Shine
 20 Year Old
Suntory The Chita Single Grain
Yamazaki 12 Year Old
Yamazaki 18 Year Old
Yamazaki 25 Year Old
Hakushu 12 Year Old
Hakushu 18 Year Old
Hakushu 25 Year Old
Nikka Taketsuru Pure Malt
 12 Year Old
Miyagikyo 15 Year Old
Miyagikyo 20 Year Old

BINCHO AT HUA BEE
Transformed from a traditional coffee shop, Bincho has a street mee pok stall and rickety wooden chairs, nodding to Singapore's past.

NEXT PAGE
This dish of mentaiko chicken features on the menu at Bincho.

BINCHO AT HUA BEE

CLUB QING
HONG KONG

Club Qing is part museum, part comfortable lounge, and part whisky shrine, with the emphasis on Japanese whisky. Owner Aaron Chan is a whisky enthusiast and collector, and he's constantly looking for new whiskies. Behind the heavy antique-style wooden front door is a cozy and well-maintained bar area. It includes an area where a complete set of Ichiro's Malt Card Series is displayed, among other rare whiskies.

The bar serves simple bar food such as fries, cheese platter, cold cuts, and snacks. "But we do not believe in food pairing with whisky at all," says Aaron. "And we do not encourage customers to drink and eat at the same time. That will simply destroy their palate, and it is a waste of whisky."

WHAT SETS THE BAR APART? "Our whisky collection is unmatched," says Aaron. "We have around 200 bottles of opened Japanese whiskies covering EVERY Japanese distillery, past and present, including some of the rarest Karuizawa single casks and [Ichiro's Malt] Hanyu Playing Cards.

"Once a rare bottle is finished, we will open another one (a different one), so customers can be sure they will find something rare every time they visit."

"One area of the bar is devoted to rare and old bottlings, some stretching back to the 1940s. The collection includes a full set of fifty-four bottles of the [Ichiro's Malt] Hanyu Playing Card Series.

"It is believed that only six sets exist on this planet, and this is the only set in Hong Kong," says Aaron proudly.

WHAT DO THEY RECOMMEND? "It's difficult," says Aaron. "Bottles get opened and finished relatively fast. In general, I would suggest that customers try rare bottles such as the [Ichiro's Malt] Hanyu Playing Cards or the Karuizawa and Yamazaki single casks from the 1980s, because there is no other place in Hong Kong where these bottles are served by the glass."

CLUB QING · 10/F, COSMOS BUILDING, 8-11 LAN KWAI FONG, CENTRAL, HONG KONG
+852 9379-7628 | WWW.CLUBQING.COM

WHAT'S ON THE BAR?

The bar has more than 200 Japanese bottles open, making it one of the largest Japanese whisky collections in the world.

Mars Komagatake
  The Revival 2011
Togouchi 8 Year Old
Togouchi 12 Year Old
Yamazaki 12 Year Old
Yamazaki 18 Year Old
Yamazaki 25 Year Old
Hakushu 12 Year Old
Hakushu 18 Year Old
Yoichi (various)
Miyagikyo (various)
Karuizawa (various)
Ichiro's Malt Card Series
Chichibu Port Pipe
Chichibu The Peated
Chichibu Chibidaru
Chichibu On The Way
Hibiki 12 Year Old
Hibiki 17 Year Old
Hibiki 21 Year Old.

CLUB QING
Described as part bar, part museum, and with an area for rare whisky.

CLUB QING 223

SOKYO LOUNGE
SYDNEY, AUSTRALIA

The Sokyo Lounge is in the foyer of The Darling Hotel, and has a casino above it, but it's one of the most chilled and relaxed spots in Sydney, and is known for elegance, sophistication, outstanding quality, and attentive but unobtrusive service. This is a laid-back and stylish dining and drinking experience. The lounge is tastefully decorated with modern Japanese paintings and furnished with plush lounge chairs. Subtle background music and a sedate ambience make this an indulgent way to eat and drink Japanese products. The Sokyo Lounge prides itself on being one of Sydney's most celebrated Japanese restaurants, and so whisky is a core part of the offering. Drinkers are increasingly tasting Japanese whisky with some of the culinary treats offered at the bar.

WHAT SETS THE BAR APART? The lounge attracts an eclectic mix, so it puts an emphasis on expert staff who know every nuance of the food and drink menu. "The staff will take a guest's likes and dislikes, and create bespoke menus for them, and whip up artisan cocktails with any ingredients they choose," says bar manager Patricia Salomo. "The customers can even elect the music they want to hear." The bar is one of the very few 360-degree-shaped watering holes in Sydney.

WHAT DO THEY RECOMMEND? Patricia says: "Nikka Miyagikyo 12 Year Old. This is such a special whisky, thanks to its delicate flavor of smokiness, flowers, and honey-sweet fruit. It's perfectly balanced, and the ultimate match for Japanese dishes.

"Hibiki Harmony is the perfect example of a young, nonaged whisky. It is light, yet complex in flavor, with notes of orange peel and white chocolate, and a little peppery spice. The best way to drink Hibiki Harmony is in a highball glass—the traditional way.

"And Nikka Taketsuru, 17 Year Old: pungent and oily on the nose, Nikka Taketsuru is full, peaty, and spicy. Some will disagree with me on pairing this with sushi, but this is one fine blend for a sipping whisky to drink at any time, anywhere, with any meal."

SOKYO LOUNGE · THE STAR, THE DARLING, 80 PYRMONT STREET, PYRMONT, SYDNEY, NSW 2009, AUSTRALIA
+61 2 9657 9161 | WWW.STAR.COM.AU/SYDNEY-NIGHTLIFE/SOKYO-BAR

WHAT'S ON THE BAR?

Sokyo has managed to pick up a few bottles that you rarely see outside Japan, as well as a full range of whiskies from the big companies.

Yamazaki 12 Year Old
Yamazaki Distiller's Reserve
Yamazaki 18 Year Old
Hakushu 12 Year Old
Hakushu Distiller's Reserve
Hibiki 12 Year Old
Hibiki 17 Year Old
Hibiki Harmony
Nikka All Malt
Nikka Whisky From The Barrel
Nikka Taketsuru Pure Malt 12 Year Old
Nikka Taketsuru Pure Malt 17 Year Old
Yoichi 10 Year Old
Yoichi 15 Year Old
Miyagikyo 12 Year Old
Suntory Kakubin
White Oak Tokinoka Blended Malt
White Oak Akashi NAS
White Oak Akashi Single Malt 14 Year Old
White Oak Akashi 15 Year Old
Rainbow Whisky
Mars Iwai
Mars Iwai Tradition
Monde Royal Crystal

SOKYO LOUNGE
In the foyer of the stylish and luxurious Darling hotel in Sydney, this bar is renowned for great food and a varied drinks menu.

SOKYO LOUNGE

UNCLE MING'S BAR
SYDNEY, AUSTRALIA

First of all you have to find it, and that's not entirely straightforward. It's actually in the basement of a suit store, and you enter it as if you're going for the clothes. Uncle Ming's is an opium-den-style underground bar in the middle of Sydney. Dark and smelling of incense, this is an irreverent, moody, and atmospheric bar specializing in Japanese whisky and Asian food, including Chinese dumplings. Ornamental lamps shed light on walls covered in pictures of Asian pinup girls, while cool music plays in the background. It's all very trendy, happening, and evocative. Japanese whisky makes up the majority of the back bar, and it's what the place is best known for. The bar also uses Japanese whisky in twists on classic cocktails in which traditionally Scotch or bourbon are used. For example, "Uncle Ming's Old-Fashioned" uses Yamazaki whisky instead of American whiskey. "There has been a huge shift over to Japanese whisky in the last couple of years in Australia," said Uncle Ming's Sharon Best in 2015. "Australians are seeing that the overall quality of master blenders and distilleries from Japan is equal to, or even better than, that of those in Scotland."

WHAT SETS THE BAR APART? As soon as you enter, you are struck by how stylish and unusual it is. Uncle Ming's claims to have one of the largest collections of Japanese whiskies in the southern hemisphere. It also specializes in Asian beers and spirits. "The kitchen serves up tasty steamed dumplings and other Asian-style snacks to be enjoyed with our drink offerings, and they offer traditional whisky cocktails with a Japanese twist," says Sharon. "The emphasis is on a fun and laid-back vibe, with the aim of providing guests with a fantastic experience every time they visit."

WHAT DO THEY RECOMMEND? Sharon says: "I would pick Hakushu 18 Year Old from Suntory, Coffey Malt from Nikka, and Chibidaru 2010 from Chichibu."

UNCLE MING'S · 55 YORK STREET, SYDNEY, NSW 2000, AUSTRALIA
+61 2 9299 8961 | WWW.UNCLEMINGS.COM.AU

WHAT'S ON THE BAR?

The whisky list here is dominated by the main Japanese whisky companies and has an impressive selection from all three, including some rare blends.

Chichibu The Peated
Chichibu On The Way
Chichibu Chibidaru
Ichiro's Malt Double Distilleries Pure Malt
Hakushu 18 Year Old
Hibiki 17 Year Old
Chichibu Port Pipe
Suntory Kakubin Yellow
Suntory Kakubin Blue
Ichiro's Malt & Grain
Ichiro's Malt & Grain Premium
Ichiro's Malt Wine Wood Reserve
Miyagikyo NAS 2015
Miyagikyo 12 Year Old
Ichiro's Malt Mizunara Wood Reserve
Nikka Coffey Grain
Nikka Coffey Malt
Nikka Pure Malt Red
Nikka Pure Malt White
Nikka Pure Malt Black
Nikka All Malt
Suntory 1981 Kioke Shiomi
Suntory The Chita Single Grain 12 Year Old
Hibiki Harmony
Yamazaki 18 Year Old
Yamazaki Puncheon 2013
Yoichi 15 Year Old

UNCLE MING'S
This cocktail, whisky, and dumpling bar is based on an opium den concept and named after one of Shanghai's legendary crime chiefs.

UNCLE MING'S BAR

WHAT'S ON THE BAR?

In addition to about fifty Suntory and Nikka expressions:

Chichibu Chibidaru
Chichibu The Floor Malted
  3 Year Old
Chichibu On The Way
Chichibu The Peated
Chichibu Port Pipe
Hakushu 18 Year Old
Ichiro's Malt Double Distilleries
  Pure Malt
Ichiro's Malt & Grain
Ichiro's Malt & Grain Premium
Ichiro's Malt Mizunara Wood
  Reserve
Ichiro's Malt Wine Wood Reserve
Mars Amber
Mars Twin Peaks
Mars Karuizawa Club
Mars Komagatake Cosmo
Mars Komagatake American Oak
  & Sherry 2011
Sasanokawa Cherry Whisky EX
Karuizawa/Yamanashi Ocean
  Bright Deluxe
Wakatsuru Shuzo Sun Shine
  20 Year Old
White Oak Testimony
White Oak 5 Year Old Single Malt
White Oak 5 Year Old Oloroso
  Sherry Cask
Yamazaki 12 Year Old

TOKYO BIRD
This venue is a combination of the best of Tokyo's yakitori-ya and classic cocktail bars, and is in an intimate and stylish Australian lounge.

Tokyo Bird is a tiny whisky and yakitori bar. It is classified as a small bar in Sydney, with a maximum capacity of sixty patrons—this ensures an intimate environment where the staff can interact with all the customers. Yakitori is a style of Japanese cuisine mainly featuring chicken served on skewers. More than 75 percent of the liquor in the back bar is Japanese whisky. This range has been growing since the owner and general manager put his personal collection up on the bar when Tokyo Bird opened in late December 2014. The bar says it has built a solid reputation, not only for its range of Japanese whisky, but also for its service and knowledge resources.

WHAT SETS THE BAR APART? General manager Jason Ang and bar manager Yoshi Onishi are both highly experienced in Sydney's bar scene and are avid Japanese whisky fans. They bring their food and drinks acumen together to create unusual evenings, such as the Japanese-flavored whisky Christmas dinner. On a normal night, they will happily chat to anyone about Japanese whiskies for hours—about anything from tasting notes and production, to the best way to import it into Australia.

WHAT DO THEY RECOMMEND? "Suntory Yamazaki 12 Year Old is the original Japanese single malt that has a defining tropical fruit and rounded spice characteristic that makes it suitable for the Japanese palate," says Jason. "It's the definition of subtle, yet elegant and refined—the quintessential Japanese whisky.

"Hakushu 18 Year Old Single Malt is a personal favorite of our bar manager. Subtle and incredibly complex, it has gentle peat with herbaceous flavors that give it a long, fresh, and delicate tone which is profoundly unique, yet very approachable.

"And Ichiro's Malt Chichibu On The Way 2013 bottling is great. Ichiro Akuto gets the most out of his ingredients to create a connoisseur's whisky that is unrivaled in approach. On The Way is a vatting of several years of Chichibu malts."

TOKYO BIRD · BELMORE LANE, SURREY HILLS,
NSW 2010, AUSTRALIA
+61 (2) 8880 0788 | WWW.TOKYOBIRD.COM.AU

WHISKY AND ALEMENT
MELBOURNE, AUSTRALIA

Whisky and Alement is a stylish bar within a bar. Its numerous bottles of whisky are given a modern backdrop of polished concrete, wood, and leather banquettes that reference whisky dens without the stuffiness and pomp. This is a bar for whisky fans: drinkers are as likely to be found taking their dram with a beer and a smoke in the courtyard as talking shop at the bar. The owners had planned a specialty Japanese whisky bar, but there are not enough stocks to sustain it, so 200 rare bottles of whisky will be sold through the main bar. The idea is to offer a rare selection of Japanese whisky at affordable prices.

WHAT SETS THE BAR APART? These guys are big hitters. The list of guest tasters from Europe reads like a who's who of the whisky industry. But Japan has a special place, too, explains owner Julian White: "One of the team specializes in Japanese whisky, and has a Japanese wife, ensuring that the bar is right up to date with what's going on in Japan. We are aiming for an affordable and unpretentious bar to help launch a new generation of whisky drinkers."

WHAT DO THEY RECOMMEND? Julian White says: "Oak Akashi 15 Year Old: on the staff's first visit to Japan, the President of Eigashima Distillery took them on a personal tour of the Eigashima (White Oak) Distillery, and brought out this. While a little too tannic for our palate, this whisky remains close to our hearts. It is the first to ever utilize another breed of Japanese oak, called konara.

"Nikka Taketsuru 17 Year Old, for its sheer breadth of flavor. The ultimate blend, delicate and subtle sweetness, developed complexity from oak, and the best integration of peat, which can woo even the newest of whisky customers.

"And finally, SMWS 132.6 Nite Nurse Nipped by Piranhas (Karuizawa 12 Year Old) 63%: an incredible palate weight! The rich, jammy fruits are offset by razor-sharp bite in the form of fresh but perfectly integrated oak. A dream dram... minus the price tag!"

WHISKEY AND ALEMENT · 270 RUSSELL STREET, MELBOURNE, VICTORIA 3000, AUSTRALIA
+61 3 9654 1284 | WWW.WHISKYANDALE.COM.AU

WHAT'S ON THE BAR?

The bar has a collection of around 200 whiskies, which will be released over time, including:

Yamazaki Sherry Cask
Yamazaki 18 Year Old
White Oak Akashi Single Malt 14 Year Old
White Oak Akashi 15 Year Old
Yamazaki The Scotch Malt Whisky Society 11 Year Old Raspberry Imperial Stout
Karuizawa The Scotch Malt Whisky Society 132.6 Nite Nurse Nipped by Piranhas 12 Year Old
Nikka Yoichi 12 Year Old
Yoichi 20 Year Old
Nikka Taketsuru Pure Malt 17 Year Old
Nikka Taketsuru Pure Malt 25 Year Old
Nikka Taketsuru Pure Malt Sherry
Nikka Coffey Grain Cask #198156
Mars Komagatake Single Cask 1985
Mars Komagatake 2012 Sherry Cask #162

WHISKY AND ALEMENT
This bar boasts a number of rare bottlings and prides itself on being up-to-date with all things Japanese.

NEXT PAGE
The cozy, atmospheric, and unpretentious interior of Whisky and Alement.

WHISKY AND ALEMENT 231

8 / 八 .

CHAPTER EIGHT

•

WHISKY COCKTAILS AND FOOD PAIRINGS

ウィスキーベースのカクテルとおつまみ

How times change. If you'd walked into a fashionable "style bar" in London in 2005 and asked for a cocktail made with a single malt whisky, the staff would probably have looked at you as if you were mad. Whisky purists regarded the idea as an insult to such a noble spirit; whisky companies had a default setting that barely accepted adding ice to a single malt, let alone pouring in a fruit drink. Bar managers couldn't afford to waste expensive spirit on such follies, and the bartenders, lacking both practice and desire, had no idea what to do with malt whisky.

Whisky Magazine staged a whisky cocktail competition, and the few brave souls who dared to weave their mixology magic were split between those who tried to show the whisky flavors off; and those who pretended they were working with vodka, and drowned the whisky taste entirely. Now that whisky companies are employing those same mixologists to come up with sexy long drinks, any style bar worthy of the name has a range of whisky cocktails, and the trendier outlets serve exciting concoctions such as Laphroaig cocktails hidden in fugs of smoke served up under glass domes. This isn't drink-making, this is art and theater combined. And few nations combine them better, and with more color and flamboyance, than Japan. The Japanese have no historical hang-ups or cultural uneasiness about mixing whisky with syrups, fruit juices, bitters, and botanicals. Their whisky cocktails are all self-indulgent fun.

Japanese bars and restaurants have also proved to be highly innovative and progressive when it comes to matching whisky with food. Not all food is suited to whisky, and no one is suggesting that every course should be matched with a different whisky, but seafood lends itself surprisingly well to malt, and spicy wasabi is also a good match.

WHISKY COCKTAILS

Whisky cocktails have become fashionable, and, given the Japanese love of color and theater, it's unsurprising that the country has thrived in this field. Some of the world's best cocktail bars are in Japan (see pp.156–81), and Japanese whisky, rich in unusual and exciting flavors, has become the spirit of choice for many bars across the world.

Cocktails made with Japanese whisky fall into two distinct camps: traditional cocktails given an Eastern twist, and modern, innovative cocktails. Japan has also brought a new dimension to even the most basic of whisky ingredients—ice. Carving ice into miniature sculptures, or serving ice as a perfect sphere in drinks, such as the highball, have become art forms.

If you've never had a highball, then try one on a hot day, or have one instead of a glass of wine with a meal—it's a refreshing and enjoyable way to drink whisky and easy to make. Here is the recipe for the highball, and some favorite Japanese whisky cocktails:

HAKUSHU SHOSHO

Shosho is one of Japan's twenty-four sekkis (seasons). Shosho means "the limit of heat," and the season begins on August 23. This is the time when the perfume from garden roses is wafted around on an autumnal breeze.

INGREDIENTS
1¾ ounces (5 cl) Hakushu 12 Year Old Single Malt
½ ounce (1.4 cl) Club soda
½ ounce (1.4 cl) rose water
Fresh mint

METHOD
1. Mix all the ingredients together.
2. Stir and serve.

HIGHBALL
The cocktail that changed whisky drinking culture in the 1950s is now once again popular with a young crowd throughout Japan.

APRÈS SKI IN FUJI,
BY UNION SQUARE CAFE, NEW YORK

The Après Ski is well established. This is a Japanese take on it.

INGREDIENTS

1¾ ounces (5 cl) Hakushu 12 Year Old Single Malt
1 ounce (2.5 cl) Antica sweet vermouth
Dashes of St. Germain, sweet elderflower liqueur
1 lemon
Some maraschino cherries

METHOD

1. Put whisky into a mixing glass or vessel and add sweet vermouth.
2. Add elderflower liqueur.
3. Add lemon peel for zest.
4. Fill a Martini glass with ice.
5. Stir the contents of the mixing glass thoroughly.
6. Discard the ice from the mixing glass, and strain the liquid into the serving glass.

THE HIGHBALL

It's thought that the highball was named after a railroad term going back to the days of steam. A glass container showed the level of water available for creating the steam. A ball floated on the top of the water, and when it was high, it meant that there was plenty of water, so the train could go full steam ahead. The term then became used for Scotch and soda, which was often served in a high glass with ice rocks floating on the surface. Its relevance to Japanese whisky came about through Suntory and the trend toward ice carving. It is considered a refreshing long drink, and has been adopted by the young set in Japan's cities.

INGREDIENTS

1½ ounces (4.2 cl) Japanese whisky
3 ounces (8.4 cl) sparkling water

METHOD

1. Stack several large cubes of ice in a highball glass.
2. Pour the whisky into the glass, and slowly stir.
3. Fill the glass with ice again, and top with sparkling water.
4. Stir three-and-a-half more times to finish the drink.

AWA HIBIKI

Alternative Whisky Academy (AWA) is a private enterprise in Osaka owned by Suntory. Hibiki 12 Year Old is one of the company's blended whiskies, but it is becoming harder to find, so feel free to replace it with Hibiki Harmony. The sweet and fragrant ingredients in this cocktail complement the fruity flavors of Hibiki 12 Year Old.

INGREDIENTS

2 ounces (5.4 cl) Strawberry Espuma
¼ ounce (0.7 cl) Hibiki 12 Year Old
¾ ounce (2.1 cl) Prosecco
½ ounce (1.4 cl) sugar cane syrup
Two dashes of Jerry Thomas bitters

METHOD

Simply add the ingredients together and stir.

LEFT_AWA HIBIKI
The sweetness of the strawberries complement Hibiki 12 Year Old or Hibiki Harmony.

BELOW_YAMAZAKI SOUR
This is a modern take on a traditional classic.

YAMAZAKI SOUR

This is a Japanese take on the traditional sour, which is made with whisky or bourbon. The sour is a classic cocktail with a history stretching back some 150 years. It is usually made with egg white, but for those who do not like it or cannot have egg white, pineapple juice can be used as a substitute. Yamazaki Distiller's Reserve makes an excellent whisky sour.

INGREDIENTS
1¾ ounces (5 cl) Yamazaki Distiller's Reserve
1⁄10 ounce (0.3 cl) lemon juice
1⁄10 ounce (0.3 cl) sugar cane syrup
1 egg white
Two dashes of lemon bitters

METHOD
1. Add Yamazaki and lemon juice.
2. Mix in the sugar cane syrup and egg white, and stir.
3. Add the lemon bitters.

JAPANESE WHISKY FOOD PAIRINGS

Over the years, there have been several attempts to match whisky with food, and there are some excellent pairings. However, most people have concluded that a whole dinner and whisky matching is a step too far. The idea that a six-course meal, with six strong glasses of whisky, would bring whisky into the same world as wine was always doomed to failure.

However, the idea of drinking whisky with one or two courses as an alternative to wine has legs, and in recent years, adventurous consumers, familiar with more demanding food, and with exotic vacation destinations on their radar, have been eager to seek out new taste experiences. Such a trend has been amply fueled by a surge in interest in Asian food in general, and Japanese food in particular.

On the face of it, Japanese food may not seem suited to pairing with strong spirits. Many Japanese dishes have delicate and subtle flavors, and whisky's strong flavors may be overwhelming, but the Japanese often do consume spirits with food. While foods such as sushi might not be suitable for such accompaniment, seafood often works well with whisky and other components of Japanese food, such as the hot radishy spice of wasabi, ginger, brine, vinegar, and malt, all lend themselves to the power of Japanese whisky.

The relationship between Japanese whisky and food is far more complex than just matching two big flavors. The subtlety and complexity of both food and drink mean that, when combined, all kinds of unpredictable fallouts occur. So the same whisky served with two different styles of Japanese food will produce totally different and unexpected tastes.

TOP_SEAWEED DISH
Whisky complements the bold salinity of seaweed and can work well with seaweed-based dishes.

ABOVE_MISO SOUP
The maltiness of certain whiskies works well alongside the savory flavors of miso soup or soy sauce.

PAIRING NOTES

SEAFOOD-BASED DISHES AND SEAWEED work well with whiskies that have a natural salinity. Perhaps Hakushu 12 Year Old, Yoichi Nonage Statement, or Nikka From The Barrel.

MISO OR SOY SAUCE works particularly well with the big, savory malts, such as several of the Karuizawas, or the aged Yamazakis.

RICH, FULL FOODS work with whiskies that have an intense mouth feel. When talking about taste and the Japanese palate, we sometimes hear the term umami—a word that combines the Japanese words for "delicious" and "taste." Umami is considered a fifth taste point alongside sweet, sour, bitter, and salty. It is normally associated with the savory taste of glutamate. The term was introduced by Japanese chemist Kikunae Ikeda, and is taken to mean "pleasant savory taste." This can be interpreted as a meaty and intensely wanting-more sensation in the mouth that could be mistaken for texture. This complements waxy, oily whiskies, such as the Hibiki 17 Year Old, and the Yamazaki 18 Year Old.

BELOW_FRIED FISH SKIN
This appears on the menu at Yusho, Chicago (see pp.186–87), and the crunchy texture would be a contrast to a smooth whisky.

BELOW RIGHT_RAMEN
One of the many tasty dishes on offer at Yusho in Chicago.

JAPANESE WHISKY FOOD PAIRINGS

LEFT_BRAISED FISH HEAD
A classic Japanese fish dish, which is as tasty as it is colorful.

RIGHT_PORK MISO RAMEN
This dish features porchetta, pickled egg, marash pepper oil, fried garlic, hijiki seaweed and scallions.

BELOW_SMOKED SALMON
An open sandwich such as this would work well with a light, delicate whisky.

NEXT PAGE_ROOSTER BALL RAMEN
A rich whisky could complement this spicy chicken dish.

While it is natural to seek to match Japanese whisky with Eastern food, it works just as well with fusion dishes, and a number of restaurants have opened in major cities across the world where foods from different parts of the East are matched with each other, including dishes such as sweet-and-sour ribs, curried chicken, and chili-dipped beef, or fused with French, American, and European food styles.

Japanese whisky also lends itself wonderfully to some of the classic whisky pairings that were put together originally for Scottish single malt whisky. Below is a selection of them.

CLASSIC WHISKY PAIRINGS

LIGHTER, MORE DELICATE WHISKIES
such as Yamazaki 10 Year Old, Hakushu 10 Year Old, Hibiki 12 Year Old:
- smoked salmon; soft, creamy cheeses.

MEDIUM-BODIED WHISKIES
with some peat influence, such as Nikka Pure Malt 17 Year Old, Nikka Pure Malt Red, and Yamazaki Mizunara Oak Cask:
- lightly smoked mackerel or seafood, duck pâté, smoked bacon, game meat.

FULL-BODIED, RICH WHISKIES
aged in sherry casks or European oak, such as Yamazaki 1984, Yamazaki 18 Year Old, or Miyagikyo 15 Year Old:
- seared or grilled steak, roast venison, rich fruit cakes, Christmas pudding, dark chocolate with ginger and cherry, strong cheddar.

STRONG, PEATY WHISKIES
such as any Yoichi, Nikka Pure Malt Black, and Chichibu The Peated:
- anchovy-based spreads or dips, strong cheddar, strong blue cheeses, especially Roquefort.

9 / 九.

CHAPTER NINE

THE FUTURE OF JAPANESE WHISKY

日本ウィスキーの未来

Having established itself on a global platform through a combination of top-quality whisky, a surge of attention from whisky writers, and a great deal of hard work from the brand owners, Japanese whisky finds itself in a potentially strong position.

However, as in many other countries that produce whisky, difficult decisions have to be made about how much money it is wise to invest in what currently seems to be a bright future. No one knows how much extra liquor is being matured across the world to meet future demand, but there are plenty of experts predicting that what goes up must at some point come down, and that one day the whisky market will crash due to a glut, as scores of producers release whiskies that have reached maturity. You get a sense of the size of the problem facing the likes of Suntory when you look at how it has tried to cope with market inconsistencies. In 2016, it released its latest version of Yamazaki Sherry Cask, but it had just 2,000 bottles to sell, each costing around $300 (£200). They were placed in a small number of prestige retailers, and they sold before they had barely touched the shelves.

To counteract the chronic shortages, Suntory invested $37 million (£26.6 million) in 2015 as part of its expansion to provide warehousing for a whopping 1.26 million casks. Meanwhile, drink distributors, starved of supply from Suntory and Nikka, are seeking to plug the shortfall by turning to lesser-known distilleries.

While, in most markets, the laws of demand and supply create a healthy environment for new producers to set out their stalls, this hasn't happened to any great extent in Japan, because of prohibitive barriers to entry. So what is next for Japanese whisky?

TRADITIONAL WHISKY FOR MODERN TIMES

The future for Japanese whisky may be a counterpoint to an economic revolution that might be sapping some of the old ways and traditions out of modern Japanese culture and society. Only time will tell whether the old rural ways of life will be swamped by modern technology and ever faster high-speed trains.

When it comes to whisky, we know that provenance and tradition are everything, and that it is the very history and heritage, the culture and personality, and its connection with the environment that make it the special drink it is. Even when you drag a twenty-five-year-old single malt into a style bar in London, Paris, or New York, and place a ridiculous price tag on it, it still keeps its story with it. Sooner or later, someone will want to hear that story once more, to take that whisky back to its roots, and learn about the people who "wrote" that malt into the whisky narrative, and the place that created it.

In other words, whisky works as a counterpoint to advanced technology. Perhaps huge economic progress is sapping the lifeblood out of loads of communities, not only in Japan, but also across the world. Perhaps the characteristics that make such places so special will survive in some form or other. The following was written by Dominic Al-Badri on Japan.Inc (www.japaninc.com):

"The Torys whisky bars set up in the '50s have almost all but disappeared, though one establishment which has managed to remain vibrant, with little time for passing fads and fashions, is located in Osaka's sleazy Juso district.

"Time has finally come full circle, however. Having never changed its decor since its opening in 1956, Juso Torys Bar is now revered for its time-capsule atmosphere as much as for its collection of Suntory whisky."

TOP AND ABOVE_OLD VERSUS NEW
Traditional and modern Japan rub against each other on a daily basis.

ABOVE_THE YOUNGER MARKET
In recent years, there has been much more interest in premium Japanese whisky in Japan, and more women and younger drinkers are discovering it.

Al-Badri says that, despite the falling prices of imported whisky in general, and of Scotch whisky in particular, and the fact that unusual single Scotch malts unavailable in Scotland are on sale at discerning liquor stores in Japan for prices unthinkable in Scotland, Japanese whisky is now holding its own:

"Cheap whisky, and Japan produces enough of that, is cheap whisky wherever you go, but no longer can Japanese malt whisky be sneered at.... The Kansai region has had few things to smile about in recent times, but knowing we make a world-class malt whisky goes some way to easing the pain. Make mine a large one."

The core process of making single malt whisky is pretty much the same wherever it is made, but, as in other parts of the world, distilleries in Japan have individual ways of executing the whisky-making process, and use distinct and individual fermentation and run times, and unique stills—as we have seen in previous chapters.

MAINTAINING THE PACE OF GROWTH

Undoubtedly, Japanese whisky remains in a state of flux, the interest levels in it remain at the top of the scale, and predicting a positive future for it would seem to be a pretty safe bet.

In many ways, Japanese whisky is catching its breath after a whirlwind period of a few years, which was unsustainable for all the reasons that have been covered in this book. The main one of these is that Japanese whisky companies cannot keep up with the pace of growth and the demand for the whisky, particularly older expressions, which they simply don't have. With some Suntory and Nikka releases keeping Japan in the public eye, and Ichiro Akuto's Chichibu providing excitement and innovation to remind everyone what Japan is capable of, Japanese whisky is quite literally taking stock and looking to the future.

What that future holds, we will see. As Nonjatta's Stefan Van Eycken says: "Where was your crystal ball when you could drive a van to Karuizawa Distillery and buy cases and cases of vintage whisky for peanuts?'"

What we can be sure of is that Suntory and Nikka are working hard to produce more whisky, and to innovate to ensure the high quality that they have become famous for. So far there has been no compromise in the country's high standards. So will we see aged Japanese whisky back on the shelves? No one knows, but it may be that both the leading companies, encouraged by the reaction to the quality on their NAS whiskies, will focus their attentions in this area, and apply all their whisky-making skills to ensure a sequence of exciting, flavorsome, but relatively young whisky.

It may be, too, that they will follow what is likely to happen in Scotland, and in a few years' time bring ten-year-old whisky to the shelves. It is likely to be promoted as premium spirit (when compared to NAS whisky), and it will carry a premium price tag. It's well possible that a small number of whiskies aged for fifteen years will also return to the market, but almost certainly they will be specifically targeted to high-end customers in affluent markets across the world.

LEFT_OUT AND OPEN
The value of a rare whisky goes up every time someone opens a bottle of it and makes it rarer still.

ABOVE_UP FOR GRABS
Many Japanese whisky collections may come back onto the market.

Moreover, both Stefan Van Eycken and investment consultancy Rare 101's Andy Simpson draw attention to the fact that scores of people are hoarding large collections of bottles. At some point, some of these collections will come back onto the market, not only making some bottles available, but potentially bringing prices down again. At some point, a degree of sanity will return to the whisky investment market.

As for new distilleries, it's going to be a long and slow process, and the obstacles to founding new whisky distilleries in Japan are immense. The high cost of setting up and equipping a distillery, specific difficulties in Japan over obtaining a distilling license, and the financial implications of waiting years before there is a sellable whisky, have discouraged many. Few new projects have been put forward, and there is no reason to think that this reluctance will change anytime soon.

Whatever the future, Japanese whisky has established itself among the world's whisky elite. Its producers have proved beyond doubt that they are a match for distillers anywhere in the world, with exciting whisky after exciting whisky. It has already been some journey, but you suspect that this is just a beginning—and there's plenty more excitement to come. So far this millennium, we have witnessed the end of an impressive beginning.

THE TREND OF UNAGED WHISKY

Japan is following Scotland down the route of promoting whisky without a statement of its age on the label. However, this does not necessarily mean that it is putting out younger whisky that is not as good as it was in the past.

When top whisky producer Nikka announced that it was to scrap its range of whiskies bearing an age on the bottle and is substituting just two bottlings with no age statements, there was a collective groan across the world of whisky. That reaction was prompted by two main factors: first, there is a commonly held view that nonage statement (NAS) whiskies represent a drop in standards, and they are an excuse for manufacturers and suppliers to sell inferior and younger whisky at inflated prices; and second, because it seemed a blatant example of Nikka copying a trend that has swept through Scottish whisky.

There has been a lot of nonsense written about NAS whiskies. While there have been inferior bottlings within the category in recent years, there have been plenty of outstanding whiskies that have not had age statements. Few would argue that the excellent whiskies from Scottish distilleries, such as Ardbeg and Glenmorangie, are not world class, even without an age on the label. In Japan, Nikka has a history of putting out quality NAS whiskies, and while Japanese prices have been in an unhealthy upward trajectory as far as the whisky drinker is concerned, at least Nikka has been able to apply the brakes while putting out some excellent whiskies—Nikka Whisky From The Barrel, Pure Malt Red, Pure Malt Black, and Coffey Grain all spring to mind. Both Suntory and Nikka have put out some excellent special releases that have been bursting with flavor, and Ichiro Akuto has shown that quality whisky making can result in acceptable and innovative malts at three and four years old, including Chichibu The First, Port Pipe, and The Floor Malted.

HIGH-QUALITY NEW WHISKIES
Ichiro Akuto's Chichibu The First, Port Pipe, and The Floor Malted are all flavorsome NAS whiskies.

YAMAZAKI DISTILLER'S RESERVE
Proof that there does not need be a drop in standards when it comes to whiskies without an age on them.

The second fear—that Nikka was merely copying an unsavory Scottish trend—doesn't bear close scrutiny, either, partly because of the historical track record referred to above, and also because the motivation was totally different. There can be no doubt that at least some Scotch whisky producers were using the trend to pump undercooked malt and to charge amped-up prices.

At Nikka, the story is different. The company was blunt: unless it managed stocks and diverted its supplies into NAS whiskies, its whisky would run out, the company would not be able to maintain its business model, and it would face closure. Nikka and Suntory have, of course, responded to the shortages by increasing output, but how much will be released in the near future and how much will be held back for aging to eighteen and twenty-five years are closely guarded secrets.

None of us should fear NAS whiskies if they're being produced by the major suppliers who have built up reputations for quality whiskies and would not sacrifice anything for short-term gain. Giants, such as Diageo, Pernod Ricard, and now Suntory Beam, will continue to make first-class whisky. When you have the ability to innovate, as Japan does, then necessity might dictate that we will start to see all kinds of exciting and wonderful whiskies. Suntory, in particular, now has access to a whole host of drinks options, and in 2015 it released a Bowmore whisky matured in a Japanese mizunara oak cask in Scotland, and the rumor mill suggests that the experiment will be reversed.

RIGHT_A YAMAZAKI CASK
The term "pure" is common in Japan, but is no longer allowed in Europe as it has been outlawed by the Scotch Whisky Association for being misleading. It is, essentially, single malt whisky. In Europe, "pot still" refers to a specific style of Irish whiskey.

WHISKY INVESTMENT

For years now, old and rare Scotch whisky has been sought after as an investment. Now, Japan's vintage bottles are commanding top prices at auction.

In retrospect, I can pinpoint when the madness with regard to Japanese whisky began. To a degree, anyway. It was sometime in the fall of 2007, on a dull midweek day. A man walks into The Whisky Shop in Norwich, England, and asks how many bottles of Yamazaki 18 Year Old are in stock.

"Four," he is told, "costing £75 ($100) each."

"I'll take all four," says the man.

The shop staff are elated. That's a lot of money for a quiet Wednesday, and to be honest, Japanese whisky, considered relatively expensive when compared to Scottish single malts of a similar age, had been sitting on the shelves for a long time. Later that same day, they receive an email from the company's head office announcing a price rise. Yamazaki is to be doubled in price to £150 ($200) per bottle to take effect immediately. That particular store has hardly seen a bottle of Yamazaki 18 Year Old since.

Since then, Japanese whisky, in general, has become the enigmatic superstar in the whisky firmament, whisky's answer to legendary rock musician Prince: not all of it is great, but when it is, it's superb, and because it's so rare to encounter it, an air of mystique and otherworldliness has grown around it. Our impression of Japanese whisky is evolving rapidly. What started as an interesting liquor category with a handful of rare gems moved swiftly to being an elusive category made up almost entirely of rare whiskies. It's thought that there is much more Japanese whisky locked in private cabinets than displayed on bar and store shelves across the world.

ABOVE_YAMAZAKI 18 YEAR OLD
One of several great Japanese bottlings that have almost disappeared from whisky store shelves, and which command high prices when they come to auction.

ABOVE RIGHT_WHISKY FROM THE SHELF
A selection of Japanese whiskies on offer in a shop — an increasingly rare sight.

RIGHT_GROWING DEMAND
Malt imports in Japan quadrupled between 2006 and 2016 due to the increase in demand for Japanese whiskies.

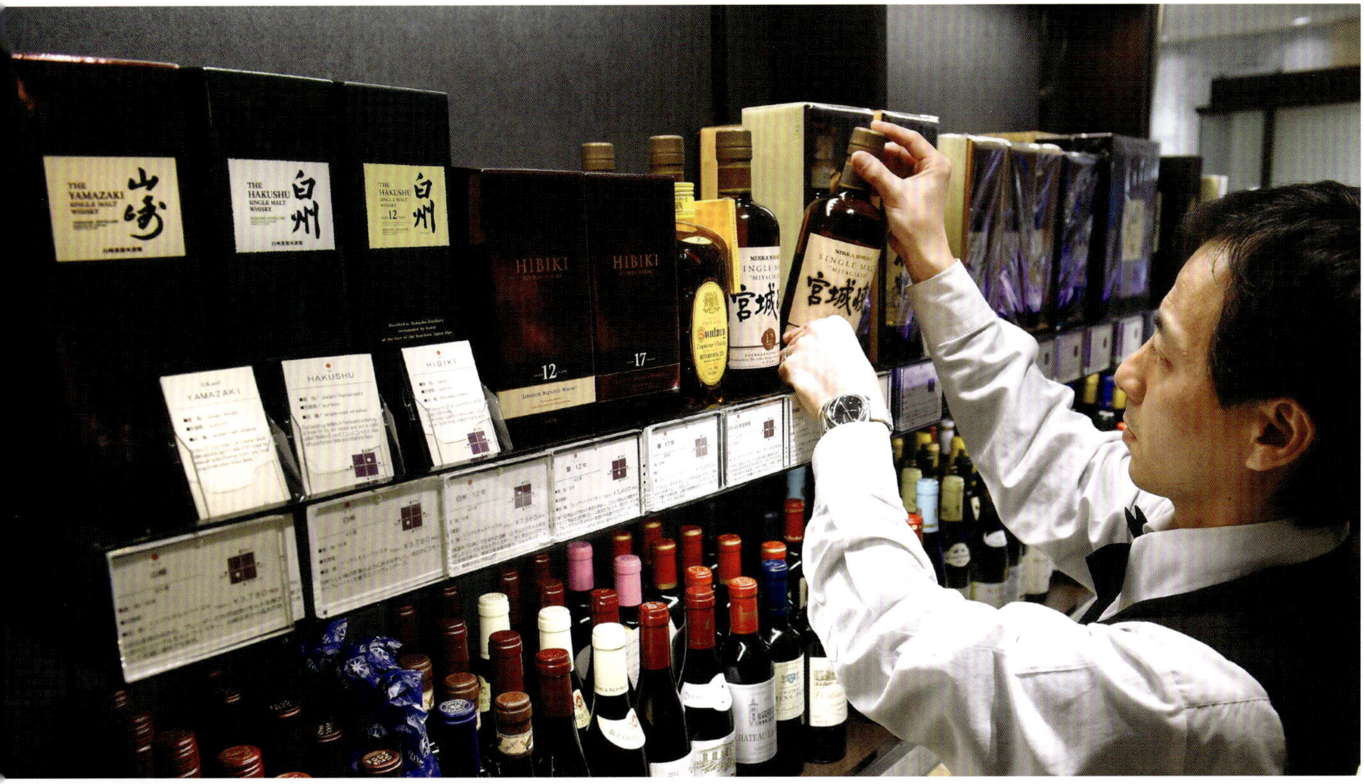
THE YAMAZAKI SINGLE MALT WHISKY
山崎
THE HAKUSHU SINGLE MALT WHISKY
白州
YAMAZAKI
HAKUSHU
HIBIKI
HIBIKI
SINGLE MALT
宮城峡

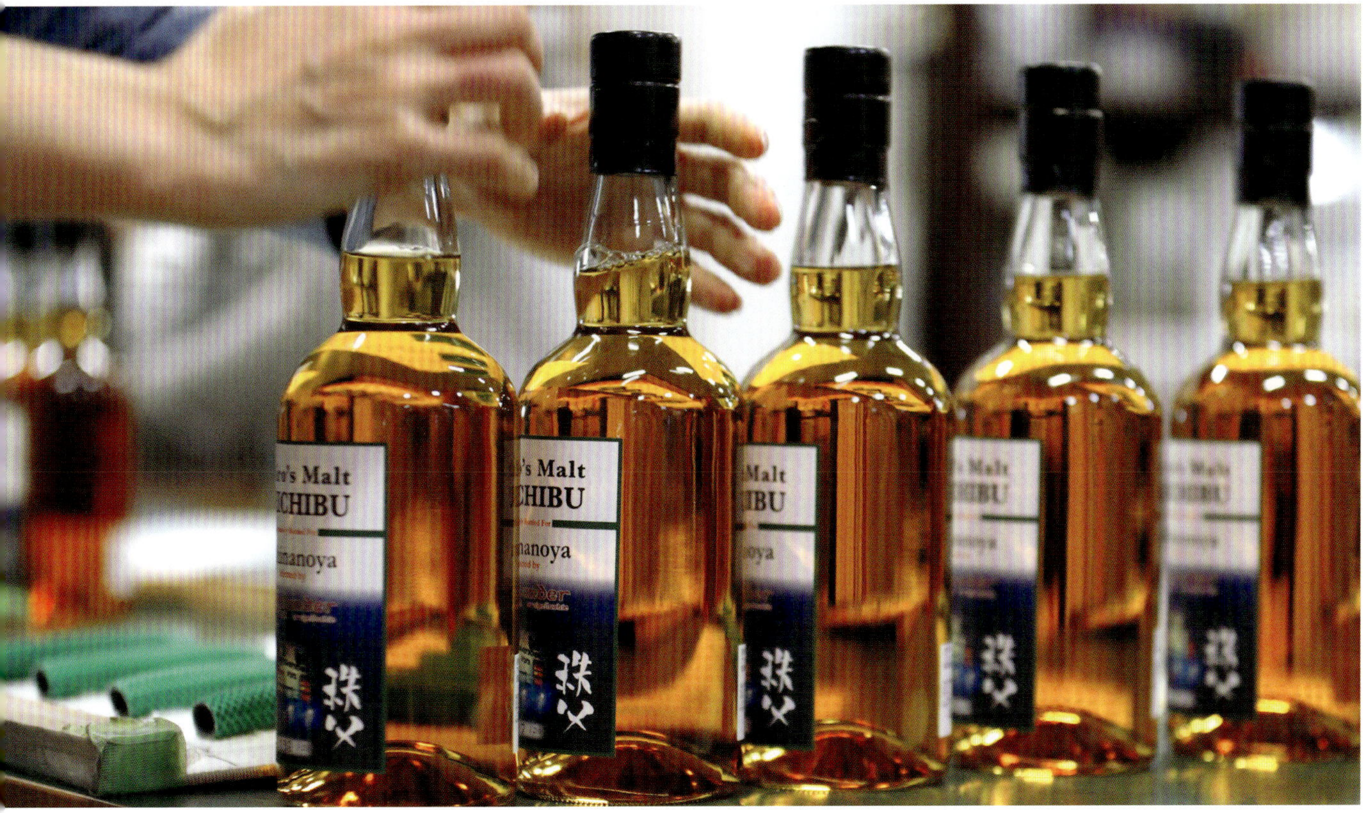
秩父

What is certainly the case, however, is that, in a short space of time, Japanese whisky went where Irish whiskey and Kentucky bourbon had never managed to go, and it was able to give Scotland a run for its money when it came to whisky as an investment. The topic of investment splits the world of whisky. Some whisky lovers reject the whole idea of it, arguing that whisky is a drink that should be drunk, not locked away in a cupboard. Collectors and investors are artificially inflating the price of whisky, say the purists, making it unaffordable by the rest of us.

This is a somewhat romantic view, and it could be argued that it doesn't really add up. As soon as the man buying the Yamazaki whisky parted with £300 ($400) for the bottles, they came off the market. Nothing wrong with that. If he drank them, they have well and truly gone forever. Alternatively, if he has stored them in a cupboard, and plans to release them to a future generation at the fair market price, then he's actually extending the life of that whisky.

The facts are these: A lot of whisky, and especially Japanese whisky, is in short supply, and facing rising demand, which has driven up the price. Sooner or later that will peak; the market will settle, and, as new stocks come on to the market, prices might actually start coming down again. For a whisky to be really worth collecting, however, it needs a perfect storm. It has to be:

- rare
- collectable
- good to drink.

All three factors apply to all aged whisky released by Suntory and Nikka, anything from Karuizawa and Hanyu, and anything from Ichiro's Malt Series. Increasingly, too, the early Chichibu bottlings are worth getting hold of. Karuizawa, in particular, has now reached levels where it is matching the rarest of the rare Scottish whisky distilleries, such as Port Ellen and Brora.

Before you rush to the bank and put your life savings into whisky, however, take a few steps back and think it through. Few investment categories react to demand and supply as sharply as whisky does. Certainly Andy Simpson, founder of whisky investment brokers Rare 101, urges caution.

"The demand for Japanese whisky for a while was almost like panic-buying," he says. "We're talking mainly about Karuizawa, and for a while it was going up at ridiculous rates.

ABOVE_SUNTORY 21 YEAR OLD
Bottles such as this tick all three boxes: rarity, collectability, and great taste.

ABOVE RIGHT_OWNER'S CASK
An example of an ultra rare and very expensive whisky.

NEXT PAGE_WAREHOUSE STOCK
A lot of whisky is in short supply, therefore demands a high price, but once new stock comes onto the market those prices are likely to settle.

There was a time in the middle of 2015 when prices may have peaked. The truth is, when you get to a certain price, it becomes unsustainable, and Japanese whisky may be in that category."

Other Japanese whiskies that have attracted interest and should have a strong future as part of a collection or as an investment are anything from Ichiro Malt range, or from the Hanyu Distillery, and especially Ichiro's Malt Card Series.

Such bottles will always be in demand, says Simpson, and he points to the large number of bars wanting to buy exciting Japanese whiskies for their customers.

"But again, prices are becoming unsustainable," he says. "You can't charge people hundreds of dollars a dram. If you came to me with thousands of dollars to buy Japanese whisky, I would argue that it might not be the best idea."

THE MOST EXPENSIVE WHISKIES

KARUIZAWA 1960 COCKEREL
HK$750,000 ($96,600/£62,750)

In all, there were forty-one bottles of this expression released, all individually named with individual netsuke ivory characters. This one sold in August 2015 at Bonhams in Hong Kong for HK$750,000 ($96,600/£62,750 at the prevailing exchange rate). It is not known how many of these bottles still exist.

KARUIZAWA 1964 48 YEAR OLD
£19,000 ($21,120)

This is the most expensive bottle of Japanese whisky that has been sold in the United Kingdom. It was one of 143 that were bottled for Wealth Solutions in Poland and was sold in September 2015. However, the Karuizawa market has since cooled down, and a bottle was bid up to £15,100 ($21,000) in January 2016, but it failed to sell. Investors are being urged to be wary of volatile price changes.

KARUIZAWA 1995 18 YEAR OLD, 36 GHOSTS
£17,500 ($24,980)

If someone said they had a 1995 vintage eighteen-year-old bottle of whisky, how much would it be worth? Maybe $200 (£150) for a bottle, if it was from a respected distillery, such as Macallan, but certainly not as much as just under £17,500 ($24,980). But that's what one of only twenty-two bottles of a Karuizawa whisky sold for in February 2016.

YAMAZAKI SHERRY CASK 2013 RELEASE
£1,500 ($2,140)

This was a not particularly expensive annual release, retailing at about $200 (£150), a price inflated by the craze for Japanese whisky, but then *Jim Murray's Whisky Bible* declared it the best whisky in the world. Within days, the bottles started selling at auction for ten times that amount. Like many other overheated bottles, the price then fell back, but they can still fetch $1,700 (£1,200) at auction.

WHISKY INVESTMENT   259

A TOURIST'S GUIDE TO JAPAN

True, there are huge differences between East and West, and the language barrier is still a major issue, not least because written Japanese doesn't give you a clue to what it means, unlike most Western languages.

The cities, and especially Tokyo, are big, busy, and noisy; the more remote parts of the country are seemingly from a different era. But everything about Japan is a blast. Every part of it, from bar culture to retail, to travel, and to food, seems to be turned up to eleven, and there are few places on the planet that are more colorful, dramatic, and exciting. The way to approach Japan is to prepare well for it—easy to do these days—and to embrace it instead of fear it.

In the following pages, I have taken the cities closest to the key distilleries (see pp. 60–111), and picked a couple of the key attractions in each city. For more in-depth information on how to get there, what to do, where to stay, and what to eat and drink, see the following pahes.

Internal travel is relatively easy in Japan. Railroads are something of a national passion, and while most of us are aware of the high-speed Shinkansen lines linking the main population centers, there is a patchwork of slower regional trains. Japan also has internal flights to many destinations, and there is a solid bus network, including overnight services. Costs are okay, too, especially if you take advantage of the train and air passes.

There are some excellent websites that can help you to plan your trip, and which explain the different train lines. They also offer excellent information on accessing English translations of essential information, and which transport services offer the best value for money.

TOKYO
HONSHU

Tokyo stretches over a vast area, is one of Japan's prefectures, and consists of multiple cities, towns, and villages, as well as Izu and Ogasawara islands. Tokyo offers a seemingly unlimited choice of shopping, entertainment, culture, and dining. The city's history can be appreciated in districts such as Asakusa, and in many excellent museums, historic temples, and gardens. Tokyo is situated on the Southern Pacific Ocean's coast of Japan's largest island, Honshu, and is ringed by distilleries: Chichibu is 67 miles (107 kilometers) away (see p. 66), Fuji Gotemba is 64 miles (102 kilometers) away (see p. 72), and Hakushu is 97 miles (155 kilometers) away (see p. 76). Tokyo also offers a number of attractive parks and open spaces within the city center and within relatively short train rides to its outskirts. It would take a book of its own to do the city justice, but here are a few of the must-see highlights:

AKIHABARA, CENTRAL TOKYO This is known as the shopping center for all things electrical, with hundreds of stores from tiny to huge. In the last decade, it has emerged as a center for Japanese otaku and anime culture, and there are now dozens of stores specializing in anime, comics, retro video games, figurines, card games and other collectibles. You'll find maid cafés here, too, where waitresses dress up and act like maids or anime characters.

UENO PARK, CENTRAL TOKYO Ueno Park is a large public space next to Ueno Station. The park grounds were originally part of Kaneiji Temple, which used to be one of the city's largest and wealthiest shrines. The temple grounds were converted into one of Japan's first Western-style parks and opened to the public in 1873. The park is famous for its museums, which include the Tokyo National Museum, the National Museum for Western Art, the Tokyo Metropolitan Art Museum, and the National Science Museum. It is also home to Ueno Zoo.

TOKYO NATIONAL MUSEUM, NORTH TOKYO The Tokyo National Museum is the oldest and largest of Japan's top-level national museums. It features one of the largest and best collections of art and archeological artifacts in Japan, made up of more than 110,000 items. At any one time, around 4,000 different items from the permanent museum collection are on display. In addition, visiting temporary exhibitions are also held regularly. Good English information and audio guides are available.

ASAKUSA, NORTH TOKYO Asakusa is the center of Tokyo's districts where an atmosphere of old Tokyo survives. Asakusa's main attraction is Sensoji, a popular Buddhist temple, built in the seventh century CE. The temple is approached via the Nakamise, a shopping street that has been providing temple visitors with a variety of traditional, local snacks, and tourist souvenirs for centuries. Explore on foot, or take a guided tour in a rickshaw.

THE TOKYO SKYTREE, NORTH TOKYO The Tokyo Skytree is a television broadcasting tower. It is the centerpiece of the Tokyo Skytree Town in the Sumida City Ward, not far from Asakusa. With a height of 2,080 feet (634 meters), it is the tallest building in Japan. A large shopping complex with an aquarium is located at its base. Its two observation decks offer spectacular views out over Tokyo. At 1,150 feet (350 meters) and 1,500 feet (450 meters), they are among the highest such vantage points in the world.

SHIBUYA, WEST TOKYO Shibuya is one of the twenty-three city wards of Tokyo, but the name often refers just to the popular shopping and entertainment area found around Shibuya Station. It is a colorful and busy area, packed with stores, restaurants, and nightclubs. Shibuya is a center for youth fashion and culture, and its streets are the birthplace of many of Japan's fashion and entertainment trends.

PREVIOUS PAGE AND BELOW_TOKYO
Tokyo has a strong claim to the title of being the world's biggest city.

RIGHT_MEIJI SHRINE
Close to Harajuku Station, the grounds of the shrine are a great place for a stroll.

MEIJI SHRINE, WEST TOKYO Meiji Shrine is dedicated to the deified spirits of Emperor Meiji and his consort, Empress Shoken. Located just beside the busy Harajuku Station, Meiji Shrine and the adjacent Yoyogi Park make up a large forested area at the heart of the city. The shrine grounds offer walking paths that are great for a relaxing stroll. Nearby, Harajuku is the magnet for trendy Tokyo youth, with a mass of teen fashion stores and cool eating places.

SHINJUKU GYOEN Shinjuku Gyoen is one of Tokyo's largest and most popular parks. Located just a short walk from Shinjuku Station, the park's spacious lawns, meandering walking paths, and tranquil scenery provide a relaxing escape from the city's hustle. In spring, it is one of the best places in the city to see cherry blossoms. The park is made up of three different types of gardens: a traditional Japanese landscape garden, featuring large ponds with islands and bridges; a formal French garden; and an English landscape garden, featuring wide lawns surrounded by flowering cherry trees. The rest of the park consists of forested areas and lawns. There is a restaurant, an art gallery, and a greenhouse with many tropical and subtropical flowers.

HOW TO GET THERE:

BY PLANE Tokyo has two principal airports: Narita and Haneda. Most international flights fly to Narita, which is about 35 miles (56 kilometers) from the city. Haneda Airport is more centrally located, and British Airways flies direct there, but there are fewer flights than to Narita.

BY BUS AND TRAIN There are JR Narita Express trains into the city and connecting with all the major stations for onward travel. Taxis from Narita are expensive and are best avoided.

- There is also a good bus service serving city hotels. For more information, go to www.limousinebus.co.jp
- For travel in Tokyo, the train system is excellent, with helpful staff, English signage, and highly punctual trains.

SENDAI
HONSHU

Sendai is north of Honshu, 3 hours and 20 minutes from Tokyo by Shinkansen. It is the ideal place to explore if you're visiting the Miyagikyo Distillery, which is just 15 miles (24 kilometers) away (see p.96). With about one million inhabitants, Sendai is the largest city in the Tohoku region. The modern city was founded in around 1600 by Date Masamune, one of feudal Japan's most powerful lords. Many of Sendai's tourist attractions are related to Masamune and his family. The 2011 tsunami destroyed Sendai's coastal outskirts, but it did not cause major damage in the city center.

DOWNTOWN SENDAI Known as the city of trees, Sendai has a compact downtown area, rich in greenery. Trees can even be found in the covered shopping area, Ichibancho Arcade. This is a shopping precinct that links a number of streets into several malls. There is a mixture of retail outlets here,

ABOVE AND BELOW_RINNOJI TEMPLE
An ideal place to relax, with beautiful gardens and ponds full of koi carp.

AOBA CASTLE
This is also known as Sendai Castle. The walls have been carefully reconstructed since World War II and the castle is now a national historic monument.

from budget stores to a state-of-the-art Apple Macintosh emporium. There is also a morning market with fresh food on sale. It's all atmospheric and special.

AOBA CASTLE Built in 1600 but destroyed by Allied carpet-bombing in 1945, Aoba Castle stands more than 300 feet (100 meters) above the city, and its remnants offer panoramic views. There is a museum outlining the castle's history on the site, featuring models of the castle as it would have looked, as well as artifacts from it. There is a also a movie, with an English translation on headphones.

RINNOJI TEMPLE Close to the center of Sendai, this temple is made special by its beautiful gardens. The temple dates back to 1441, and the gardens have several paths, a three-storied pagoda, and a large number of ponds containing koi carp. It is the perfect place to relax in Sendai.

HOW TO GET THERE:

BY SHINKANSEN Sendai is connected with Tokyo by the JR Tohoku Shinkansen. Hayabusa, Hayate, and Komachi trains take 100 minutes to travel between Sendai and Tokyo, and they require seat reservations. Yamabiko trains have some unreserved seating and take about 2 hours. The whole journey is covered by Japan Rail Pass and JR East Pass.

BY LOCAL TRAIN By local trains along the JR Tohoku Line, the one-way trip from Tokyo to Sendai takes about 7 hours and typically involves about three to four transfers of trains.

BY HIGHWAY BUS Multiple bus companies, including Willer Express, offer direct highway bus service between Tokyo and Sendai during both the day and night. Travel duration is about 5½ hours.

OSAKA
HONSHU

Osaka is south of Tokyo, on the Pacific coast. With a population of 2.5 million, Osaka is Japan's third largest, and second most important, city. It has been the economic powerhouse of the Kansai region for many centuries. While in Osaka, why not pop in to one of the city's whisky bars (see pp.176–78), where, given the proximity of Yamazaki Distillery (see p.82), you'll find a large number of rare and exciting Suntory bottlings. Yamazaki distillery is just 20 miles (33 km) away from Osaka, White Oak is 25 miles (40 km) away (see p.102), and Miyashita Shuzo is 112 miles (180 km) away (see p.93).

SHINSEKAI as an area was developed after the 1903 National Industrial Exposition, with Paris and New York serving as influences. Tsutenkaku Tower was constructed in 1912 to emulate Paris's Eiffel Tower. It's here you'll find the best kushikatsu, one of Osaka's best-known specialties—skewers, traditionally using battered and deep-fried fish, but now often made with chicken, beef, vegetables, or even fruit. Many of Shinsekai's kushikatsu restaurants are open for twenty-four hours, but they truly come alive only when the lights are switched on at night. Shinsekai is also home to Spa World, where natural hot spring water is pumped from under the earth's surface to a number of baths. People bathe naked here in gender separated pools.

OSAKA CASTLE has a checkered history, having been totally destroyed on more than one occasion. The current reconstruction is made of concrete and iron and was built in 1931; it survived heavy bombing raids in World War II. It was further modernized in the 1990s and houses an informative museum about the castle's history. Osaka Castle Park has plenty of green space, sports facilities, a multipurpose arena (Osakajo Hall), and a shrine.

ABOVE_SHINSEKAI
A popular center for leisure and recreation. Here, you'll find traditional food and public hot spring baths.

ABOVE RIGHT_BUNRAKU THEATER
This is one of the few places you can see this traditional Japanese puppet theater performed.

NATIONAL BUNRAKU THEATER Bunraku is traditional Japanese puppet theater and has been an immensely popular form of entertainment for many centuries. Osaka is its capital, and the National Bunraku Theater is one of the few places where you can see it performed. Performances are usually held in three-week runs in January, April, June, July/August, and November, and there are English performances and headphones available.

HOW TO GET THERE:

BY SHINKANSEN Tokyo (Tokyo and Shinagawa stations) and Osaka (Shin-Osaka Station) are connected with each other by the JR Tokaido Shinkansen. Journey time is between 2½ and 4 hours and the distance is around 312 miles (500 kilometers).

BY HIGHWAY BUS Tokyo to Osaka by highway bus takes around eight hours. There are daytime and overnight buses. Fierce competition on the Tokyo–Osaka route has produced a wide variety of comfort levels and an abundance of low-priced offers.

BY AIR Multiple airlines operate between Tokyo and Osaka. A majority of flights use Tokyo's Haneda Airport and Osaka's Itami Airport, but a smaller number of flights also serve Tokyo's Narita Airport and Osaka's Kansai Airport. Flight duration is one hour.

OKAYAMA
HONSHU

Okayama is the capital of Okayama Prefecture, and the largest city in the Chugoku region after Hiroshima. The city is an important transportation hub, developed as a castle town during the Edo period (1603–1867), and became a significant regional power. Okayama's most famous attraction is Kōrakuen Garden, which is ranked as one of the best landscape gardens in Japan. Okayama serves as the location for the popular fairy tale of Momotaro (the Peach Boy), so visitors will notice many references to the legendary hero. If Miyashita Shuzo Distillery starts producing whisky spirit regularly, this will be within easy reach, just 20 miles (32 kilometers) away (see p.93).

KŌRAKUEN GARDENS Kōrakuen is Okayama's main attraction. It is ranked as one of Japan's three best landscape gardens, and is located just beside Okayama Castle. The local feudal lord ordered the construction of Kōrakuen in 1687. In 1884, it became the property of Okayama Prefecture, and was opened to the public. It is a spacious garden that incorporates a large pond, streams, walking paths, and a hill that serves as a lookout point. It also has spacious lawns, as well as plum, cherry, and maple groves, tea and rice fields, an archery range, and an aviary.

INUJIMA ISLAND Inujima is a small island off Okayama. It has become known in recent years as a site for modern art, and serves as a venue for the Setouchi Triennale modern art festival. Due to its small size, the island can be explored entirely on foot. The island was once an industrial site with a copper refinery, and the ruins still remain. In 2008, these were converted into the Inujima Seirensho Art Museum. A gallery is located mostly underground. Among the artworks on display is an intriguing tunnel of mirrors.

KURASHIKI Kurashiki is 10 miles (16 kilometers) from Okayama. It has a pretty canal area that dates from the Edo period, when the city was a rice distribution center. Many of Kurashiki's former storehouses have been converted into boutiques, cafés, and museums, including the Ohara, which houses a large collection of works by famous Western artists.

ABOVE_KŌRAKUEN GARDENS
The popular landscaped gardens, which sit on the north side of the Aashi River.

ABOVE RIGHT_KURASHIKI
A bridge over the canal in the historic city of Kurashiki. Distinctive white-walled houses like this were originally built for storing goods.

BELOW RIGHT_OKAYAMA
The evening December sun over the Okayama Prefecture.

HOW TO GET THERE:

BY SHINKANSEN Tokyo and Okayama are two major stations along the JR Tokaido/Sanyo Shinkansen. The trip takes approximately 3½ to 4 hours by Hikari train. The journey would be around 415 miles (660 kilometers) by road.

BY AIR JAL and ANA operate multiple flights per day between Tokyo's Haneda Airport and Okayama Airport. Flight duration is 75 minutes.

BY OVERNIGHT BUS Several bus companies, including Ryobi, Odakyu, and JR Bus, operate night buses between Tokyo (Tokyo and Shinjuku Stations) and Okayama (Okayama Station). The trip takes 10 hours.

SAPPORO
HOKKAIDO

Sapporo is not the closest city to Nikka's Yoichi Distillery—Otaru is, but since the visitor can practically reach Otaru only through Sapporo, we deal with the latter first. There's plenty to see here—it should not be missed. Way up north on the island of Hokkaido, Sapporo is 36 miles (58 kilometers) away from Nikka's Yoichi Distillery (see p.106). While in the city, why not stop in the Nikka Bar, to test some of the whisky company's rarer malts? The new distillery at Akkeshi is on the opposite coast, around 200 miles (320 km) away (see p.64).

SAPPORO is the capital of Hokkaido, and Japan's fifth largest city. It was chosen as the island's administrative center and enlarged with the help of foreign specialists. For this reason, its street system is based on a North American-style grid. Sapporo became world famous in 1972, when the Winter Olympics were held there. Today, the city is well known for its ramen, its beer, and for the annual snow festival, which is held in February.

SUSUKINO is Japan's largest entertainment district outside Tokyo. It is a bustling, colorful, and busy mixture of stores, bars, restaurants, karaoke shops, and red-light establishments. You can also play pachinko here—a game that mixes slot-machine technology and pinball. Also visit Ramen Yokocho, a narrow lane lined with shops serving Sapporo's ramen. Every February, the snow festival is held here.

THE SAPPORO SNOW FESTIVAL (Sapporo Yuki Matsuri) is held in February and lasts a week. It has been held for more than sixty-five years, and has grown into a large event, featuring spectacular snow and ice sculptures, and attracting more than two million visitors a year. The snow festival is staged on three sites: Odori, Susukino, and Tsu Dome. The main site is Odori, which is close to the center of Sapporo. The festival's famous large snow sculptures are exhibited there, as well as more than 100 smaller snow statues. Concerts and events are held in the evening. The nearby Sapporo Television Tower, which has extended opening hours throughout the festival period, offers fabulous views over the whole event.

HISTORIC VILLAGE
The Historic Village is a collection of sixty buildings from Hokkaido's past. Sapporo is the place to come for skiing and is home to the annual winter Snow Festival.

THE HISTORIC VILLAGE AND MUSEUM OF HOKKAIDO The Historic Village is an open-air museum in the suburbs of Sapporo. It is made up of around sixty typical buildings from all over Hokkaido, dating from the Meiji and Taisho periods (1868 to 1926), the era when Hokkaido's development was carried out on a large scale. There are four different sections: a town, a fishing village, a farm village, and a mountain village.

The Historical Museum documents the history of Hokkaido's development. It is located about a ten-minute walk from the Historical Village. The museum has eight areas that chronologically cover the region's history from its first occupation by humans about 20,000 years ago to the postwar years after 1945 and into the future.

SAPPORO TEINE The largest of several medium-sized ski resorts, Sapporo Teine is about 40 minutes outside Hokkaido. It features a variety of ski trails, from wide, gently sloping hills to long and fast advanced courses, including two runs used for ski events at the 1972 Winter Olympics. The trails are spread out over two zones and connected by a gondola lift. The upper one features medium-to-advanced courses, off-trail runs, and a snow park with jumps, boxes, and rails. The lower Olympia Zone has wider, less steep trails suitable for beginners, as well as a family park offering sledding and tubing.

MOERENUMA PARK The grounds owe their bold design to Japanese American sculptor Isamu Noguchi, whom the city commissioned in 1988 to create a park from an old landfill.

HOW TO GET THERE:

BY AIR Tokyo–Sapporo is the world's busiest air route, with dozens of flights per day. The majority of flights go from Tokyo's Haneda Airport and fly to Sapporo's New Chitose Airport, but quite a few flights also go from Narita Airport.
➤ Flight duration is around 90 minutes.

BY DAYTIME TRAIN Take the JR Tohoku Shinkansen from Tokyo to Shin-Aomori Station (3½ hours), then take the JR Hakucho limited express to Hakodate (2 hours) and, finally, the JR Hokuto limited express to Sapporo (3½ hours).
➤ Counting transfers, the whole trip takes around 10 hours.

BY NIGHT TRAIN The Cassiopeia night train operates on selected days between Tokyo's Ueno Station and Sapporo.
➤ Travel time is 16–17 hours.

OTARU
HOKKAIDO

Otaru is the closest city to any whisky maker in Japan, lying just 12 miles (20 kilometers) from Yoichi Distillery (see p.106). Otaru is a small harbor city, 24 miles (38 kilometers) northwest of Sapporo, and 30 to 45 minutes from it by train. It boasts a pretty canal area and unusual buildings. It has a long history as a major trade and fishing port, and has many old warehouses and former shipping and trade company offices that give the downtown area a traditional feel.

OTARU CANAL The Otaru Canal was a central part of the city's busy port in the early twentieth century, but it became a victim of technological progress. Local people helped to restore part of the canal in the 1980s, and the old warehouses were transformed into museums, stores, and restaurants. Now artists present their works to passing tourists during the day, and in the evenings old-fashioned gas lamps are lit to create a special atmosphere.

THE OTARU SNOW LIGHT PATH FESTIVAL This is a winter festival held every February in Otaru, normally at the same time as the Sapporo Snow Festival. The city is decorated in lights and small snow statues for ten days. There are two main official festival areas that get lit up daily. The festival takes place within a 15-minute walk of the train station.

THE OTARU CITY MUSEUM The Otaru City Museum comprises a conventional history museum beside Otaru Canal, and a less centrally located railroad museum in the grounds of a railroad yard. Housed in a former warehouse next to the canal, the Canal Building is located within the city's main tourist area. The museum covers the history of Otaru, from the time of Hokkaido's native Ainu people to the preservation movement during the 1970s. The story is told by models and displays, which are explained in an English pamphlet.

The Railway Museum is located outside the main tourist area on the former site of the terminal of Hokkaido's first railroad line. Full-sized trains from various periods are exhibited here, while the history of Otaru's railroads is explained with exhibits.

ABOVE_OTARU SNOW LIGHT PATH FESTIVAL
Otaru's stunning light festival is held in February at the same time as Sapporo's Snow Festival.

RIGHT_OTARU CANAL
Spectacularly lit up for the light festival, Otaru Canal is also a great place to walk during the day.

HOW TO GET THERE:

BY TRAIN Travel to Sapporo, then go from Sapporo to Otaru. There are several trains every hour between Sapporo and Otaru. The one-way trip takes 30 minutes by rapid train, or 45 minutes by local train.

WHISKY DIRECTORY

This is a guide to the major Japanese whiskies that are available on the market. The whiskies are first categorized by the company that owns them, and within that, they are listed by distillery. Single malts are always made in one distillery, but blended and blended malts are made up of whiskies that have come from several different distilleries and are not always blended at the same distillery. Therefore, the blended whiskies are listed underneath their parent company rather than a distillery (except for Rainbow Whisky, which is always blended at Aioi Unibio Distillery).

AIOI UNIBIO CO., LTD.
AIOI UNIBIO DISTILLERY
Blended and blended malt whisky:
Rainbow Whisky, 37%

CHUGOKU JOZO CO., LTD.
Blended and blended malt whisky:
Togouchi 8 Year Old, 40%
Togouchi 12 Year Old, 43%
Togouchi 18 Year Old, 43%

EIGASHIMA BREWING CO., LTD.
Blended and blended malt whisky:
White Oak Akashi, 40%
White Oak Akashi Blended Grain, 40%
White Oak Akashi Blended Malt, 40%
White Oak Tokinoka Blended Malt, 40%

WHITE OAK DISTILLERY
Single malts:
White Oak Akashi NAS, 46%
White Oak Akashi Single Malt 14 Year Old, 56%
White Oak Akashi 15 Year Old, 58%
White Oak Testimony, 50%
White Oak 5 Year Old Single Malt, 45%
White Oak 5 Year Old Oloroso Sherry Cask, 50%

HOMBO SHUZO CO., LTD.
Blended and blended malt whisky:
Mars Iwai, 40%
Mars Iwai Tradition Wine Cask Finish, 40%
Mars Amber, 40%
Mars Maltage Cosmo, 43%
Mars Maltage Komagatake Pure Malt 10 Year Old, 40%
Mars Twin Peaks, 40%
Mars Karuizawa Club, 39%
Mars Komagatake Cosmo, 43%
Mars The Lucky Cat, 39%
Monde Royal Crystal, 40%

SHINSHU MARS DISTILLERY
Single malts:
Mars Malt Gallery American White Oak, 58%
Mars Komagatake Single Cask 24 Year Old, 58%
Mars Komagatake Single Cask 25 Year Old, 46%
Mars Komagatake The Revival 2011, 58%
Mars Komagatake American Oak & Sherry 2011, 57%
Mars Komagatake Cognac Cask #1041 23 Year Old, 63.5%
Mars Komagatake Sherry Cask #162 27 Year Old, 60.7%
Mars Komagatake 2012 Sherry Cask #1436, 58%
Mars Komagatake 2012 Sherry Cask #162, 60.7%
Mars Komagatake Single Cask 1985, 60.7%
Mars Komagatake Single Cask 1988 25 Year Old, 46%
Mars Maltage Komagatake 10 Year Old Wine Cask Finish, 40%

KIRIN

FUJI GOTEMBA

<u>Single malts:</u>

Fuji Gotemba 15 Year Old, 43%

Kirin 18 Year Old, 43%

<u>Single grains:</u>

Fuji Gotemba Single Grain Blender's Choice, 46%

MONDE SHUZO CO., LTD.

<u>Blended and blended malt whisky:</u>

Isawa Blended Whisky, 40%

MONDE SHUZO DISTILLERY

<u>Single malts:</u>

Isawa Malt Vintage 1983 25 Year Old, 43%

Isawa Single Malt 10 Year Old, 43%

NIKKA WHISKY DISTILLING CO., LTD.

<u>Blended and blended malt whisky:</u>

Nikka Coffey Grain, 57%

Nikka Fortune 80, 43%

Nikka Hokkaido 12 Year Old, 43%

Nikka Malt 70th Anniversary 12 Year Old, 40%

Nikka Pure Malt Cask Strength, 55.5%

Nikka Pure Malt 12 Year Old, 40%

Nikka 40 Year Old 43%

Nikka All Malt, 40%

Nikka Gold & Gold Samurai, 43%

Nikka Super Genshu, 55.5%

Nikka Super Revival, 43%

Nikka 8 Year Old Black Pure Malt, 40%

Nikka Pure Malt 17 Year Old, 43%

Nikka Pure Malt 21 Year Old, 43%

Nikka Pure Malt Black, 43%

Nikka Pure Malt Red, 43%

Nikka Pure Malt White, 43%

Nikka Rare Old Super, 45%

Nikka Whisky From The Barrel, 51.4%

Nikka Taketsuru Pure Malt NAS, 43%

Nikka Taketsuru Pure Malt Sherry, 43%

Nikka Taketsuru Pure Malt 12 Year Old, 40%

Nikka Taketsuru Pure Malt 17 Year Old, 43%

Nikka Taketsuru Pure Malt 21 Year Old, 43%

Nikka Taketsuru Pure Malt 25 Year Old, 43%

Nikka Taketsuru 35 Year Old, 43%

Nikka Tsuru 17 Year Old, 43%

<u>Single grains:</u>

Nikka Coffey Grain Cask #198156, 60%

<u>Single malts:</u>

Nikka Coffey Malt, 45%

MIYAGIKYO DISTILLERY

<u>Single malts:</u>

Miyagikyo 10 Year Old, 45%

Miyagikyo 12 Year Old, 45%

Miyagikyo 15 Year Old, 45%

Miyagikyo 20 Year Old 1988, 50%

Miyagikyo 20 Year Old 1990, 48%

Miyagikyo Single Cask 1986 Cask #80283, 63%

Miyagikyo Single Cask 1988 23 Year Old Cask #55, 57%

Nikka Miyagikyo Single Cask 1989, 61%

Miyagikyo Single Cask 1989 Cask #105419, 60%

Miyagikyo Single Cask 1990 Cask #36385, 61%

Miyagikyo NAS 2015, 45%

Nikka 1991 Single Cask, 58%

YOICHI DISTILLERY

<u>Single malts:</u>

Yoichi 10 Year Old, 45%

Yoichi 12 Year Old, 45%

Yoichi 15 Year Old, 45%

Yoichi 20 Year Old, 52%

Yoichi 20 Year Old 1988, 55%

Yoichi 20 Year Old 1989, 55%

Yoichi 20 Year Old 10th Whisky Live Tokyo, 62%

Yoichi 18 Year Old Single Cask #1299374, 58%

Yoichi 19 Year Old Single Cask #36385, 61%

Yoichi 23 Year Old Single Cask #112814, 59%

Yoichi NAS, 43%

Yoichi The Scotch Malt Whisky Society, 23 Year Old, 57.1%

SASANOKAWA SHUZO CO., LTD.

Blended and blended malt whisky:
Sasanokawa Cherry Whisky EX, 40%

YAMAZAKURA DISTILLERY

Single malts:
Yamazakura 15 Year Old Pure Malt, 43%

SUNTORY

Blended and blended malt whisky:
Hibiki 12 Year Old, 43%
Hibiki 17 Year Old, 43%
Hibiki 21 Year Old, 43%
Hibiki 30 Year Old, 43%
Hibiki Harmony, 43%
Hibiki Deep Harmony, 43%
Hibiki Mellow Harmony, 43%
Hokutu 12 Year Old, 40%
Suntory 1981 Kioke Shiomi, 43%
Suntory 1991 Furudaru Shiage, 43%
Suntory 2000 Millennium, 43%
Suntory Reserve Whisky Silky, 43%
Suntory Royal Whisky, 43%
Suntory Whisky Excellence, 43%
Suntory Kakubin, 40%
Suntory Kakubin Blue, 43%
Suntory Kakubin Yellow, 40%
Suntory Rolling Stones 50 Year Old, 50%

Single grains:
Suntory The Chita Single Grain, 43%

HAKUSHU DISTILLERY

Single malts:
Hakushu 10 Year Old, 40%
Hakushu 12 Year Old, 43%
Hakushu 18 Year Old, 43%
Hakushu 25 Year Old, 43%
Hakushu 1989, 60%
Hakushu Single Cask Osaka 3rd Anniversary, 55%
Hakushu Distiller's Reserve, 43%
Hakushu Heavily Peated, 48%

YAMAZAKI DISTILLERY

Single malts:
Yamazaki 10 Year Old, 40%
Yamazaki 12 Year Old, 43%
Yamazaki 18 Year Old, 43%
Yamazaki 25 Year Old, 43%
Yamazaki 10 Year Old Cask Strength, 57%
Yamazaki 15 Year Old Cask Strength, 58%
Yamazaki 1984, 48%
Yamazaki 1993, 62%
Yamazaki Bourbon Barrel, 48.2%
Yamazaki 1979 Mizunara Oak Cask, 55%
Yamazaki Sherry Cask, 48%
Yamazaki The Scotch Malt Whisky Society 16 Year Old, 54%
Yamazaki The Scotch Malt Whisky Society 11 Year Old Raspberry Imperial Stout, 53.9%
Yamazaki Single Cask Whisky Live Tokyo 2012, 58%
Yamazaki Distiller's Reserve, 43%
Yamazaki Puncheon 2013, 48%
Yamazaki 1986 Owner's Cask, 60%

VENTURE WHISKY LTD.

Blended and blended malt whisky:
Ichiro's Malt & Grain, 46%
Ichiro's Malt & Grain Premium, 50%
Ichiro's Malt Double Distilleries Pure Malt, 46%
Ichiro's Malt Mizunara Wood Reserve, 46%
Ichiro's Malt Wine Wood Reserve, 46%
Karuizawa/Yamanashi Ocean Bright Deluxe, 42%

CHICHIBU DISTILLERY

Single malts:
Chichibu On The Way, 58.5%
Chichibu Single Cask Bourbon Barrel 3 Year Old, 62.2%
Chichibu Peated Bottled 2015, 62.5%
Chichibu Chibidaru, 53.5%
Chichibu Chibidaru 2009 Cask #286, 53.5%
Chichibu Port Pipe, 54.5%
Chichibu The First, 61.8%
Chichibu The Floor Malted 3 Year Old, 50.5%
Chichibu The Peated 2010, 59.6%
Chichibu The Peated, 2011, 62.5%
Chichibu Newborn 2009 Heavily Peated, 61.4%

HANYU DISTILLERY

Single malts:

Hanyu 2000 Zuma Roka Single Cask #919, 57.6%
Hanyu 1988 Single Cask #9501, 55.6%
Hanyu 1991 Single Cask, 57.3%
Hanyu 1990 "The Wave" Cask #9305, 53%
Hanyu 1988 "Nice Butt" Cask #9307, 55%
Hanyu Noh Whisky 21 Year Old Cask #9306, 55.6%
Hanyu Single Cask Whisky Talk Fukuoka 2011, 60.1%
Ichiro's Malt & Grain Premium, 50%
Ichiro's Malt Hanyu 2000–2010 The Final Vintage, 59%
Ichiro's Malt Hanyu 2011 Tokyo Whisky Live, 60.9%
Ichiro's Malt Whisky Talk 12 Year Old, 60.1%
Ichiro's Malt Card Series:
* Eight of Hearts, 56.8%
* Six of Hearts, 57.9%
* Five of Spades, 60.5%
* Ace of Clubs 2000, 59.4%
* Eight of Clubs 1988, 56%
* Ten of Clubs, 52.4%
* Ace of Diamonds, 56.4%
* Four of Diamonds Cask #9030, 56.9%
* Cask Strength 23 Year Old, 58%
* The Joker, 57.7%

KARUIZAWA DISTILLERY

Single malts:

Karuizawa 17 Year Old, 59.5%
Karuizawa Single Cask 2725 Taiwanese Release, 59.6%
Karuizawa 1967 Single Cask #6426, 58.4%
Karuizawa 1968 Single Cask #6955, 61.1%
Karuizawa 1970 Single Cask #6177, 64.3%
Karuizawa 1971 Single Cask #6878, 64.1%
Karuizawa 1973 Single Cask #6249, 56%
Karuizawa 1976 Single Cask #6719, 63%
Karuizawa 1967 42 Year Old, 58.4%
Karuizawa Vintage 1981 Cask #2634, 55.2%
Karuizawa 1964, 57.7%
Karuizawa 1981, 63.4%
Karuizawa 1981 #103, 54.5%
Karuizawa 1981 Noh Series 31 Year Old, 56%
Karuizawa 1982 Bourbon Cask 29 Year Old, 58.8%
Karuizawa 1985 Single Cask 7017, 60.8%
Karuizawa 1986 Single Cask 7387, 60.7%
Karuizawa Noh 29 Bourbon, 58.8%
Karuizawa Noh 31 Sherry, 63.9%
Karuizawa Spirit of Asama, 48%
Karuizawa 19 Year Old, 10th Whisky Live, *Whisky Magazine*, 60%
Karuizawa 1988 Vintage. 60.6%
Karuizawa Kohaku 1995 Vintage 10 Year Old, 59.9%
Karuizawa Sherry Cask 30 Year Old, 58.2%
Karuizawa The Scotch Malt Whisky Society 132.6 Nite Nurse Nipped by Piranhas 12 Year Old, 63%
Karuizawa The Colors of Four Seasons 13 Year Old, 64.2%
Karuizawa Fuji Mountain Single Cask #7982, 54.5%
Karuizawa TWE 10th Anniversary Sherry Cask #2748, 56.1%
Karuizawa 1999 14 Year Old Last Bottling, 60.5%
Karuizawa 1999 14 Year Old Cask #2316 (For HST), 61.3%
Karuizawa Rare Flat Bottle 1981 13 Year Old, 58%
Karuizawa 1984 Blue Wave Cask #3657, 59.7%
Karuizawa 1997 Spirit Safe Cask #3312, 60.2%
Karuizawa The Bar Show 2013, 62.4%
Karuizawa 1984–2012 International Bar Show, 61.6%
Karuizawa Cask Strength 1st Release, 61.7%
Karuizawa Cask Strength 2nd Release, 61.7%
Karuizawa Cask Strength 3rd Release, 60.5%
Karuizawa 2000 12 Year Old Dragon Label, 64.3%
Karuizawa Memories of Karuizawa 16 Year Old, 61.8%
Karuizawa Multivintage, 59.1%
Karuizawa Martins Selection Vintage 1973, 56%

KAWASAKI DISTILLERY

Single malts:

Kawasaki, 1981 / Bot. 2009, 62.4%

Single grains:

Kawasaki 1976 33 Year Old Ichiro's Choice Grain, 65.6%
Kawasaki 1980 Single Cask Grain, 59.6%
Kawasaki 1982 Whisky Live Tokyo 29 Year Old Single Grain, 65.5%

WAKATSURU CO., LTD.
WAKATSURU SHUZO DISTILLERY

Single malts:

Wakatsuru Shuzo Sun Shine 20 Year Old, 59%

GLOSSARY

ABV
An abbreviation for alcohol by volume. This is the standard way of measuring how much alcohol (ethanol) is in an alcoholic drink.

AMONTILLADO
A type of sherry that is named after the Montilla region of southern Spain where the style originated.

AMOROSO
A dark, rich, and sweet sherry, which is similar to Oloroso sherry.

"ANGELS' SHARE"
The name for the small volume of whisky that is lost to evaporation during the maturation process.

AWAMORI
An earthy flavored alcoholic beverage made only in Okinawa, Japan. It is similar to sake but has several major differences: it is distilled like a single malt scotch, is stronger than sake, and is made with a different strain of rice.

BONDED WAREHOUSE
A place where stock, including whisky, is stored "under bond" before duty is due to be paid on it.

BUTT
A wine cask that contains around two hogsheads (about 125–126 gallons, or 475–480 liters) of liquid.

CARAMEL
A dark brown sugar-based confectionery used by some whisky makers as a coloring agent.

CASK STRENGTH
The alcohol-by-volume (abv) level of a whisky once it has completed the maturation process. The cask strength of whisky is typically around 60 to 65 percent abv before dilution.

CHARRING
Part of the barrel-making process whereby the inside is toasted with flame. This means that the taste of the whisky will change as it matures in the barrel.

CHILL-FILTERING
A cosmetic method of removing residue from a whisky by cooling and passing the whisky through a filter.

CONGENERS
Chemical compounds formed during fermentation, distillation, and maturation of whisky that affect its taste and smell.

DRAM
A Scottish term for a measure of whisky. A dram is typically around 25 ml.

FINO
A dry and very pale sherry from Spain.

FIRST-FILL CASK
The term used for an oak cask that is filled for the first time with new-make whisky after it has been emptied of its previous contents.

GRIST
A coarse flour of malt and other grains that is used to make a whisky.

HIGHBALL
A cocktail of whisky mixed with club soda or ginger ale and served with ice in a tall glass.

HOGSHEAD ("HOGGIE")
A cask holding approximately 55 gallons (208 liters) of liquid.

MADEIRA
A fortified Portuguese wine made in the Madeira Islands in several different styles.

MARSALA
A wine made in the area around Marsala, Sicily.

MASH BILL
The misture of different grains that go into a whisky, also known as a grain bill.

MASHING
The process whereby grain(s) and water is combined and heated.

MASH TUN
The large vessel used for mashing. It typically features a stirring mechanism, known as a mash rake, and a heating device.

MIZUNARA
Japanese oak: barrels made of this are often used to mature Japanese whisky in.

MIZUWARI
A drink made with whisky and lots of water and ice.

MOUTH-COATING
Moving the whisky around the mouth to coat the four taste receptors and help release flavors.

MOUTHFEEL
A way of assessing a whisky's intensity by holding it on the center of the tongue for a few seconds.

NONAGE STATEMENT (NAS)
Whisky that is sold without a specific age on the label.

NEW-MAKE
The spirit produced by a distillery prior to maturation.

OLOROSO
A dark and nutty variety of sherry produced by oxidative aging.

PEDRO XIMÉNEZ
A type of white grape that is grown in certain parts of Spain.

PHENOLS
Chemical compounds introduced to a whisky through a peat-heated fire. Phenols add a smoky aroma and flavor to the spirit.

RAMEN
A Japanese noodle soup with vegetables and meat or fish, often seasoned with soy sauce and miso.

SAKE
A brewed alcoholic drink that is made from fermenting rice. It is usually matured for between nine and twelve months.

SALADIN BOX
A nineteenth-century French invention in which barley germinates while being mechanically turned.

SHŌCHŪ
An alcoholic drink distilled from rice, barley, or sweet potatoes.

SOLERA
A process for aging liquids by fractional blending in such a way that the finished product is a mixture of ages.

STAVES
The pieces of wood that form a barrel.

WASH BACK
A large vat, usually made of wood, in which distillers ferment the wort to form wash.

WASH
The liquid produced at the end of the fermentation of the wort, after the yeast has been added.

WORT
The sugary liquid obtained during the mashing process. The sugars will ferment to form alcohol.

INDEX

A

ABV definition 280
advertising 145, 146–7, 149–50, 153, 154
Aioi Unibio Co., Ltd. 276
Aioi Unibio Distillery 276
air temperature 52
Akadama 24
Akashi, Honshu 102
Akashi White Oak 102
Akihabara 263
Akkeshi Distillery 62–3, 64
Akuto, Ichiro 66–7, 70–1, 91, 92, 140–2, 168, 253
 see also Chichibu Distillery; Hanyu Distillery
Al-Badri, Dominic 248–9
amontillado 280
amoroso 280
"angels' share" 52, 280
Après Ski in Fuji 237
Ardbeg 253
Argentina 30
Asahi Brewery 96, 106
Auld Alliance, Singapore 216, 217
Australian bars 224–30
AWA Hibiki 238
awamori 14, 28, 280

B

Bar Argyll, Shinjuku, Tokyo 167
Bar Augusta Tarlogie, Osaka 177
Bar Black Sheep, Shibuya, Tokyo 173
Bar Caol Ila, Shibuya, Tokyo 172, 173
Bar Cordon Noir, Kyoto 179
Bar Evita, Ginza, Tokyo 163
Bar High Five, Ginza, Tokyo 162

Bar Jackalope, Los Angeles 184, 185
Bar K, Osaka 178
Bar Kitchen Tenjin, Fukuoka 180
Bar Lupin, Ginza, Tokyo 163
Bar Plastic Model, Shinjuku, Tokyo 168
Bar Rock Rock, Osaka 178
Bar Society, Minato-ku, Tokyo 161
barley
 Golden Promise 90
 imports 14
 Japan 68, 93
 malting 46
 mugicha 14
barrels see casks
bars
 Australia 224–30
 Chicago 186
 France 209–10
 Fukuoka 180
 Germany 213
 Hong Kong 222
 Kyoto 179
 Los Angeles 184
 New York 191–6
 Norway 199
 Osaka 177–8, 248
 overview 28, 157, 183
 Poland 214
 Sapporo 181
 Singapore 216
 Tokyo Ginza District 162–3
 Tokyo Minato District 158–61
 Tokyo other areas 174–5
 Tokyo Shibuya District 172–3
 Tokyo Shinjuku District 166–9
 Toyko Ginza District 155
 U.K. 200–6

beer 14, 28, 45, 181
Bincho at Hua Bee, Singapore 218, 219
blended whisky
 demand 77
 imports 17, 57
 Japanese methods 14–17, 57–8
 Nikka 57–8, 110
 overview 56
 Scotland 57
 Suntory 57–8, 77, 88
bonded warehouse 280
bourbon casks 51, 52
The Bow Bar, Sapporo 181
Bowmore 51, 154, 254
Broom, Dave 29, 30, 95, 108, 139, 142, 152
Bunting, Chris 144–7, 151, 152
butt 280
Buxrud, Ulf 152

C

Campbelltoun Loch, Chiyoda-ku, Tokyo 155, 175
Canada 17
caramel 280
Cask Strength, Minato-ku, Tokyo 160
cask strength 280
casks 50–2, 53–5
charring 280
Chicago bars 186
Chichibu 2009 148
Chichibu Chibidaru 226
Chichibu Distillery 19, 47, 62–3, 66–8, 142, 250, 258, 278
Chichibu On The Way 140, 196, 229
Chichibu Port Pipe 114, 252, 253

Chichibu Single Cask Bourbon Barrel 200, 213
Chichibu The First 66, 114, 194, 252, 253
Chichibu The Floor Malted 3 Year Old 115, 252, 253
Chichibu The Peated 243
chill-filtered 280
Chugoku Jozo Co., Ltd. 276
climate 36, 38–40, 52
Club Qing, Hong Kong 222, 223
cocktails
    Après Ski in Fuji 237
    AWA Hibiki 238
    Hakushu Shosho 236
    Highball 237
    overview 235–6
    Yamazaki Sour 239
Coffey stills 52, 96–9
Coldicott, Nicholas 152–5
color, maturation 50
Compass Box 57
congeners 280
consumer perception 19–20, 142–3, 145–6, 152
copper 48
Copper and Oak, New York 194, 195
Cowan, Rita 27, 30, 32
Croll, David 142
culture 12, 28, 139, 145–6, 248
cut 48

D

Dainipponkaju 31, 106
Diageo 154
distillation 48, 52
distilleries
    future developments 143, 251
    location map 62–3
Dom Whisky, Warsaw, Poland 214, 215
Dr. Jekyll's Pub, Oslo, Norway 198, 199
Dubliners, Shinjuku, Tokyo 167
Dutch traders 29

E

Eigashima Brewing Co., Ltd. 276
Eigashima Shuzo 102–4

F

fermentation 47
fino 280
first-fill cask 280
The Flatiron Room, New York 192, 193
flavor
    blended whisky 58
    maturation 50
    mizunara oak 51
flavor wheel 113
food pairings 235, 240–3
foreign influence 33, 139, 149, 152
France, bars 209–10
Fuji 36, 41
Fuji Gotemba 15 Year Old 115
Fuji Gotemba Distillery 62–3, 72, 277
Fujisanroku 72
Fukuoka bars 180
Fukuyo, Shinji 88–9
future
    consumer perception 19–20
    demand 143
    distilleries 143, 251
    export 147
    international growth 154
    investment 256–9
    nonage statement (NAS) whiskies 155, 250, 253
    pricing 150, 247, 249, 251
    shortages 143
    tradition 248

G

Gaia Flow 100
gai-atsu 33
geography 36
Germany, bars 213
Glenmorangie 253
Gotemba, Honshu 72
grain 45
grist 280

H

Hakushu 10 Year Old 78, 116, 243
Hakushu 12 Year Old 78, 116, 144, 184, 192, 236–7, 241
Hakushu 18 Year Old 78, 117, 196, 226, 229
Hakushu 25 Year Old 78, 117
Hakushu 1989 118
Hakushu Distillery 37, 62–3, 76–81, 278
Hakushu No Age Statement 144
Hakushu Shosho 236
Hanyu 1988 Single Cask #9501 118
Hanyu 1990 "The Wave" Cask #9305 209
Hanyu 1991 Single Cask 119
Hanyu Distillery 62–3, 66, 70, 92, 142, 258, 259, 278
Hanyu 2000 Zuma Roka Single Cask #919 191, 205
Helmsdale Bar, Minato-ku, Tokyo 160
Hibiki 12 Year Old 132, 184, 196, 214 238, 243
Hibiki 17 Year Old 132, 140, 200, 206, 228, 241
Hibiki 21 Year Old 133
Hibiki Harmony 87, 89, 184, 224
Hibiya Bar Whisky-S, Ginza, Tokyo 163
Highball 145, 149, 154, 184, 237, 280
Highball Bar Umeda 1923, Osaka 178
The Highlander Inn, Speyside 200, 201
Hiraishi, Mikio 105
history see also Taketsuru, Masataka; Torii, Shinjiro
    American whiskey introduction 14, 29
    culture 28
    downturn 32
    Dutch traders 29
    early whisky 30
    first distilleries 14, 31
    gai-atsu 33
    military status 32
    Nikka 23, 24, 27
    Suntory 23, 24
hogshead ("hoggie") 280
Hokkaido see also Otaru; Sapporo
    Akkeshi Distillery 64
    climate 38, 40, 41
    peat 64, 108
    Yoichi Distillery 106–9

Hokuto 12 Year Old 133
Hombo Shuzo 94–5, 276
Hombo Shuzo Co., Ltd. 276
Hong Kong bars 222
Honshu *see also* Okayama; Osaka; Sendai; Tokyo
   Chichibu Distillery 66–8
   climate 40, 41
   Fuji Gotemba Distillery 72
   Hakushu Distillery 76–81
   Hanyu Distillery 92
   Karuizawa Distillery 90–1
   Mars Shinshu Distillery 94–5
   Miyagikyo Distillery 96–9
   Miyashita Shuzo Distillery 93
   Shizuoka Distillery 100
   White Oak Distillery 102–4
   Yamazaki Distillery 82–7
Horigami, Atsushi 146, 147, 154, 167
The Hub, Shinjuku, Tokyo 168
humidity 52

I
Ichiro's Malt Card Series Ace of Clubs 218
Ichiro's Malt Card Series Ace of Diamonds 140
Ichiro's Malt Card Series 92, 149, 154, 155, 258
Ichiro's Malt Card Series Eight of Hearts 119
Ichiro's Malt Card Series Five of Spades 120
Ichiro's Malt Double Distilleries Pure Malt 206
Ichiro's Malt Mizunara Wood Reserve 194
impersonation 14
imports, blending 14, 17, 57
India 17, 52
ingredients 45, 48
investment whiskies 256–9
Islay 51, 173
The Itten Bar, Shinjuku, Tokyo 168
Iwai, Kiichiro 94, 95

J
Jackson, Michael 139, 142, 145, 152
ji-whisky 20
Juso Torys Bar, Osaka 248

K
K6, Kyoto 179
Kakubin whisky 24
Karuizawa 17 Year Old 120
Karuizawa 30 Year Old #5347 Sherry Cask 203
Karuizawa 1960 Cockerel 259
Karuizawa 1964 48 Year Old 90, 148, 259
Karuizawa 1967 Single Cask #6426 121, 199
Karuizawa 1969 209
Karuizawa 1971 Single Cask #6878 121
Karuizawa 1976 Single Cask #6719 122
Karuizawa 1981 Single Cask #103 140, 205
Karuizawa 1985 Single Cask #7017 122
Karuizawa 1986 Single Cask #7387 123
Karuizawa 1995 18 Year Old 259
Karuizawa Distillery 62–3, 90–1, 140–2, 148–9, 250, 258, 279
Karuizawa Scotch Malt Whisky Society 132.6 Nite Nurse Nipped by Piranhas 230
Kawasaki 1980 Single Cask Grain 148
Kawasaki Distillery 279
Kenny's Bar, Shinjuku, Tokyo 169
Kenton Company, Ltd 64
Kentucky blending 52
Kirin
   Fuji Gotemba Distillery 72, 74–5, 277
   Karuizawa Distillery 90–1, 279
Kishi, Hisashi 163
konara oak 104
Koshimizu, Seiichi 57
Kotobukiya 24, 31
Kyoto bars 179

L
La Maison du Whisky, Paris 92
Laphroaig 16–17
Le Gamin de Bastille, Paris 210, 211
Le Sherry Butt, Paris 208, 209
London bars 203–6
Los Angeles bars 184
lyne arm 48

M
Madeira 280
Malt House Islay, Nerima-ku, Tokyo 174
malting 46
manufacturing method
   distillation 48
   fermentation 47
   ingredients 45
   malting 46
   mashing 46
   maturation 50–2
   overview 44
maps 40, 62–3
Mars Komagatake Single Cask 25 Year Old 216
Mars Shinshu Distillery 62–3, 94–5
Marsala 280
mash bill 280
mash tun 281
The Mash Tun, Shingawa-ku, Tokyo 175
mashing 46, 280
maturation 50–2
May, Sir William 29
McEwan, Jim 30
Melbourne bars 230
Miller, Marcin 140–3
Miyagikyo 10 Year Old 123
Miyagikyo 12 Year Old 124, 224
Miyagikyo 15 Year Old 124, 243
Miyagikyo 1989 Single Cask 125
Miyagikyo Distillery 62–3, 96–9
Miyamoto, Mike 8, 20, 163
Miyashita, Buichiro 93
Miyashita Shuzo Distillery 62–3, 93
mizunara oak 51, 52, 68, 254, 281
mizuwari 70, 281
Monde Shuzo Distillery 277
Morrison Bowmore 154

Mount Echigo-Komagatake 41
mouth-coating definition 281
mouthfeel definition 281
mugicha 14
Munich 213
Murray, Jim 139, 142, 143, 154, 259
museums
    Hakushu Distillery 81
    Yamazaki Distillery 87

N

Nakamura, Taiko 100
New York bars 191–6
new-make, definition 281
Nikka
    casks 51
    Dainipponkaju 31, 106
    future 250, 253, 254
    history 23, 24, 27
    Miyagikyo Distillery 96–9, 277
    supply issues 19, 99, 109, 110, 253, 254
    Yoichi Distillery 106–9, 277
Nikka 40 Year Old 148
Nikka Yoichi 1991 Single Cask 125
Nikka Bar, Sapporo 181
Nikka Blender's Bar, Minato-ku, Tokyo 161
Nikka Coffey Grain 96–9, 192, 206, 214, 218, 253
Nikka Coffey Malt 206, 214, 218, 226
Nikka Pure Malt 17 Year Old 243
Nikka Pure Malt Black 135, 243, 253
Nikka Pure Malt Red 135, 243, 253
Nikka Pure Malt White 136
Nikka Rare Old Super 136
Nikka Taketsuru 35 Year Old 216
Nikka Taketsuru Pure Malt 137
Nikka Taketsuru Pure Malt 12 Year Old 134
Nikka Taketsuru Pure Malt 17 Year Old 224, 230
Nikka Taketsuru Pure Malt 21 Year Old 134
Nikka Whisky From The Barrel 137, 191, 199, 203, 253
nonage statement (NAS) whiskies
    definition 281
    future 155, 250, 253, 254
    Nikka 19, 96, 99, 109, 110–11, 253

Nonjatta 20, 144, 148, 151
Norway, bars 199
Number One Drinks Company 91, 140–2, 149, 154

O

oak 50, 51
Off the Rails: A Journey Through Japan 12
Okayama
    Miyashita Shuzo Distillery 93
    travel guide 270–1
oloroso 281
Ono, Takeshi 76
Osaka
    bars 177–8, 248
    climate 40, 41
    travel guide 268–9
Oslo 199
Otaru, travel guide 274
oxidization 50

P

Paper Moon, Shinjuku, Tokyo 169
Paris 92, 209–10
peat 38, 46, 64
Pedro Ximénez 281
Pernod-Ricard 154
Perry, Commodore Matthew 29
phenols 281
plum wine 51, 214
Poland, bars 214
port pipes 52
pot stills 48, 49
pricing 150, 247, 249, 251, 256–9

Q

Quercus Bar, Shinjuku, Tokyo 168

R

rainfall 41
ramen 181, 241, 243, 281

S

SakaMai, New York 196, 197
sake 14, 70, 93, 281
Sakuma, Tadashi 110–11
saladin box 281

salarymen 32, 145
Sapporo
    bars 181
    climate 40, 41
    travel guide 272–3
Sasanokawa Shuzo 70, 92, 278
Scotland
    bars 200
    humidity 52
    influence on Japan 27, 29, 30, 35, 155, 253–4
    Speyside 45, 47
sea currents 40
seafood 235, 240, 241
Sendai
    Miyagikyo Distillery 96–9, 277
    travel guide 266–7
Sexy Fish, London 202, 203
sherry casks 51, 52
Shimamoto, Honshu 82
Shinano, Kiyomitsu 177
Shinshu Mars Distillery 276
Shizuoka Distillery 62–3, 100
shōchū 14, 180, 281
Shōchū Lounge, London 204, 205
shortages
    international availability 23
    investment whiskies 258
    Nikka 19, 99, 109, 110, 254
    Suntory 150, 247, 254
Shot Bar Zoetrope, Shinjuku, Tokyo 143, 147, 154, 167
Simpson, Andy 251, 258
Singapore bars 216
single malts definition 57
snow 40
Sokyo Lounge, Sydney 224, 225
solera 281
Spain 17
Speyside 30, 47, 200
Speyside Way, Meguro-ku, Tokyo 174
Spincoaster Music Bar, Shibuya, Tokyo 173
Spirit of Asama 91
spirit still 48
Star Bar, Ginza, Tokyo 155, 163

INDEX 285

staves 281
stills 19, 48, 49, 96–9
sulfur 48
Suntory
  blended whisky 88, 155
  casks 51
  foundation 14
  future 250, 254
  growth 12, 154
  Hakushu Distillery 76–81, 278
  Highball 145, 149–50, 154
  history 23, 24
  Osaka 177
  supply issues 19, 150, 247, 254
  Torys bars 32
  Yamazaki Distillery 82–7, 278
Suntory 21 Year Old 258
Suntory Royal 77
Suntory Whisky Shirofuda 24, 145
Sushi & Soul, Munich, Germany 212, 213
Sydney bars 224–9

T
Taka Bar, Osaka 178
Taketsuru, Masataka
  Dainipponkaju 31, 106
  Kotobukiya 31
  Miyagikyo Distillery 96
  Nikka 32
  Scotland 14, 27, 30
  Yamazaki Distillery 82, 94
Taketsuru 17 Year Old 224, 230
Taketsuru 35 Year Old 216
Taketsuru Pure Malt 96
Tanaka, Jota 74–5
tasting notes overview 53, 113
terroir 36
Toita, Keichi 64
Tokyo
  bars, Ginza District 155, 162–3
  bars, Minato District 158–61
  bars, other areas 174–5
  bars, Shibuya District 172–3
  bars, Shinjuku District 166–9
  climate 40
  travel guide 263–5
  Whisky Live Japan 140, 142, 143

Tokyo Bird, Surrey Hills, Australia 228, 229
Tokyo Loose, Shinjuku, Tokyo 168
Tokyo National Museum 264
Tonkotsu, London 15, 206, 207
Torii, Shinjiro
  Japanese palate 8, 17
  Kotobukiya 14, 24, 31
  photographs 26, 27
  Yamazaki Distillery 82, 94
Torys bars 32, 145, 248
trains 12
travel guide 262
Tsuji, Hiromitsu 83

U
Ueno Park 263
U.K. bars 200–6
umami 51, 241
Uncle Ming's Bar, Sydney 226, 227
United States
  American whiskey 14
  Chicago bars 186
  Kentucky blending 17
  Los Angeles bars 184
  New York bars 191–6
  Suntory 12
Usuikyou 1983 Vintage 218

V
Van Eycken, Stefan 148–50, 151, 250, 251
vanillins 51
Venture Whisky 66–8, 278

W
Wakatsuru Shuzo Distillery 279
Warsaw 214
wash 47, 281
wash back 46, 47, 281
water
  Japan 38, 41, 78, 89
  mineral content 45
  River Spey 45, 47
  softness 45
websites 20, 144, 151, 279
Whisky and Alement, Melbourne 230, 231–3

Whisky Magazine 140, 142
whisky styles 19
White Oak Akashi 15 Year Old 230
White Oak Distillery 62–3, 102–4, 276
Wodka Tonic, Minato-ku, Tokyo 150, 160
wort 46–7, 281

Y
Yamazaki 10 Year Old 126, 154, 243
Yamazaki 12 Year Old 13, 51, 126, 152, 191, 192, 229
Yamazaki 18 Year Old 127, 200, 203, 205, 210, 214, 241, 243, 256
Yamazaki 25 Year Old 127
Yamazaki 1979 85
Yamazaki 1984 128, 144, 199, 243
Yamazaki 1986 Owner's Cask 148, 150
Yamazaki 1990 Sherry Butt 216
Yamazaki 1993 128
Yamazaki Anniversary Bottling 84 199
Yamazaki Bourbon Barrel 129
Yamazaki Distiller's Reserve 239, 254
Yamazaki Distillery 31, 56, 62–3, 82–7, 278
Yamazaki Mizunara Oak 87, 129, 243
Yamazaki Sherry Cask 247
Yamazaki Sour 239
Yamazakura Distillery 278
yeast 44, 45, 47
Yoichi 10 Year Old 130, 140, 149, 209
Yoichi 12 Year Old 130, 186
Yoichi 15 Year Old 131, 144, 152, 184, 186
Yoichi 20 Year Old 131
Yoichi 1991 210
Yoichi Distillery 31, 32, 62–3, 106–9, 277
Yoichi NAS 205, 241
Yusho, Chicago 186, 187

Z
Zuma, New York 190, 191
Zarifeh, Ramsay 12

ACKNOWLEDGMENTS

Many authors start their acknowledgment section with a comment about how their book wouldn't have been written if it hadn't been for the help of someone special. But in the case of Marcin Miller, it's absolutely true: he employed me as editor of *Whisky Magazine* and set me on a whisky obsession that will last a lifetime. Marcin was not only a crucial source of information for this book, but he offered me encouragement and support when I needed it most. I would also like to give a big thank you to Stefan Van Eycken, Chris Bunting, and Nicholas Coldicott, for being generous with their time and knowledge. I would also like to thank the following people: Gemma Albone, Sarah Belize-Butler, and the rest of THRSXTY Communications, Didier Ghorbanzadeh, Yumi Yushikawa, Ichiro Akuto, everyone at the Japan National Tourism Organization, Dominic al-Badri and Japan.Inc, and Leah Alexander. I'd also like to pay credit to three people who didn't contribute to this book but who cast a shadow over all work on Japanese whisky: the writers Jim Murray and Dave Broom, and the late and great Michael Jackson, who loved Japan, its whisky, and its people with a passion. And finally, a big thank you to my long-suffering family: my wife Sally, and children Jules, Louie, and Maddy. This book is dedicated to them because it is the most beautiful whisky book I've written.

BOOKS

The World Atlas of Whisky
Broom, Dave (Mitchell Beazley, 2014)

Drinking Japan
Bunting, Chris (Tuttle Shokai Inc, 2011)

Japanese Whiskies: Facts, Figures and Taste, The Definitive Guide to Japanese Whiskies
Buxrud, Ulf (DataAnalys Scandinavia AB, 2008)

Whiskey: The Definitive World Guide
Jackson, Michael (DK, 2005)

Jim Murray's Whisky Bible 2016
Murray, Jim (Dram Good Books Ltd, 2015)

Malt Whisky Yearbook 2016
Ronde, Ingvar (MagDig Media Ltd, 2015)

1001 Whiskies You Must Taste Before You Die
Roskrow, Dominic (ed) (Universe, 2012)

The World's Best Whiskies: 740 Unmissable Drams from Tennessee to Tokyo
Roskrow, Dominic (Jacqui Small LLP, 2010)

Whisky Opus
Roskrow, Dominic, and Smith, Gavin D. (eds) (DK, 2012)

WEBSITES

Dekantā, Tokyo: www.dekanta.com
Nonjatta: www.nonjatta.com
Whisky Mizuwari: www.whiskymizuwari.blogspot.co.uk
Whisky Magazine: www.whiskymag.com
Whisky Live: www.whiskylive.com
Whisky Advocate: www.whiskyadvocate.com
whisky-pages: www.whisky-pages.com
Malt Madness: www.maltmadness.com
Whiskyfun: www.whiskyfun.com
Malt Maniacs: www.maltmaniacs.net
The Number One Drinks Company: www.one-drinks.com
The Whisky Exchange Blog: blog.thewhiskyexchange.com
Japan Whisky Reviews: japanwhisky.blogspot.co.uk

PICTURE CREDITS

The publishers would like to thank the distilleries, bars, picture libraries, and photographers for their kind permission to reproduce the works featured in this book. Every effort has been made to trace all copyright holders but if any have been inadvertently overlooked, the publishers would be pleased to make the necessary arrangements at the first opportunity.

9 Bloomberg/Getty Images **10** Bloomberg/Getty Images **13** Bloomberg/Getty Images **15** Courtesy of Tonkotsu **16** Cephas Picture Library/Alamy Stock Photo **18t** Bloomberg/Getty Images **18bl** JUAN CEVALLOS/AFP/Getty Images **18br** Jeremy Sutton-Hibbert/Alamy Stock Photo **19l** Hemis/Alamy Stock Photo **19r** Drambox Media Library **21** Courtesy of Suntory Holdings Limited **24** Courtesy of Suntory Holdings Limited **26** Courtesy of Suntory Holdings Limited **27l** Courtesy of Suntory Holdings Limited **27r** El Español **28l** JTB MEDIA CREATION, Inc./Alamy Stock Photo **28r** Matthias Merges **29t** North Wind Picture Archives/Alamy Stock Photo **29b** Universal Images Group/Getty Images **30t** Miss Whisky **30b** Courtesy of Suntory Holdings Limited **31** Courtesy of Suntory Holdings Limited **32** David Lefranc/Corbis **33** Bettmann/Getty Images **36t** The Asahi Shimbun/Getty Images **36b** JTB Photo/Universal Images Group/Getty Images **37** KAZUHIRO NOGI/AFP/Getty Images **38** Drambox Media Library **39** Drambox Media Library **40l** JTB Photo/Universal Images Group/Getty Images **40r** JTB Photo/Universal Images Group/Getty Images **41** JTB Photo/Universal Images Group/Getty Images **42** JTB Photo/Universal Images Group/Getty Images **44t** Alexey Kopytko/Getty Images **44b** WorldPix/Alamy Stock Photo **45l** Philip Dickson/Alamy Stock Photo **45r** AAron Ontiveroz/Getty Images **46l** Drambox Media Library **46r** Hemis/Alamy Stock Photo **47** Drambox Media Library **48** Bloomberg/Getty Images **50tl** Drambox Media Library **50tr** Drambox Media Librar **50b** Drambox Media Library **51** JTB Photo/Universal Images Group/Getty Images **52t** Drambox Media Library **52b** James Bullock **53** Drambox Media Library **54** Drambox Media Library **56** Drambox Media Library **57t** Jeremy Sutton-Hibbert/Alamy Stock Photo **57b** Courtesy of Suntory Holdings Limited **59** Courtesy of Suntory Holdings Limited **63** Shutterstock **64** Clint Anesbury, Akkeshi Distillery Project Team **65** Clint Anesbury, Akkeshi Distillery Project Team **66** The Whisky Exchange **67** Drambox Media Library **68** Bloomberg/Getty Images **69** Bloomberg/Getty Images **71** Drambox Media Library **72** Courtesy of Kirin Company Limited **73** Courtesy of Kirin Company Limited **75** Courtesy of Kirin Company Limited **76** KAZUHIRO NOGI/AFP/Getty Images **78l** Courtesy of Suntory Holdings Limited **78cl** Courtesy of Suntory Holdings Limited **78cr** Courtesy of Suntory Holdings Limited **78r** The Whisky Exchange **79** Associated Press **80** James Bullock **81** James Bullock **82t** Courtesy of Suntory Holdings Limited **82b** Drambox Media Library **83** KAZUHIRO NOGI/AFP/Getty Images **84** Bloomberg/Getty Images **85t** PAUL J. RICHARDS/AFP/Getty Images **85c** Courtesy of Suntory Holdings Limited **85b** James Bullock **86** James Bullock **87** Bloomberg/Getty Images **89** Courtesy of Suntory Holdings Limited **90** WhiskyTimes **91** Number One Drinks Company **92** The Whisky Exchange **93** Tomohiro Ohsumi/Getty Images **94** James Bullock **96** The Whisky Exchange **97t** Courtesy of Asahi Breweries Limited **97b** Courtesy of Asahi Breweries Limited **98t** dash101 **98b** Spirit and Beer **99t** Courtesy of Asahi Breweries Limited **99b** The Whisky Exchange **100** JTB Photo/Universal Images Group/Getty Images **102** Courtesy of the White Oak Distillery **103** Chris Bunting **104** Chris Bunting **105** Chris Bunting **106** JTB Photo/Universal Images Group/Getty Images **107l** James Bullock **107r** Bloomberg/Getty Images **109l** Bloomberg/Getty Images **109r** Courtesy of Asahi Breweries Limited **111** Courtesy of Asahi Breweries Limited **114t** Number One Drinks Company **114b** The Whisky Exchange **115t** The Whisky Exchange **115b** The Whisky Exchange **116t** Courtesy of Suntory Holdings Limited **116b** Courtesy of Suntory Holdings Limited **117t** Courtesy of Suntory Holdings Limited **117b** Courtesy of Suntory Holdings Limited **118t** The Whisky Exchange **118b** Number One Drinks Company **119t** The Whisky Exchange **119b** The Whisky Exchange **120t** Number One Drinks Company **120b** The Whisky Exchange **121t** The Whisky Exchange **121b** The Whisky Exchange **122t** Number One Drinks Company **122b** Number One Drinks Company **123t** The Whisky Exchange **123b** Number One Drinks Company **124t** The Whisky Exchange **124b** The Whisky Exchange **125t** The Whisky Exchange **125b** The Whisky Exchange **126t** The Whisky Exchange **126b** Courtesy of Suntory Holdings Limited **127t** Courtesy of Suntory Holdings Limited **127b** Courtesy of Suntory Holdings Limited **128t** The Whisky Exchange **128b** Courtesy of Suntory Holdings Limited **129t** The Whisky Exchange **129b** Courtesy of Suntory Holdings Limited **130t** The Whisky Exchange **130b** Courtesy of Asahi Breweries Limited **131t** The Whisky Exchange **131b** The Whisky Exchange **132t** The Whisky Exchange **132b** The Whisky Exchange **133t** The Whisky Exchange **133b** The Whisky Exchange **134t** The Whisky Exchange **134b** The Whisky Exchange **135t** The Whisky Exchange **135b** The Whisky Exchange **136t** The Whisky Exchange **136b** The Whisky Exchange **137t** The Whisky Exchange **137b** The Whisky Exchange **141** Marcin Miller **142** Metric Design Studio, Oslo, Norway **143t** Jeremy Sutton-Hibbert/Getty Images **143b** Jeremy Sutton-Hibbert/Getty Images **145t** Chris Bunting **145b** Chris Bunting **146** Jeremy Sutton-Hibbert/Alamy Stock Photo **147** Bar Zoetrope **149** Stefan Van Eycken **150** The Whisky Exchange **151** Nonjatta **152** Nicholas Coldicott **153t** Courtesy of Rockfish Bar **153b** Keith Tsuji/Getty Images **154** Courtesy of Suntory Holdings Limited **155l** The Whisky Exchange **155cl** The Whisky Exchange **155cr** The Whisky Exchange **155r** The Whisky Exchange **158** JaCZhou 2015/Getty Images **160t** Jeremy Sutton-Hibbert/Alamy Stock Photo **160b** Jeremy Sutton-Hibbert/Alamy Stock Photo **161l** Park Hotel Tokyo, Shiodome **161r** Park Hotel Tokyo, Shiodome **162t** Sandro Bisaro/Getty Images **162b** Shutterstock **163t** Gurunavi, Inc. **163c** Japan National Tourism Organization **163b** Bar Lupin Ginza **164** Luca Rossini/Getty Images **165** Shutterstock **167** The Dubliners' Irish Pub, Shibuya **168** Alexander Spatari/Getty Images **169** Alexander Spatari/Getty Images **170** kokoroimages.com/Getty Images **172** Jeremy Sutton-Hibbert/Alamy Stock Photo **173l** Courtesy of Spincoaster Music Bar **173r** Shutterstock **174t** huzu1959/Getty Images **174b** Chris Bunting **175l** THE MASH TUN TOKYO **175r** Toru Suzuki & THE MASH TUN TOKYO **176** Shutterstock **178t** Bar K **178b** German F. Vidal-Oriola/Getty Images **179** Gerhard Joren/Getty Images **180t** Shutterstock **180b** Bar Kitchen Tenjin **181t** Nikka Bar **181b** THE BOW BAR Sapporo **185t** Allen J. Schaben/Los Angeles Times/Getty Images **185b** Bar Jackalope **187tl** Matthias Merges **187tc** Matthias Merges **187tr** Matthias Merges **187cr** Matthias Merges **187br** Matthias Merges **187bl** Matthias Merges **188–9** Matthias Merges **190t** Nicole Franzen **190b** Nicole Franzen **193t** The Flatiron Room **193b** The Flatiron Room **195tl** Copper and Oak **195tr** Copper and Oak **195cr** Copper and Oak **195br** Copper and Oak **195bc** Copper and Oak **195bl** Copper and Oak **195cl** Copper and Oak **197t** Sakamai **197b** Sakamai **198t** Dr Jekyll's **198b** Dr Jekyll's **201** Highlander Inn **202t** Paul Winch-Furness **202cr** Paul Winch-Furness **202cl** Sim Canetty-Clarke **202br** Sim Canetty-Clarke **202bl** Mark Brumell **204t** Shochu **204bl** Shochu **204br** Shochu **207t** Tonkotsu **207br** Tonkotsu **207bl** Tonkotsu **207cl** Tonkotsu **208t** Le Sherry Butt **208b** Le Sherry Butt **211t** Le Gamin **211b** Le Gamin **212t** Sushi & Soul **212br** Sushi & Soul **212bl** Sushi & Soul **215** Dom Whisky **217t** James Bullock **217b** James Bullock **219t** Edmond Ho **219br** Edmond Ho **219bl** John Heng **219cl** Edmond Ho **220–1** John Heng **223t** Club Qing **223br** Club Qing **223bl** Club Qing **225tl** Sokyo Lounge **225tr** Sokyo Lounge **225bl** Sokyo Lounge **225cl** Sokyo Lounge **227t** Uncle Mings **227tr** Uncle Mings **227cr** Uncle Mings **227br** Uncle Mings **227bl** Uncle Mings **228** George Hong **231t** Tokyo Bird **231br** Tokyo Bird **231bl** Tokyo Bird **232–3** Tokyo Bird **236** Courtesy of Suntory Holdings Limited **238t** Courtesy of Suntory Holdings Limited **238b** Courtesy of Suntory Holdings Limited **239t** Courtesy of Suntory Holdings Limited **239b** Courtesy of Suntory Holdings Limited **240t** ZenShui/Laurence Mouton **240b** Michael Ventura/Alamy Stock Photo **241t** Matthias Merges **241b** Matthias Merges **242** Matthias Merges **243t** haoliang/Getty Images **243b** Matthias Merges **244–5** Matthias Merges **254** The Whisky Exchange **255** Courtesy of Suntory Holdings Limited **256** Courtesy of Suntory Holdings Limited **257t** Yannick Luthy/Alamy Stock Photo **257b** TORU YAMANAKA/AFP/Getty Images **258** Courtesy of Suntory Holdings Limited **259** KAZUHIRO NOGI/AFP/Getty Images **260–1** Bloomberg/Getty Images **262** Nuno Santos **264** Nuno Santos **265** Christian Kober/Getty Images **266t** Japan National Tourism Organization **266b** Japan National Tourism Organization **267** Japan National Tourism Organization **268** Yannick Luthy/Alamy Stock Photo **269** epa european press photo agency b.v./Alamy Stock Photo **270** Japan National Tourism Organization **271t** Getty Images **271b** JTB Photo/Universal Images Group/Getty Images **272** Iain Masterton/Alamy Stock Photo **274** Japan National Tourism Organization **275** Shutterstock

(Key: top = t; bottom = b; left = l; right = r; center = c; top left = tl; top right = tr; center left = cl; center right = cr; bottom left = bl; bottom right = br)

ABOUT THE AUTHOR

Dominic Roskrow is the former editor of *Whisky Magazine*, *The Spirits Business*, and *Whiskeria*. He has written eight books on whisky including *The World's Best Whiskies*, *1001 Whiskies To Try Before You Die*, and *The Whisky Opus* (for which he was nominated for the 2013 Fortnum & Mason Drinks Writer of the Year award), and has contributed to several more, including every edition of *The Whisky Yearbook*. He specializes in world whisky and whisky from non-traditional whisky-making regions, and he has had work published in newspapers and magazines across the world including *Drinks International*, *Harpers Wine & Spirits Trade News*, *Whisky Advocate*, *The Times*, *The Sunday Times*, the *Daily Telegraph*, and the *Wall Street Journal*. He has visited more than 100 distilleries across the world, most recently in Israel and Taiwan. He has been made a Keeper of The Quaich and a Kentucky Colonel for his contributions to Scotch whisky and bourbon respectively, and he was named the 2015 Fortnum & Mason Drinks Writer of the Year.